The Long and Winding Road

The Long and Winding Road

LESLEY PEARSE

MICHAEL JOSEPH

PENGUIN MICHAEL JOSEPH

UK | USA | Canada | Ireland | Australia
India | New Zealand | South Africa

Penguin Michael Joseph is part of the Penguin Random House group of companies
whose addresses can be found at global.penguinrandomhouse.com

First published 2024
004

Every effort has been made to trace copyright holders and to obtain their permission
for the use of copyright material. The publisher apologizes for any errors or
omissions and would be grateful to be notified of any corrections that
should be incorporated in future editions of this book

Page 12 'Lovin' you' by Minnie Riperton and Richard Randolph

This book is a work of non-fiction based on the life, experiences and
recollections of the author. In some cases names of people, places, dates,
sequences and the detail of events have been changed
to protect the privacy of others

Set in 15.5/18pt Garamond MT Std
Typeset by Jouve (UK), Milton Keynes
Printed and bound in Great Britain by Clays Ltd, Elcograf S.p.A.

The authorized representative in the EEA is Penguin Random House Ireland,
Morrison Chambers, 32 Nassau Street, Dublin D02 YH68

A CIP catalogue record for this book is available from the British Library

HARDBACK ISBN: 978–0–241–45320–9
TRADE PAPERBACK ISBN: 978–0–241–70150–8

www.greenpenguin.co.uk

While writing this autobiography, again and again people
who had meant a great deal to me popped into my head.
Some of them made only a brief but memorable contribution
in my life. Others were around longer, enriching and bringing
happiness, yet sadly they all disappeared far too quickly.
Back in the day before mobiles and email addresses we
had to make a far more concerted effort to hold onto
people, and I, like many, failed in that.

But I wish to dedicate this book to all those friends and lovers
who coloured my life, made me laugh, comforted me in the
bad times and shared the good. I haven't forgotten you,
just mislaid you. And I want to thank you now for
your contribution to my life.

I

I can remember exactly where I was when I first heard the Beatles' song 'The Long and Winding Road'. It was early June in 1970. I was twenty-five, sitting in London's Richmond Park, listening to a transistor radio, and the song made me cry because I felt I'd been on that winding road for ever. Had I known then just how fraught with drama and disappointment it would continue to be, I might have wished to step off it. But I'd always been an optimist.

I was born in Rochester, Kent, in February 1945, just as Churchill, Roosevelt and Stalin were winding up their talks on the future of Europe after the expected defeat of Germany. These took place in Yalta, Crimea. Apparently, Stalin wanted to meet in Moscow, but Churchill said it was too damn cold there in February. Two months later Roosevelt died, and despite the discussed plans, Stalin took over a huge amount of Europe, including Poland.

Of course I wasn't aware of any of that, but as a kid I certainly felt it was a curse to be born in freezing February. My birthday always fell at half-term too, and I'd be shoved out to play in the snow. I still prefer looking at snow through a window in a warm room!

My mother, Marie Glynn, was an Irish nurse from Roscommon, and my father, Sergeant Arthur Geoffrey Sargent (yes, really), was in the Royal Marines, stationed in Chatham. My brother Michael was two when I was born, a very pretty little boy with a mop of blond curls. I resembled Winston Churchill.

I don't know when my parents bought the house in Grafton Avenue, Rochester. It was typical of the late 1930s terraced houses, with a keyhole-style front porch and a large back garden.

I assume as the address was on my birth certificate that they must have bought it in 1937 or 1938 when they got married and Dad was seconded to the New Zealand Navy. He was there until the Second World War broke out when his ship sailed away to fight.

The next part of my story is legend and hearsay. I could never get adults to verify or explain, and mostly they didn't wish to discuss what had happened or really didn't know. But the undeniable fact, proved years later by my mother's death certificate, was that in early January of 1948 she died of septicaemia following a miscarriage. My father was away at sea, and Michael and I were seen out in the garden in the snow with no coats on. When Michael was asked by our neighbour where our coats were, he said he couldn't reach them, and Mummy was asleep. She'd been asleep for a long time.

She had been dead, it seems, for a few days.

Michael was five, I was three, but if my brother remembered anything about that time, he never said. It doesn't bear thinking about, two small children being alone in the house for so long with no heating or food and thick snow outside. I think it was possible that Michael attempted to light the gas to get warm or try to cook something for us, but we were afraid of the popping sound the Ascot water heater made when it was turned on and of lighting the gas stove. To this day I have an absolute hatred of gas cookers.

I don't remember anything of this, and in fact I didn't discover what our mother had died of until I got married at twenty and had to show her death certificate. There it was in black ink. The truth.

We had been told various stories over the years — one was that our mother tripped over our toys on the stairs. What sort of person puts the blame for a mother's death on her children? On Coronation Day, when we were crowded round a neighbour's television to watch the ceremony, I heard some old lady ask if we were the 'Tragic Children'.

Meanwhile, back in 1948, Michael and I were too

young to be aware of all that. I believe my father came home on leave shortly afterwards and employed a housekeeper for a while, but she turned out to be useless, or maybe Michael and I were difficult because we were traumatized. Uncle Jim, Dad's brother, and his wife, Auntie Sybil, wanted to take me in apparently, but they had a son, Malcolm, and couldn't manage both of us. Dad didn't want us split up. Our mother had a huge family in Ireland, and her sister Anne lived on a farm and had no children of her own. I was told as a child that our Irish relatives didn't offer to help because they were all Catholic and Dad was a Protestant. Later in this memoir I will explain that that was a lie. It was only recently, aged seventy-seven, that I was told the truth.

People forget that there was no help for single fathers in those days, so the Catholic Church stepped in and put us into orphanages run by nuns. Despite Dad's wish that we were to be kept together, Michael was sent somewhere in Gloucestershire and I went to Grove Park in south London, so we didn't even have the comfort of one another.

My earliest memory is of my first night in St Joseph's — well, I think that's what the place was called. A rather grand house with big chilly rooms, and a huge staircase with oak panelling. I was the youngest child there and, I believe, the only one with a parent, but my experience on that first night has never left me.

I was in a dormitory on the ground floor, and I woke in the night wanting to go to the loo. I suppose I lost my way and ended up in the hall. On the turn of the stairs there was a life-sized statue of Jesus, with night-lights all around him. It was so scary that I wet myself and cried. A nun appeared, grabbed me by the scruff of my neck and rubbed my nose in the pee. As if I was a dog. Had she never heard the line from the Bible, 'Suffer the little children to come unto me'? And she was a woman who professed to be a Bride of Christ!

I have to admit, despite that baptism of fire (or pee), I got off considerably lighter than the other girls. I expect it was because I had a father, a respectable, forceful one who was likely to kick up a stink if I was ill-treated. I was also young and hadn't yet learned to answer back. The other girls went to a nearby school every day and I played alone in the garden. Sometimes a nun took me to the bakery to collect the bread and she'd buy me a penny bun. That was a good memory.

Apart from the penny buns, the food at St Joseph's was disgusting, and we had to stay in the refectory until we'd eaten every scrap. Even if it was congealed on the plate. At least it gave me the ability to eat absolutely anything! During mealtimes we were not allowed to talk, and the nuns sat at a table, with their nice food and real butter, on a raised platform keeping an eye on us.

The punishments at the convent were severe, the worst being locked in what the girls called 'The Dark Place'. It was an old icehouse lined with lead, and girls were often locked in there for twenty-four hours, with no food, no blanket and in pitch darkness. I was never put in there, but as I got older I was aware of its effect on those who were. They had blank expressions when they came out, and one girl developed a terrible tic under her eye. They all had nightmares.

Another punishment was being forced to kneel on gravel and recite the rosary. I had that a few times. It was excruciating after just a few minutes. But my abiding memory of awfulness was the cold. Weekends and holidays, we had to stay outside, which was all right in summer, but in winter it was grim. There were no tights in those days, and we had grey ankle socks and a gabardine raincoat, no gloves, scarves or hats. More reasons for me to hate snow. My legs were chapped and stung, and we had nothing to play with. No swing, skipping ropes or balls. We were just herded out there like sheep.

The older girls worked in the laundry. I used to wish I was in there, but those girls often showed us burn marks from an iron on their arms, inflicted purposely by the nuns because they had dared to talk or sing. In winter, when it got dark, we were allowed in and we'd run to the playroom to get a seat on the hot pipes that ran round it. Calling it a playroom was a joke: a box of broken toys, dolls with missing arms and legs, and books in pieces. But it was warm.

My father came to see me a couple of times. He couldn't come more often, and he never managed to visit Michael, as it took six hours by train to reach Gloucester. I would go down to the gate to wait for him, and my excitement at seeing my tall handsome daddy in his Marines uniform was off the scale. The moment he stepped inside the gate, all the other girls would swarm out and surround him. He was a kind, gentle man, even though he was a sergeant and people imagined him to be super-tough, but he'd hug and talk to all of the children. I can remember standing back and thinking, but that's my daddy, and really that distance between us was never breached, even years after I'd left there.

We all used to talk about leaving St Joseph's, and the dream for most of the girls was that someone would come and take them away to foster or adopt them. It rarely happened, I believe, and when the girls were fifteen, they were sent to some menial live-in job. But I had a father, so I put all my trust in him.

Quite rightly, as it turned out. I was to learn, years later, that Dad was so desperate to get Michael and me back that he signed up at a marriage bureau. There he was introduced to forty-seven-year-old Hilda Cant, SRN, who had recently left Queen Alexandra's Royal Army Nursing Corps where she worked on hospital ships and in military hospitals in Egypt, India, Africa and many other places. Her finest hour was at Dunkirk where she hauled the wounded men onto a hastily converted cross-Channel ferry, which stood in for a real hospital ship.

When she put her name down with the marriage bureau she was working as a school nurse in Catford and was foster-mother to Selina, aged nine, whom she wanted to adopt. Hilda said she gave her requirements for a husband as 'a man who is preferably officer class, but I'll settle for an NCO. He must have his own house, at least two children and be artistic.'

Dad ticked every box.

Apparently, they got married at St Mildred's Church near Grove Park, a whisper away from where I was, just a couple of months after their first meeting. The wedding took place on 6 December 1951 so that they could have us home for Christmas.

Just a few days later I was called down to Mother Superior's sitting room in the early evening. In there I saw this plump posh lady in a midnight blue coat and matching hat. She told me she had married my father and was my new mother. Furthermore she would be back the next morning to take me home. She said my father had gone to collect Michael and I would have an older sister called Selina.

Needless to say, I was thrilled and far too excited to pick up on any tension in that room. I had a dim memory of Michael, but I don't think I actually understood what a brother meant, being closeted with just girls for three years. Nor did I know where home was. But as soon as I skipped out of that room and up the stairs to the bathroom the dreaded Sister Agnes, the nastiest nun of all, advanced on me and said, 'Your new mother said you smell.'

The smell, I assume, was a kaolin poultice they had wrapped around my so-called 'weak' chest. The sister hauled off my clothes, yanking the end of the poultice from under my vest, like ripping off a plaster. She picked up a copper stick and beat me with it, then flung me into the bath. We always had to keep a vest on – you couldn't be naked in the sight of the Lord. She pushed me under the water, washed my hair roughly with carbolic soap, making sure she got plenty into my eyes, then got a jug of cold water and poured that over me. If anyone heard my screams no one came. Then I had to try to dry myself with the wet vest still on, crying my eyes out. The weals on my back from the beating stung, and I can remember wondering why at one moment everything could be so wonderful, and the next I was back in Hell.

It transpired that Mother Superior had asked Hilda if I was to be kept 'in the Faith'. Hilda had said no, quite reasonably: she and my father were Protestants. My beating was revenge.

The next day, I was dressed in a too-short tartan kilt and a shrunken jumper. Hilda and I had to stay the night in a guesthouse. I couldn't get the jumper off as it was stuck to the weals on my back. I can remember Hilda's shocked face as she helped me. She didn't say much but found some ointment to put on the sores. Despite my back, I was in seventh heaven and got to sleep with my new mother.

Many years later she told me she didn't sleep a wink as I latched onto her like a barnacle, so needy for affection. And Hilda wasn't a cuddly person, not then or ever.

The next day I met Selina, my new sister. She was very pretty with shiny chestnut hair in two perfect plaits and big blue eyes. She seemed as thrilled to have a sister as I was. I had no real memory of the house in Grafton Avenue where my mother died, but in my new home, I was taken aback by a very plush traditional red-patterned hall and stair carpet. In those post-war days, with shortages of everything, shabby was the norm. Our new mum had bought it and used to joke that it was like being at the Ritz cinema. That carpet lasted for some thirty years.

Dad arrived home with Michael the next day and soon the three of us children were pressed into making Christmas decorations, mainly paper chains. There were lots of intriguing things in the house. First there was a hand-carved nativity scene, which Mum had brought back from Egypt. Dad had made a stable for the characters, and year after year it had pride of place in the window. There were shelves full of books, and fascinating pictures that were not religious and scary as I'd been used to. Above all, I remember a roaring fire, and I was warm at last. Mum had made me a dressing-gown from the red wool lining in her Queen Alexandra's uniform cloak. She made Michael one from the grey outer part. Selina and I had pretty winceyette nighties, too. Once we were in bed Selina always reached out for my hand across the gap between us. I loved her for making me feel so secure. Although I've never told her that!

Years later Mum told me that Michael had been treated very badly at the place he had been sent to. He weighed half of what an eight-year-old should, and had worms, weeping sores on his legs and terrible nightmares. He was very pale, and had been made to wear boots several sizes too small so his toes were all scrunched up. He never talked about it but, then, none of us three kids spoke of 'before'. I suppose we were just happy to be together and safe.

We bonded very quickly. Dad painted sea scenes with sailing ships on the walls of the front room, and that became our playroom. Mum had a wind-up portable record player she'd taken all round the world with her, and Selina and I would dance to 'The Legend of the Glass Mountain'. Well, Selina danced – she was graceful. I was more like a hippopotamus.

That first Christmas, just a couple of weeks after I'd left St Joseph's, was far more than I had dared dream of. My first-ever stocking, with a tangerine at the toe, a sugar mouse, and we each had boxes of pencils with our names printed on them. Mum had made me a knitted doll, which I loved, but best of all, Selina and I were given matching red coats with hoods. To be dressed the same as my new big sister was the best thing in the whole world.

After Christmas we had to go to school. On the first day of term it snowed, and Michael and Selina had to take me to the Infants before they went on to the Juniors. As we walked out onto the road, Mum said, 'Michael, hold Lesley's hand.' And he did, until we went into the Infants' playground. I think that was when I discovered what having a big brother meant.

Michael was a very bright kid. Later it became apparent that he was gifted. He could read anything, do complicated sums in his head, and made crystal sets, a kind of primitive radio – or wireless, as it was called then. He would fiddle with what looked like a bunch of wires, give us an earpiece to listen with and we could hear *Friday Night is Music Night* or *Journey into Space*.

Selina was also pretty bright, but I couldn't get the hang of reading. Years later I found out I had mild dyslexia, but it wasn't understood back then. Mum had little patience with me over this. I can remember her batting me round the head with Jane Austen's *Sense and Sensibility* when I got words wrong, but Selina and Michael read to me, so I very soon acquired a passion for books. It forced me to try harder at reading because I was hungry for stories, but I was nine or ten before I mastered it.

Dad had retired from the Royal Marines and joined the General Post Office after he married Mum. When he wasn't working, he was always in his shed at the bottom of the garden, making model boats and other things. Michael liked to get in there and poke about, often mixing up potions that he got me to try. Back then he said he wanted to be a doctor, but the adults pooh-poohed that idea as his hands were always dirty. I was very proud when he got his doctorate years later. He wasn't a medical doctor, but a scientist is every bit as valuable to humanity.

By 1953 the three of us kids had become very close. We put on plays and Selina was always the princess, Michael the prince, and I was the witch. I thought up most of the stories but we all made the costumes and painted the scenery on cardboard boxes. Dad was good at designing things and made us a fantastic cart, a sort of super soapbox one, with old pram wheels. It had a seat for Michael on the front to steer and one for Selina on the back, where she had to push us along with her feet. I got the best seat inside it, just riding! Its rails were painted bright colours and we were the envy of every kid in the area. In the summer holidays and on Saturdays the three of us would go for miles in it, right out into the country.

In darkest February of 1953, Mum went off to London on the train and came home with baby Paul in her arms. She and Dad planned to adopt him and Selina at the same time. Selina and Paul shared a birthday, 5 January, but ten years apart. As far as I was concerned, Mum had brought baby Paul home for my delight. I adored him, and Mum was very happy to let me give him his bottles. He was better than a doll.

It was, of course, the year of Queen Elizabeth II's

Coronation. We spent hours at school learning 'I Vow to Thee My Country'. The sadness of the previous year, when King George VI died, was put aside in the excitement of the parades and other events that were planned.

Mum was very good at making fancy-dress costumes. She turned Michael into King Arthur with sacking painted silver for chain mail. I was to be a hula-hula girl as Dad had brought the costume back from somewhere, and a little geisha outfit for Selina. But the day of the Coronation arrived with heavy rain, and although we got dressed up in the hope it would stop and we could go on the floats, the cocoa-and-water mix Mum had rubbed on me to make me look tanned grew streaky. And Selina's painted chalk-white face had tracks down it.

Dad had hung red, white and blue streamers down the front of the house, and as we couldn't go to the parade, we went to the neighbours' house, which had a TV. That was where I learned we were the 'Tragic Children' and what odd remarks adults could make when they were together. The woman seemed to be obsessed with how on earth the Queen could possibly use the loo in all that Coronation regalia.

When we arrived home later that afternoon, our once white house was permanently striped, as the dye had come out of the crêpe paper. We got indoors to find that the Coronation coach decoration, on the special cake Mum had made had sunk through the icing right up to its roof. She burst into tears, the first and last time I ever saw her cry. Of course, years later, as a mother myself, I realized she'd planned painstakingly for the day but everything had gone horribly wrong.

Those early years in Rochester were mainly good, despite Mum being fierce and undemonstrative. But one occasion is engraved in my memory. Mum was a terrible cook, even though our standards were extremely low after the orphanages. The meat was the worst thing, fatty with gristle. Us kids had made a shop in the playroom and Mum had given us empty food packets and tins to stock it. As we had our meals in there too, we came up with the idea of cutting off the offending bits of fat and gristle and shoving them into the boxes.

One evening Mum appeared at our bedrooms, ordered us out of our beds and to come downstairs. She had found the stash in the playroom. Amazingly she told me to go back to bed because I was too young to be responsible. Possibly the real reason was that she knew I was such a gannet I'd eat anything. But Michael and Selina were made to eat every scrap of the mouldy rank meat. Poor Selina always gagged at even the thought of fat. I have never been able to understand why a nurse would make children eat rotten meat.

I was also a little puzzled as to why Mum could spend ages playing with Paul, but we never got a cuddle. I recall one time trying to sit on her lap and she ejected me as if I was a poisonous snake. I certainly didn't feel jealous of Paul, I loved him, we all did, but to feel some affection for me now and then would have been nice.

Whenever we did anything wrong, the punishment was usually being sent to bed without any tea to await a smacked bottom. We didn't have to do much to earn it, playing Knock Down Ginger (knocking on doors and running away), going down to the River Medway instead of to Sunday school, and other such things. Selina was brave. She'd lie on her bed insisting it wouldn't hurt but I'd be crying even before I heard the sound of Mum's footsteps on the stairs. At least the smacking wasn't like a cane or a copper stick. The sting wore off quickly.

Mum's sister, Auntie Celia, was a children's officer and often arranged for foster children to come and stay with us. They all brought joy, some on their arrival, but more when they left. One girl, Mary, I absolutely detested. She was eight, the same age as me, and pretty but had screaming tantrums. I didn't hate her for that – it was fascinating to see her in full flight, her face purple, nose streaming with snot. I hated her because I felt Michael liked her more than me. But he was a kind boy and I guess he felt he had to be especially nice to her. Mary hit me on the head once with a garden rake, piercing the skin. I had to go to hospital and have it stitched up along with an anti-tetanus injection. I planned to repay her in kind, but luckily for Mary, she had worn out Mum's patience and was moved on to another family. I couldn't have been happier.

The village of Borstal wasn't far from where we lived, and we got used to seeing 'Borstal Boys' digging sugar beet for farmers and doing other menial jobs. They were held up as an example of what could happen if you strayed from the straight and narrow.

One day Michael and I had gone to a place called Fort Horsted – Selina wasn't with us. It had been built in the 1800s to protect Chatham dockyard when there was fear of a French invasion. As I remember, it was a huge ugly concrete place with a deep moat around it. We used to look down into the moat and see trees growing at the bottom. During both world wars they kept artillery there but it has since been given scheduled historic status. We kids knew nothing about that – I don't think anyone did back in the early fifties. But we'd been told not to play there because there was no fence and we believed the moat to be bottomless! But that made it even more attractive.

We'd no sooner got there than some boys we instantly recognized as runaway Borstal Boys surrounded us and herded us into a kind of camp they'd made in the bushes. They wanted Michael to go to the shop and buy them chocolate, cake and matches. Michael refused, so they grabbed me, pulled off my dress and said they would kill me if Michael didn't do as they said. I remember the horror on Michael's face as he rushed off with the warning that he wasn't to tell anyone presumably ringing in his ears.

To be fair to the boys, they never laid a hand on me. In fact they told me to stop crying and gave me a couple of sherbet lemons, but wouldn't let me put my dress back on.

When Michael came back with their shopping, they immediately threw my dress at me and said we could go. We ran away and hid to watch the police arriving later to round the boys up. Michael didn't say much about it, only that he'd told the shopkeeper the boys were threatening to kill his little sister and he had to get back to me before the shopkeeper could ring the police.

That was clever of him, but I don't think we ever told Mum and Dad. If we had we would undoubtedly have been punished for being at Fort Horsted.

The good times seemed to end for our little gang of three when Michael won a scholarship to the Royal Hospital School near Ipswich. It was founded in 1712 for the sons of seagoing men, to teach the boys navigation and arithmetic. It was originally in Greenwich and called Greenwich Hospital, now the Maritime Museum. Michael had passed his eleven-plus exam with such high marks that he could have had a scholarship to any one of the most prestigious schools in England, but our father chose the Royal Hospital School because of its naval tradition.

Michael went alone on the train from London's Liverpool Street station, wearing a full naval uniform, and he was so small that Mum kept his first pair of serge bell bottoms as a souvenir. The boys were not allowed to take with them any personal items, and that included a stuffed panda he was very attached to. He was brave and didn't cry, but I did as I waved him off with Mum, because I could see he was really scared.

Whether he loved the school or hated it I never knew. Michael wasn't one for complaining or boasting. But I do know that ultimately it was good for him: there were masters who realized how gifted he was and stretched his abilities.

Selina had gone to the senior school a year earlier, too, before Michael went away. It was evident to me that the somewhat idyllic times the three of us had shared were now over. There would be no more long treks out into the countryside with the cart or lighting fires to half-cook sausages or scrumping fruit from orchards. We'd lost the cart anyway because Michael and Selina had hurtled in it down a steep grassy bank and broken it. Dad refused to mend it because they could have been killed. There would also be no more climbing over the wall of the bakery to see the horses that pulled the bread vans or Saturday-morning pictures in Chatham, followed by visiting the dungeon beneath the Tudor museum in Rochester high street. Although the dungeon freaked me out, with its guillotine and torture instruments, Michael and Selina loved it, so I pretended I did too.

I had to go off to junior school alone and became wrapped up in fantasy. A favourite one was that my real mother was not dead but locked up somewhere, like Rapunzel, and I told the kids at school that my stepmother was responsible. Another was that I'd run away from home and was living under a bush in a field. I embellished this one and it became an almost daily serial to be told at playtime. Some of the kids brought me cake to live on. No one asked why I looked clean and my hair was plaited.

To my mind, the best stories I ever told were in my news book. They were about my fictitious adventures in India. I was a fan of Rudyard Kipling, so there were threads from his books, but more from Mum, who often talked about her time in military hospitals there. She showed me pictures of banyan trees that she'd done in pastels and told me stories about all the animals and snakes she'd seen.

One afternoon I spotted Mum coming into the school assembly hall – our classroom had windows that gave onto it. She stopped to look at a display of work on the table, and at that point I got a sense of foreboding. Sure enough, just ten minutes or so later, I was summoned to Miss Goad the headmistress's office (a great name for a headmistress!).

My mother was in there with her, the two of them puffed up with anger as Mum picked up my news-book and proceeded to read aloud: 'In India we lived in a white marble palace. We had an ayah to look after us, and servants who brought us fruit and drinks. Mongooses often came up on the veranda and a few times we had to yell when we saw a cobra there too. My daddy rode a black stallion.'

That was as far as Mum got before she exploded. 'The only thing your father ever rode was his bike!'

I got ten strikes of the ruler on the knuckles of both hands, and Mum said, 'You can lock up from a thief but not a liar.'

My hands stinging, I went to my classroom, biting back tears. I didn't see writing stories as lying. If that was the case surely all books were lies, yet we were encouraged to read.

Throughout my school days I received corporal punishment many times, mostly the cane. As a matter of pride I wouldn't cry. Sometimes I wondered if I was caned more because of that. But I liked my reputation for being tough.

Fortunately my teacher at the primary school was a kinder soul than Miss Goad and Mum. She took me to one side and said, 'If I tell you to write news, you must stick to what really happened, but if I say it's a story, you can write anything you like.'

I didn't bother to ask what the point of writing news was when it was just 'Got up, went to school, came home, had tea and went to bed.' My life was so uneventful it bored me to think about it, never mind write it down. But I think Mum should have been more appreciative of my writing. After all, she was the one who had filled my head with stories about India. It was unusual in those days for women to have travelled as widely as she had. Nowadays I wish I'd pumped her for more stories and written them all down. I have killed her off in two of my books, a bit of spite for her being such a fire-eating dragon, but I owe her a great deal. She was inspirational – even though as a child what I really wanted was a cuddle.

*

The year I was due to take my eleven-plus, Kent County Council in their wisdom decided to abandon the normal exam and replace it with an intelligence test. I believe I did remarkably well, though I learned that much later from a teacher, not Mum or Dad.

During the Christmas holidays of 1955, we went to New Cross in London to stay with a fearsome friend of Mum's, Auntie Eleanor. None of us kids liked her or her house, where her cats peed everywhere. But I suppose Mum missed London and adult conversation. I think she and Eleanor had met while doing their nursing training.

Also during this holiday, she took us to Hither Green, where she had lived as a child. To her delight, her childhood home was empty as the previous owner had died. In what seemed like the blink of an eye, she and Dad bought it. It must have taken longer than I imagine, as Dad had to transfer from the Post Office in Rochester to Mount Pleasant in London. Selina and I had to go to new schools too.

I don't know what Selina made of the move, she never said, but Michael and I hated the idea. Leahurst Road was one of those typical Edwardian terraces that are all over London. It was treeless and the front garden was about three feet wide, just enough space for a bike and a dustbin. But whether we liked the idea or not, we moved on 24 February

1956, my eleventh birthday. Paul was four, Selina fourteen and Michael thirteen. Early that new year, I had been sent to London with Dad, so I could start at my new primary school. Dad and I had to stay with Mum's aged aunts, Patty and Emily, both in their eighties. Their tiny terraced house was in a Victorian time warp, still with gas lighting and an outside lavatory.

I liked Patty. She had been a governess and was nearly blind, so she would get me to read to her. I can remember perching on a chair under the gas light, straining my eyes to see. Patty loved it that I would read her Dickens and Rudyard Kipling. Emily, her younger sister, had good eyesight but when she was asked to read she chose the obituary column in the local paper. Patty would sigh with a mixture of disappointment and resignation.

My new school was Lee Manor, which was three doors away from the new house. Mum had been to this school until she was fifteen. She might have had fond memories of it, but I have none. It was pretty terrifying, having to go there alone on the first day, with Mum, Selina and Paul all in Rochester. I was not yet eleven and the other girls picked on me from the start. They claimed I spoke posh. Well, I suppose I did. Mum was always correcting our speech and I hadn't got the South London twang. Day after day the girls played nasty tricks on me. They tied my coat sleeves in knots, filled my pockets with rice, smeared sticky stuff on my desk and called me names.

One day I had had enough. As I was walking across the playground to go home, a group of girls surrounded me, jeering at me. In a fury I launched myself at the ringleader and whacked her, then proceeded to attack the rest until they all ran away. Unknown to me, Dad was coming past the school gates, possibly going to the new house to do some small jobs. He heard the racket and walked into the playground. Years later he told me I was crying my eyes out, but punching left and right at my tormentors. He could see I was in control so he left me to it.

Maybe it was as well that he didn't interfere: that fight did wonders for my reputation of being tough and it followed me to senior school.

On my eleventh birthday in February, Mum, Selina and Paul were coming up from Rochester in the removal van to move into the new house at Hither Green. It was a freezing cold day, a foot of snow lying in the garden at the old house. I was really excited to see Paul and Selina, and was told by the aunts I was to go straight to the new house when I finished school. In my naivety, I expected there would be a birthday tea and presents there.

But there was nothing. The house was as cold and

cheerless as a morgue. Mum was stressed out because she'd left her fur coat in a wardrobe and it had been put on the van before she could retrieve it. She'd been like a block of ice all day. There was no central heating, of course, but Dad lit a fire in what became known as the breakfast room at the back of the house, then got us all fish and chips from the shop.

As we sat down to eat there was a kind of roaring noise and, to our horror, filthy brown water cascaded down the chimney breast. It transpired the boiler that heated the water, unused and cold for years, had caused the main pipe and tank to burst.

In the chaos of Mum and Dad rushing to mop up the water, I wailed, 'It's my birthday and everyone's forgotten!'

I got no sympathy, only a clout. That day marked the start of a miserable period that lasted until I left home at sixteen.

As a much wiser adult looking back, I can now understand what made Mum so nasty to me and Selina. She had become bored with her life as wife and mother to four kids who were not her own and missed nursing where she had been someone important. She ought to have been happier once we moved house as she, her sister Celia and several other nursing friends were within walking distance of each other. Michael was off at boarding school, and Paul was now four and not so dependent on her. She arranged for Selina to go to Kidbrooke Comprehensive, but it was extremely odd that she didn't send me there too. The conclusion I've come to was Divide and Rule. She didn't want Selina offering me any protection in a big school.

If I put my kind head on, I can believe she thought it would be good for me to be toughened up. But over the years I saw more of her Divide and Rule policy, and I'm sure she didn't want any of us four to gain comfort from each other. She had been an officer in the army, treated with respect and waited on. Marrying a man and taking on his motherless children while adopting two more was immensely kind and generous, but she probably didn't think it through. She had no real experience with children, especially ones as damaged as we three older ones were.

She didn't know that children needed more than food, sleep and play to thrive. The nearest thing to affection I got was when she told people how good I was at darning socks. And I suspect that was to make sure I would always do it and save her the bother. Money was short and she had no real outlets for her talents in painting or music. Worst of all she probably found Dad terribly dull. He was always tinkering in his shed or working. He didn't know how to communicate with us kids, and probably couldn't begin to understand a complicated woman like Hilda – her name means 'warrior maiden', which describes her pretty well.

But back to me. In the previous year, London kids had taken the eleven-plus but as I hadn't done it I couldn't be counted. In September I was sent to Catford County, a girls-only comprehensive, known to everyone as Catford Cowshed. To be fair I was put in the top stream, but I found that huge school pretty terrifying. Bullying abounded, and it was quite a long bus ride.

But a new church school was being built close to our home and it was to be called Northbrook. Rumour had it that the original idea was to take in very bright kids. Whether that was true, and I can pat myself on the head, or not, I don't know. But the following year, after the Easter holidays, I was there in the playground, one of the first sixteen pupils. The plan was that each year the school would fill with younger children.

Standing in that playground alongside me were two old adversaries: Madeline from Juniors, whom I'd fought with, and Christine Diamond. She went to Holbeach Road School and we'd had a few run-ins on the bus as we used to try to push each other off. I remember feeling sick with apprehension. But Madeline avoided looking at me, remembering, I suppose, that I could be dangerous. However, Christine spoke as if we'd always been friends, and that was what we became and still are, even after all these years.

With only sixteen kids in a school it was like having a spotlight on you all the time. Our teacher, the deputy head, Mrs Hinton, was young and very glamorous. She'd been brought up in France and had the *je ne sais quoi* that French women have. Although only in her twenties, she commanded respect and obedience.

Sadly I was neither good nor obedient. I remember Mrs Hinton once saying to me, 'Lesley, you have a monkey on your shoulder. He sits there quietly enough for most of the time, but then he prods you into being silly, or breaking rules, and you go along with it.'

How right she was! That monkey is with me to this day. If there's a rule to be broken, a dare to be taken, or a chance to lark around, I'm up for it. Being my own analyst for a moment, I think this was because I was kept down so much at home. I was afraid of Mum, so I did exactly as I was told, creeping round her by cleaning, mending and ironing clothes, anything to curry favour. Not that it worked. I also used to try to get her attention by telling her a lie, something like 'I saw Mrs Hall get taken away in an ambulance. I think she was run over.'

I can't believe I was so dumb as to tell a lie that was so easily disproved. She was brilliant at catching me out. But perhaps I worked on the idea that any attention, even a good hiding, was better than being ignored.

She was spectacularly brilliant at ignoring, which I know now to be a form of abuse. She'd ask everyone round the table if they would like seconds at dinner but bypass me. I'd say hello when I got in from school and she'd act like she couldn't hear or see me. I found it very distressing. I can't count the nights I lay in bed crying.

At school, I suppose I wanted everyone to know me and like me. I was a real-life Jekyll and Hyde and played to the crowd. I was given the job of changing the pictures each week in the foyer. The works of art were in a big folder and I could choose which ones to put in the frames. I loved that job, even if I couldn't paint and draw: Mum had opened our eyes to art, taking us to galleries and telling us about artists. At first I played the job straight, picking out the beautiful Monets, Degases, or Toulouse-Lautrecs. But the monkey on my shoulder prodded me, and soon I was putting out the nudes, the ruder the better.

I entertained the whole school, which, of course, had been my aim, but in doing so I lost the job I loved. I got the cane too, but what hurt me more was that someone else would now be responsible for picking out wonderful works of art. And I'd disappointed Mrs Hinton.

Yet I didn't really learn. One day in an art class we were put in groups of four, with a huge piece of paper and were told to do a 'cave' painting. We had to imagine what we would illustrate on the walls of our home if we had lived in those times.

The art teacher left the room, and I soon encouraged my group to follow my lead. We painted men peeing against the walls, ladies with extra large breasts and pubic hair to their knees. We were all giggling and the rest of the class came to look and found our painting hilarious.

Our teacher returned, saw what we'd done and was furious, knowing immediately I was the instigator. He accused me of leading other children astray and told me he didn't want me in his art class ever again. Instead I would do maths in the library.

Again I wished I hadn't done it. Clowning around might have made me admired by my classmates, which sort of made up for the bleakness of my home life, but I'd liked art, even if I wasn't very good at it. I hated maths. Worse still I knew a letter about this would be sent to my home, and Mum's punishments were much more severe than missing the art class.

But she didn't need a letter from the school about my bad behaviour as an excuse to punish me, she had her own set of rules, and Heaven help anyone who broke them. An example was time-keeping. She timed me coming home from school. Not to teach punctuality, but to prevent me walking home with Christine Diamond. If I arrived later than four twenty, she knew I'd gone round the slightly longer way where Christine lived. She would strike me with a cane for this. Without knowing anything at all about the Diamonds, she would say, 'They aren't our sort.'

I loved the Diamonds, and wished I could live with them. Ironically Christine rose to a top position in Barings Bank. So much for Mum's snooty ideas. I took great pleasure many decades later in telling her that, and even driving her past Chris's lovely house to make my point. Mrs Diamond did so much to help me too, both then and after I'd left home.

People often ask why my dad didn't intervene, but I don't think he really knew what was going on, or maybe he didn't look too hard. Even Mum was fond of saying, 'He took the line of least resistance.'

Selina was much braver than me. She dared to answer back. I admired her so much for that. Mum once threw something at her, and Selina threw it right back. My heroine. But even Selina's courage didn't stop her being punished: at sixteen she was five minutes late getting home one evening, and Mum wouldn't let her in. She spent that cold winter's night curled up on the doorstep. Who would do that to a teenage girl?

It was hardly surprising that, soon after, Selina moved into a bedsitter in Lewisham. She worked in a bank, but it must have been a struggle financially. I wished so much I could go with her because things grew worse once she'd gone. Paul was the only ray of light. When I was fourteen he was seven and I often took him out to parks and other places with me at weekends and during the holidays. He would snuggle up to me on buses, and it made up for the bleakness at home. Needless to say I was never allowed to go to friends' houses, and certainly wouldn't have asked them back to mine. But I hatched my plans for leaving home as soon as I could.

Selina got married when she was just eighteen. In Jack's family she had found the love and security she didn't get in ours. She and I often talk about her wedding day, and her embarrassment at what Mum did. Selina was beautiful – I thought she was like the young Elizabeth Taylor. I was a bridesmaid and I still cringe at the vision of me in a yellow flock nylon dress, a lot taller than the other two bridesmaids. Mum had insisted the reception was to be at our house, but I'm sure Selina never imagined she would provide only

Marmite sandwiches and absolutely no alcohol, not even a sweet sherry to toast the bride and groom. Our dear mother disapproved of drinking.

I'm sure Jack's family had some booze in their car, but even they weren't brave enough to bring it in. I remember Jack's dad spotted the piano, a baby grand no less, and was just about to sit down and play something jolly, when Mum whisked away the stool. She wasn't going to let people she considered to be riff-raff touch her beloved ivories.

While this was going on, I was out in the garden with Andy, a very new boyfriend, having a sly gulp of vodka from a bottle he'd brought with him. It was a miracle he was there, but he'd phoned that morning while I was having my hair done, and Mum invited him. To this day I don't know why. He was a bit of a thug but she was always nice to men, and perhaps she liked his voice. So he came, which left me shaking in terror.

The wedding breakfast must have been one of the shortest in history. Jack's father ushered his family and Selina out to his car and on to a right royal knees-up at his house. I was eating leftover Marmite sandwiches for days.

That summer, Michael was set to leave the Royal Hospital School to go on to Nottingham University. He was only seventeen as he'd taken his A levels a year early and done astoundingly well. Dad asked me to go with him for Michael's last speech day: as head boy Michael would be escorting Lord Mountbatten around the school. I'd never been to Michael's school before, or on such a long train ride with Dad. It was a very hot day, and when we arrived all the boys were out on the parade ground in their naval uniforms and standing to attention. Every now and then one would faint with the heat, but he'd have water splashed on his face and be made to stand up again.

Finally a helicopter came down on the playing field, and Michael marched forward to meet and escort Lord Mountbatten to the school. My heart nearly burst with pride that he had been chosen for that prestigious job, and no man had ever looked more splendid than Mountbatten did with all his gold braid and medals, to say nothing of his sword, glinting in the sunlight.

With Selina married and Michael going to university, there was absolutely no reason for me to stay either. At sixteen I got a copy of the *Lady*, applied for a nanny's job near Hastings and was accepted.

It proved to be one of the smartest moves of my life. The people I worked for were lovely, as were their two children and their home. I learned such a lot from them.

2

My life in Hastings was happy. I did some nursery training and had a few boyfriends, including one called Brian, who wanted to marry me. He was nice enough, but too boring for me to contemplate spending the rest of my life with him so we parted ways. Sorry, Brian!

It was 1963 when my life started to get interesting. In midsummer of that year, now eighteen, I decided to put my head into the lion's den once again and return home to London.

Big mistake! Mum didn't want me at home, and was scathing that I wasn't going on to another nannying job. I hadn't ruled it out, but the big city lights beckoned, and I wanted to see what else was out there. Once when I was younger and had said I wanted to be a nurse, she had snorted with derision and said, 'You have no sense of responsibility.' Clearly, she didn't think a sense of responsibility was necessary for childcare. Needless to say, I didn't say so.

My sketchy plan for the future was to do office work for a bit while I considered my options. I was old enough now to apply for nurse training, but I didn't mention it to Mum for fear of her scorn. I got a job immediately at Pawson & Leaf, a warehouse by St Paul's Cathedral. When I say 'warehouse', it wasn't like Amazon, with forklifts and shelf units, more like an old-fashioned department store but wholesale, with lingerie, haberdashery, gents outfitting, household linens and anything else you can think of, in a four- or five-storey ancient, dusty, dark building. I think the starting pay was four pounds a week. Mum took two pounds ten shillings for my keep, and my season ticket on the train was ten shillings, leaving me with a pound. I'd earned that much at school by doing a paper round. But it wasn't just the lack of spending money that made me want to run away again: it was my stepmother's endless carping, belittling, and wearing me down with her nastiness. By then Selina had had her first baby, Karen, or I might have been tempted to ask to stay with her. One day I mentioned Selina and, quick as a flash, Mum said, 'She won't want you turning up on her doorstep.' Of course I believed her.

I liked the job at the warehouse. I was put in haberdashery, filling orders for rolls of Sylko, lengths of hair ribbon and bias binding. As I'd always been a keen dressmaker, I knew what everything was for and enjoyed working with it. My workmates were fun too,

38

except the fusty old departmental managers, who were like characters from *Are You Being Served?* But many of them dropped off to sleep after lunch, so we underlings were free to visit other departments.

My favourite person at Pawson's was an Anglo-Indian girl whose name I can't remember. She lived in the East End, and said she was the love child of Sabu the Elephant Boy. Whether that was true or not I didn't care, though I hope it was: we used to watch Sabu at Saturday-morning pictures. She was the telephonist, sitting in her switchboard kiosk to plug in callers to the right extension. I was in awe of that. It looked terribly difficult, but another couple of girls and I would often slink into her kiosk to chat. She got married during that time, and when she came back from her honeymoon, we were all agog to hear what 'It' was like. I can't speak for the others, but I was a virgin, and although I'd had a few close shaves with too eager boyfriends, I was determined to wait until I married.

She said it was all right, but she didn't like it when he made her kiss his 'thing'. I was nearly sick at the thought of that. A boy had once taken me to the pictures, and during the film he pushed my head down onto his opened trousers. I was so horrified I ran out! She laughed at my appalled expression. 'It wasn't his thing I minded so much,' she said. 'It was the attachments!'

I've laughed at those words so often since, that

I even had one of my characters say it. But back then I was very naive about almost everything.

My parents were teetotal, so I was brought up to think of public houses as places of evil. My early Roman Catholic memories had been replaced by staunch Church of England ones. I'd go to church both for Morning Prayer and Evensong most Sundays and until I was about ten there had been Sunday school too. Add to that going to a church school and I could probably be a contestant on *Mastermind* with my specialist subject the Bible. We were not allowed to go out to play on a Sunday. Toys and games were banned and reading had to be something Godly.

So, of course, I certainly didn't intend to kiss any man's willy. Ever.

The only reason I knew the basics about sex was because when Mum brought baby Paul home from London she felt she had to make sure we didn't get the idea you went on a train to London to get a baby. So, although I knew the rudiments of how babies were made, I was unsure of the technicalities. Mum, ever one for quite florid explanations, once told me, 'God made humans fall in love to separate them from the beasts of the field.' To be fair, I always liked that image and thought that once Cupid's dart had hit you marriage came next and then you'd be transported to something wonderful that made babies. So I was waiting for that special someone and a sign from the heavens that this was what He ordained.

I got a pay rise at Pawson's, and decided I earned enough now to live in a shared flat. God knows I couldn't take Mum any longer. I scoured the *Evening Standard* nightly looking for a likely home and finally found one I thought sounded right: 'Fifth girl to share flat in Earl's Court. £2 per week.' There was a phone number too, which I later learned was a shared pay phone on the ground floor.

The four girls at Warwick Road were not very welcoming when I went to meet them. At eighteen I was three or four years younger than they were, and they probably didn't want to wet-nurse some kid. But it seemed they had no other takers, and I could see why. The flat was crummy, on the top floor, and had damp patches on the wall. It had very little to recommend it to anyone but a desperate teenager needing a very low rent.

They told me their boyfriends were all rugby players, but I knew nothing about that species. I moved in on a Saturday, and they informed me their men usually stayed over. I had to share a room with two of the girls, and apart from being told there was a rota for taking the rubbish out, there was no encouragement to become friends.

I had been asleep for some time when they all came

rolling in with their men, drunk, noisy and totally unaware of their new flatmate. But it got worse. Once the lights were out and my two roommates had retired to their beds I was subjected to sounds of loud, bestial rutting. At times I was scared for the girls' lives. This was re-enacted on many other nights, and had there been some sort of communication between those girls and me I might have been less fraught about it. But they ignored me until they wanted something done. Then it was 'Your turn to take out the rubbish', 'You clean the bathroom.' What I'd heard convinced me that sex was painful, nasty and to be avoided at all costs.

One Friday night the other girls said they'd be throwing a party and asked if there was someone I'd like to invite. As I didn't think anyone at Pawson's would fit in with their rugby-playing men, I didn't ask anyone. The girls got in the drink, eight-pint tins of beer and cider, while the food consisted of crisps, and all the light-bulbs were changed to red ones.

I thought I looked really good on the night, my dark hair backcombed within an inch of its life and flicked up on my shoulders. I wore a white, silky, button-through shift dress with ruffles down the front. With my Cleopatra eye make-up and high heels, I probably looked as if I was in my mid-twenties, and after a couple of ciders I lost my nerves.

A very handsome man called Steven, with fair hair and blue eyes, wearing a smart, pale grey suit, took a great deal of interest in me, dancing with me, getting me drinks, and generally being lovely. By the early hours we'd been smooching for some time, and he asked me if I'd like to go to Brighton with him right then. He said he had an appointment there early on Saturday morning and afterwards we could explore the city. In my naivety I imagined it would take all night to drive to Brighton, or maybe my brain was clouded by cider, but I agreed and off we went.

When we arrived, no longer than an hour and a half later, he took me straight to a hotel. I assume he told the desk clerk I was his wife, and I couldn't refuse to go to his room without making myself look very foolish. I couldn't walk away either: I had no money on me and it was tipping down with rain. All I can say about that night is that I really believed we hadn't done the deed. I had always imagined that once you did, it when you were married, it would be wonderful. I wasn't married, it wasn't wonderful and it hurt. I thought of the motto 'Act in haste and repent at leisure.'

I woke the next morning to find myself in a seedy room. There were no ensuites in those days, you had to go down the landing to a bathroom, and I didn't have anything with me, not a toothbrush or face flannel. I was still wearing my party frock. It was such a cliché too: people were always joking about taking girls to Brighton to seduce them.

To be fair to Steven he was quite nice to me. He was at least twenty-five, maybe older, and he had the kind of confidence boys of my own age lacked. He had an appointment at a building site and I waited in his car feeling very glum. Afterwards, as it was still raining, he suggested we go back to London.

There was a weird atmosphere when I got back to the flat. The other girls kept looking at me and whispering. When one asked what the hotel was like I had a flash of insight and knew that they'd set me up. I felt sick for the remainder of the weekend. If any friend of mine had told me she was planning to drive off to Brighton in the middle of the night with a man she knew nothing about, I would have told her not to go. When I thought over the events of the previous evening I recalled Steven arriving and getting into a huddle with Judith, the nastiest of the girls, who pointed me out. She'd almost certainly encouraged him to drag me off to Brighton. So, I forced myself to smile and, through gritted teeth, I claimed my trip to Brighton had been lovely.

To my surprise Steven phoned me that week and asked me out to dinner. I went, because I guessed he had realized I was naive and felt bad at using that for his own ends. And, of course, a second date sent a silent message to my flatmates that I wasn't such a loser. He was different that evening, attentive and caring in as much as he said I should move somewhere with nicer flatmates. He'd only got to know them through rugby-playing friends. When he dropped me home in Warwick Road, he kissed me and wished me well. He didn't suggest meeting me again.

Two weeks later, and no period, I became very scared. I was sure I was overreacting, I couldn't be pregnant after just once, so I tried to ignore it. But one morning I had to rush to the bathroom to be sick. Judith saw me and told me I'd better find somewhere else to live as they didn't want someone like me there.

I wish I'd been brave enough to point out it was 'There but for the grace of God' that none of them were in the same situation, but I wasn't even sure I was pregnant. However, I knew I didn't want to stay sharing with such mean girls.

Shortly afterwards I found a better-paid job at a photographic laboratory in Holborn. From the start it was a laugh. The staff there were a wonderfully eclectic mix of people who, I came to realize many years later, wouldn't have fitted in anywhere else. The boss was another Hilda like Mum, a fire-eating dragon with a face like an uncooked currant bun, who shouted her orders and insulted us. Kathy, a petite, flame-haired girl with a huge bust, owned up to me that she'd been a hostess in a nightclub. Axel was from the Seychelles, played calypso songs on his guitar and sang; his then girlfriend Katy wasn't as smitten as he was and would soon disappear. There were others too, all equally entertaining, and as we took rolls of film from envelopes to be processed, we would fire paper clips at each other on rubber-band catapults.

As long as Hilda was out of the office there was so much laughter. A lot of films came in from laboratories: studied over a light box, they revealed nasty operations. A cry would go up when the film-cutters had something gruesome for us to see and we'd rush over. There was also a bit of porn, equally exciting but destined never to get back to the photographers: the law then stated that obscene pictures could not be sent via Her Majesty's Royal Mail. They would be sent a curt letter telling them to come in person to collect their prints. As you can imagine, few people called to claim them.

Meanwhile the Warwick Road girls began to ramp up their nastiness, especially when they caught me running for the bathroom to be sick again. 'You've got to go,' Judith said spitefully. 'If you don't go willingly we'll throw your stuff out on the street.'

I knew they would too, so I confided in Kathy at work. She was instantly concerned and told me she'd got pregnant at seventeen and her parents had blackmailed her boyfriend into marrying her. The baby was stillborn and her husband disappeared, not even going to the hospital to comfort her. Sad as her story was, Kathy was a fun-loving, big-hearted woman. I had instinctively told the right person. She comforted me, and said I had to wait a little longer to be sure, but she would help with getting me to a doctor. As for my flatmates, she said I must find somewhere else to live as soon as possible: they would only get more unpleasant.

One evening Steven turned up. I was on the doorstep, looking for my key and he stopped his car and beckoned to me. He took me to a nearby pub. Just the smell of beer and cigarette smoke made me feel faint. He saw how pale I'd gone and asked what was wrong and I said I was afraid I might be pregnant. Quick as a flash, he said, 'Well, don't expect me to help. I'm married.' A real charmer!

As I hadn't expected to see him again after the last date, I didn't for one moment think he was the honourable type, but a bit of sympathy and a kind word might have helped.

The very next evening when I came in from work, my four flatmates were lined up on the landing like an execution squad. 'You can pack your bag now and go,' Judith snarled. 'We don't want someone like you here.'

I was brave enough to point out what hypocrites they all were. In 1963 there was no Pill, so any one of them could have ended up pregnant. I added they were a filthy bunch too, that not one of them had a clue about hygiene, and I wondered how their boyfriends could stand the stench of them. Or the filth in the flat.

I packed my case and left, rushing over to Kathy's. She lived in Ladbroke Square in Notting Hill. In those days that area was pretty rough, and she shared with a much older woman she knew from her nightclub-hostessing days. That night Kathy told me she had wanted to move for a long time, and perhaps we could get a flat together. She said that Axel and Birdie at work were also looking for somewhere.

My first weekend with Kathy I tried the gin-and-boiling-hot-bath treatment. I was very sick and felt terrible, but nothing happened. She said we must make preparations, and a decent flat was a start. I found the flat for us, and if we lived there now the rent would be astronomical, as it was on the corner of Holland Park Avenue and another road, not too far from Holland Park tube station.

I was exploring the area that first Saturday, and as

I was about to walk down towards Shepherd's Bush, I saw a well-dressed man sticking a 'Flat to Let' notice on the front door. I leaped forward and, with a big smile, told him my friends and I were looking for a flat. He introduced himself as B. B. Brown, a name I've never forgotten, and he said if I called up my friends immediately, and we were prepared to sign a tenancy agreement, we could have it.

I rang Kathy to tell her and she answered so fast I wondered if she'd been sitting by the phone. She said she would run down to meet me. She must have done too, as she was there in the twinkling of an eye. B. B. Brown was sorting out mail in the hall.

The flat was great, sparsely furnished, but that didn't bother us. The sitting room was round, like a tower, there were two bedrooms, a bathroom and a small kitchen. It was no palace but, compared with most rented places in London at that time, it was fine.

Kathy flirted with B. B., and in the months to come I was to see her use her wiles on many men. He got out a tenancy agreement. Kathy signed it, and gave him a cheque for a month's rent in advance. When he left, we danced around the flat whooping and laughing. Neither of us could believe we'd found somewhere so nice so easily. I could only offer to give her my share of the rent each week, but she said we'd sort it out if Birdie and Axel moved in.

That was one of Kathy's wonderful traits. She was generous, kind and motherly, along with being something of a sex-bomb. To my sadness I lost contact with her many years ago. The last I heard of her she'd married a waiter called Graham. But she was there for me when I most needed a friend.

Birdie and Axel were only too happy to move in with us. Kathy and I had the bigger bedroom with two single beds, overlooking Holland Park, leaving the other room with a double bed for Axel and Birdie. I owned two sheets, a pillowcase, a towel and that was it, but Kathy filled the taxi with her stuff. That night she showed me her knickers collection. I kid you not, she must have had at least fifty pairs and, except for a few, they were all saucy. Her best pair was two red hearts with black lace, joined by red ribbons. She said she'd bought them for Valentine's night back in February when she had a hot date. He disappeared shortly after, and Kathy came out with my favourite of her sayings: 'I can get any bloke I want, but sadly I can't keep them.'

She could too. Just as she'd charmed B. B. Brown into letting us the flat without any references, she could lure any man.

You must remember as you read this how innocent, gullible and trusting I was at eighteen. I hadn't encountered Real Life. Home was middle class and almost Victorian, then my nannying job had been with rich people who had a beautiful home. There was so much I didn't know, and when Kathy told me about her life as a nightclub hostess, I was shocked. She said she had to ask the man she spent the evening with for ten pounds, that was her fee, and she encouraged him to drink a great deal, for the benefit of the club. The men often asked for more after they left and she would fix a price for sleeping with them. I was horrified, but managed to hide it. After all, in theory she was taking care of me now. Later she told me that our flat would be ideal for her to make some money on the side. Some evenings, she would go out into Holland Park Avenue and wait by a phone box, and if she brought a man back, I was to go into the sitting room.

She made it clear it wasn't her plan to involve me in this. Thankfully. After my one nasty experience I would have signed a pledge never to sleep with another man. And then she said the next thing we had to do was take me to a doctor. I thought for a minute she was aiming to get me a backstreet abortion – after all, she had recommended the gin and the hot bath – but that wasn't her plan. She was a truly good person, protective of weaker souls, and she sensed I needed a stand-in mum. Or a big sister.

Birdie and Axel moved in the following week, by

which time Kathy had found there were two Australian men upstairs, both very good-looking. The one she fancied was a surfing champion.

But the four of us had hardly got settled in the flat when our boss at the film laboratory sacked us, with most of the rest of the staff. Her excuse was that she was overstaffed. She gave us an extra week's money in lieu of notice, but we were out of the door on Friday afternoon.

It was a real blow. I was quietly confident I could get a clerical job when the employment agencies opened on Monday, while Kathy could do shorthand and typing so she'd be okay too. But Axel had a problem. People were not kind to men and women of colour back then. We all got drunk that weekend, and Kathy invited the Aussies upstairs to come down and join us. Norman was the one she fancied, though I don't recall him wanting her. The other was Peter, a good-looking, dark-haired man of twenty-three, rather serious and reserved.

I don't remember much about that evening, except I trod on some broken glass and cut my bare foot. Peter took me upstairs to clean the wound and put a plaster on it. Maybe it was his kindness to me, but I started to cry and told him my father and stepmother couldn't care less about me.

Monday came round and off I went to scour the

agencies for a job, and by the time I got home I'd landed one as a filing clerk at a solicitor's chambers in Chancery Lane. If Kathy could pull any man she wanted but not keep them, I could chat myself into any job but not keep it. Sometimes I've been sacked, others I just walked away from, but in the sixties there was plenty of work. CVs hadn't been invented, or if they had they hadn't worked their way down to the lowly jobs I went for.

Kathy and Birdie both signed on as temps, and Axel got a job as a chef in a Wimpy Bar, a forerunner of McDonald's. As it turned out Axel's job was good for all of us: he'd smuggle home eggs, bacon and frankfurters, and fed us when we'd run out of money. He had a sunny disposition that kept us going when winter arrived and the flat was freezing and we didn't have enough money for the electricity meter.

I kept putting off going to a doctor, why I don't know. Maybe I imagined if I didn't think about it, my problem would go away. Meanwhile, I was having fun with Kathy. She knew an American airmen's club called the Douglas House, in Bayswater. The airmen stationed at places like Lakenheath were paid fortnightly and would rush to London for a night out. On those weekends, Kathy and I glammed ourselves up and off we went. We had to get someone to sign us in, but that was never a problem, though ditching them once we got inside often was. Kathy always signed herself in as Katharine Hepburn, after the actress. I don't know why I didn't use a false name but I was plain Lesley Sargent.

The Douglas House had a great cabaret, and quite famous names played there, including Georgie Fame and the Blue Flames. There were tap dancers, comedians, magicians, all sorts. Kathy even ensnared Georgie Fame one night. I had to sleep in the sitting room. The airmen were very gentlemanly, at least the ones I met were, but I hated that the Black men had to sit on one side, segregated from the whites.

On 22 November 1963, I finally plucked up the courage to let Kathy take me to a doctor. It was foggy, the street just off Westbourne Park was squalid and the doctor's surgery on the corner equally nasty. As we walked into the dark green waiting room, which smelt of mould, it seemed just the sort of place where they would do abortions. I nearly ran out, but Kathy had a tight hold of my arm, and I suppose I knew now that this wasn't something I could run from.

The doctor was small, rotund and wore thick glasses. He told me to go behind the screen, take off my knickers and get on the couch. Kathy sat on the chair, waving a finger at me to warn me to behave. She hadn't told me I'd have an internal examination, and I was so shocked I was rigid. Kathy told me afterwards she'd noted that my toes, visible at the end of the screen, were screwed up.

'Yes, my dear, you are definitely expecting a baby,' the doctor said. His tone was kindly, and when I began to cry he patted my shoulder. 'I take it this wasn't the news you wanted, then?'

He gave me a prescription for iron pills, told me he reckoned my due date to be in July and hastily wrote a letter for me to take to Hammersmith Hospital's antenatal department. He told me the almoner would be there to talk to me as I wasn't married.

We left that surgery with me in shock. It was real now. There was a baby inside me, and I couldn't pretend otherwise any more. Kathy said she would stand by me and help, and she was sure Birdie and Axel would too. Then she suggested we go home and change to head out to the Douglas House as that would cheer me up. I wasn't convinced that anything short of sudden death would do that, but I agreed.

I remember I went to great pains with my appearance that night. I wore a red sheath dress, reminding myself that very soon I wouldn't be able to get into it. I put my hair up in a French pleat and stuck on false eyelashes. We hopped on the tube to Queensway and walked down the road, but as we got to the Douglas House we were amazed to see the windows blacked out and more black material draped around the double doors.

A burly airman in uniform stood at the door. His stance and expression told us something had happened.

'What is it?' Kathy asked.

'The President is dead,' he intoned, as if struggling with his emotions. 'He was assassinated today in Dallas.'

I'm ashamed to admit my first thought was not for Kennedy, or his wife and family, but that I couldn't get blotto and forget the doctor's words. But Kathy and I managed to say how sorry we were, and beat a hasty retreat to a cellar bar just around the corner. I was a rarity in those days in that I didn't smoke – it was another thing Mum had warned me off, saying it made girls look cheap. Back then smoking and drinking weren't frowned upon for pregnant women too. But that cellar bar was incredibly smoky and in no time at all, even before I'd finished my first rum and blackcurrant, my eyes were running and the smoke was affecting my false eyelashes.

A chap came over to me and asked why I was crying. To my eternal shame, I said, 'Because President Kennedy is dead. It's so very sad.'

He gave me a hug and said it was nice that an English girl had such compassion for America. Over his shoulder I saw Kathy smirk.

People often said for donkey's years after that everyone remembered where they were when the President was killed. Each time I've heard it I feel ashamed that I'd been so shallow. But to me the date is linked inextricably with the confirmation of my pregnancy.

I managed to block my 'problem', as I thought of it then, from my mind until well after Christmas and New Year 1964. I didn't show and I felt well. Life was fun at the flat, except in really cold weather when we'd huddle round the one-bar electric fire with our coats on. My new job at the solicitor's was very interesting, and while I was filing papers I read everything. The wife of a Yeoman of the Guard at the Tower of London with five children was petitioning for a divorce because of his cruelty: that was a case I followed avidly. I had never really imagined Yeomen to be real men – to me they were like Disney characters – but this one had thrown his wife downstairs, locked her out in the cold and beaten her till she had to be hospitalized. The poor lady had no one to turn to, and life in the Tower of London must have been pretty claustrophobic.

There was also a great deal of correspondence coming in about the Profumo affair. I don't know if Mr Alton, the solicitor who employed me, was acting for someone in the case or just had a professional interest in it, but Mandy Rice-Davies came to the office one day, and I made her some tea. She was truly gorgeous, just as they said, 'a walking wolf whistle'.

There was also quite a lot of stuff about Peter Rachman, the slum landlord with whom Mandy and Christine Keeler had been up to no good. I read, appalled, about the way he treated his tenants, packing them in, several families to one room, and sending heavies round to silence them if they complained. I even went to the addresses of places he had owned in the Paddington area and marvelled that anyone could live anywhere so ghastly.

Much of what I learned in that period came in useful years later when I began writing. I think I was born with a social conscience, but to discover so much about inequality, that some rich and privileged people were treating the poor and disadvantaged so badly was a real eye-opener.

Meanwhile, back at our flat, Kathy popped out to the telephone box now and then to pick up a punter. I never saw these men: she told me to stay in Axel and Birdie's room with them, or the sitting room, until she called the all-clear. She had one regular who liked her to walk around the bedroom naked with just the light of the street lamps on her. That was something to giggle at.

She not only protected me from what she was doing, but also spent her earnings on us three. Money went into the electricity meter, we had fish and chips quite often, and she bought me some clothes from Shepherd's Bush Market and a few baby items. Axel was of the opinion she was a nymphomaniac. That was the sort of thing men said in those days. I doubt there was any truth in it. But there was an element of needing sex in her behaviour – she seemed to crave it. Maybe she mistook it for affection? She was always waylaying poor Norman upstairs. On occasion she'd go into his flat and climb into his bed to wait for him to come home. Peter, his flatmate, who had become my friend, was concerned for my safety and really didn't approve of what Kathy got up to.

Christmas arrived and I went home to Kathy's parents. Only then was I to realize what had caused some of her behaviour. They had one of those pristine bungalows where nothing is out of place – even the spare toilet roll was covered by a doll with a crocheted crinoline. Her father said very little and her mother was like a glacier. Over the two days we were there she made many disparaging remarks about Kathy as a child, sharp, nasty comments about her looks, her lack of ambition and drive, and her inability to settle down with a nice man. I took that to mean she wanted Kathy to have a man like her father, a yes-man who worked hard, got no affection at home, and let her rule the roost. It was no wonder Kathy was always searching for love. Naive as I was, I realized her promiscuity was probably preventing the kind of man she wanted and needed from seeing the kind, generous, loving woman she was.

Just after Christmas I took in a box for the couple who lived on the ground floor, and had gone away. We threw a party on New Year's Eve, Chuck Berry's 'Memphis Tennessee' and the Beatles' 'Twist and Shout' blaring from Kathy's portable record player. I don't know who opened the neighbours' box, but it was a case of champagne, and soon everyone was swigging it like there was no tomorrow.

Peter and Norman had come down from upstairs to join in, just before we greeted the New Year. At about two in the morning Peter took my hand and dragged me unwillingly out and up to his flat. He made me a cup of tea, and then came the lecture. 'You can't carry on like this, Lesley,' he said very firmly. 'You are having a baby and I think it's time you looked at what that means.'

I was flabbergasted. No one else had guessed, not at work or anywhere. Even Kathy's mother hadn't sniffed it out.

'I've got sisters,' he said, by way of an explanation. 'I can't sit back and watch you act so irresponsibly.

Are you booked into hospital for the birth? Where do you think you're going to live? And what are you going to live on?'

Needless to say, I burst into tears. These questions often popped into my head at night, but by day I could forget them. I admitted that the baby was due in early July and I hadn't yet been to the hospital as instructed by the doctor. Peter asked about my parents. Of course I knew I'd get no assistance from them, and I told him that Steven, the baby's father, was long gone.

'You must go to the hospital. They'll put you in touch with someone to help you. There are hostels for unmarried mothers – at least, there are in Australia. I'm sure they have them here. I know it must seem very scary but, Lesley, it'll be a whole lot worse if you wait till the very last minute and haven't made any plans.'

I slept in his bed for the rest of the night, no sex, he just cuddled me, and from downstairs the din of the party carried on. His brotherly kindness made me see he was right.

January was the month of reckoning. First, our downstairs neighbours came back and asked for their champagne. I had to admit, to my shame, that it had been drunk at a party. I expected them to go mad and insist we pay them for it, but maybe the sight of me quaking in my boots softened them so they forgave us. How kind that was of them, and how generous. More than thirty-five years later, when my girls had a party while I was away, their friends saw a box of champagne and drank it all. I wasn't so kind, especially as I had to grovel to my neighbours because of the terrible noise from the party.

But back to January 1964. I took a morning off work and went to the antenatal department at Hammersmith Hospital. I was given a due date of 4 July, and saw the almoner, who dealt with social problems. She said she'd put me in touch with someone from the Moral Welfare Association.

'It would be wisest to have your baby adopted,' she said crisply. 'Without parental help, it is impossible for unmarried mothers to bring up a child alone. Best that you don't even consider it.'

Just telling me the due date put a thousand images into my head. My 'problem' was gone. Now it was a real-life baby in my tummy. I imagined pushing a pram in the park, cuddling him by the fire, giving him a bath, and if he turned out to be she, dressing her in frilly pink things. I wanted to give my baby the childhood I hadn't had, for him or her to know that they were loved. I wanted to keep my baby and I vowed to myself that I would.

Next came the dreaded visit from Miss Hammick, a social worker. I had the windows open in the flat for a whole day to get rid of the smell of the New Year's Eve party. I scrubbed the carpet, put some flowers in a vase, and left a copy of the *Nursery World* with some baby knitting patterns on the coffee-table to prove I was committed.

Miss Hammick was just what I expected, a woman very like some of Mum's old nursing pals: dried up and disapproving, probably in her late fifties with a thin, lined face, wearing a tweed coat and a brown velour hat. When she spoke it was like hearing Mum with her plummy voice, and a similar note of disapproval. She told me a well-brought-up girl like me would be offered a place in Swiss Cottage, north London. I would go there six weeks before the birth and stay until six weeks afterwards. At that point I would hand over my baby to his or her new parents at the adoption society's offices. 'You won't meet them, of course. They'll be in another room. Later you'll get letters and photographs to let you know how Baby is progressing. At six months the adoption will take place and you will have no more contact with the new parents.'

'But I want to keep my baby,' I ventured.

She looked at me as if I was something she'd trodden in. There was no compassion in her eyes, and her mouth was set in a straight line. I think if she'd been able to she'd have liked to take a stick to me too.

'For a girl in your position it is virtually impossible to keep your baby,' she said, in a harsh tone. 'Now we will fill in the forms and get this all going.'

Another humiliation was being given a card for the 'special clinic'. I had no idea what that was.

When I arrived I saw a sign saying, 'No names are used here. You will be given a number.'

Suddenly it dawned on me that this was the department that dealt with venereal diseases, and I was even more horrified to think anyone would imagine I had one of those.

I didn't tell anyone at work about my situation, just wore a roll-on, as they were called, a kind of light-weight corset with suspenders to attach your stockings to. My nineteenth birthday arrived in February and Peter gave me a toy koala bear. I thought it was the best present I'd ever had. Then, in early March, Kathy became ill. She thought it was German measles and, of course, that is dangerous for pregnant women. Peter was about to move into a bedsitter in Earl's Court and said I was to go with him to keep safe.

As it turned out Kathy had more than German measles: she had shingles too, and her father came and took her home. Soon after, Birdie and Axel went to a room in Kentish Town and the flat was abandoned.

Peter's room in Barkston Gardens was small and

horrible, with a one-ring gas burner to cook on and a gas fire along with peeling, stained wallpaper. We had to share the bathroom with other tenants, and had only a single bed. But Peter was planning to go on a tour around France, Germany, Austria, Italy and Spain, as all visiting Aussies did at that time. He agreed he would give me money for the rent while he was away, so his stuff could stay with me. He pointed out it was far cheaper to live here, and I'd be warmer and safer on my own once he'd gone. He promised he'd be back before the end of May when I had to go to the mother-and-baby home. He spoke to the boys in the room next door and asked them to keep an eye on me, but I didn't know that until the one time I needed some help.

Peter worked for a shipping company, and he was always very smartly dressed. I would take his clothes and mine to the launderette one evening a week. I borrowed an iron from the landlady in the basement and ironed his shirts on the bed.

In those days Earl's Court was known as Kangaroo Valley on account of the hordes of Aussies and New Zealanders doing their customary trip to England. On Saturdays and Sundays Peter would take me sightseeing all around London, snapping endless photographs. We went to St Paul's, the Tower, Greenwich and many more places. Later I was to wonder what his family would think when he got home and showed them the pictures and saw him with a pregnant English girl. But Peter was forthright. He knew he wasn't responsible for my pregnancy and I suppose he felt he didn't need to hide me because he was doing the right thing in looking after me.

I took him to visit my sister in Plumstead one day. In his forthright manner he said, 'They wouldn't keep animals in a house so small back home.' Needless to say, my sister was really offended. I don't think I told her I was pregnant as I didn't want my parents to know. But maybe she guessed.

I became quite adept at cooking Peter and me a meal on that gas ring. Only simple things like chops and mashed potato. Peter often said I was a miracle worker. But all too soon he was preparing to leave for the continent. I made him a pile of Marmite sandwiches to take with him. He wrote from France to say he had been eating them for nearly a week. He also called me his English rose and said he'd never met anyone with so much courage. That meant a lot to me.

I tried not to cry when he left. In fact, I made jokes about having the bed all to myself, but I felt as if my heart had been torn out. I had plans for things to do to fill the evenings and weekends. I had a portable Singer sewing machine so I could make some maternity dresses and things for the baby. And I bought enough dark brown wool to knit Peter a cardigan.

I nearly didn't survive long enough to make anything. The gas must have run out in the morning before I went to work, and when I got home I put some money in the meter. Then I lay down on the bed for a rest. I fell asleep and the gas tap was open. Furthermore the sash window had been sealed with Elastoplast to keep out draughts. We hadn't taken it off as it was so cold, which meant the room was virtually airtight.

The boys in the next room smelt gas, and when I didn't open the door at their knock, they broke in, dragged me out unconscious and called an ambulance. I spent two nights in hospital. I remember a vicar came to speak to me. He must have thought I'd gassed myself on purpose. But it transpired that a previous tenant in the room had committed suicide and that was why she'd sealed the window.

My mind often turns to that nasty room in Earl's Court. I was terribly alone at that time. I went to work and came home, didn't see anyone as I was saving every penny I could. I made two maternity dresses, some nightdresses for my baby, and I knitted Peter's brown cardigan. It was like a prison cell, that room, with no comforts, no armchair or TV. I didn't even have a radio. The weekends were the worst, though. I'd walk for miles so I could sleep when I got home. All around me people were laughing and talking together, and I had no one. I was absolutely terrified at what lay before me, and there was no one I could share it with.

Mr Alton, the solicitor I worked for, finally spoke up as my pregnancy became apparent to everyone. He asked me what I was going to do and was really kind. I've always found Jewish people far less judgemental than others – the couple whose champagne we'd drunk were Jewish too. He even brought me a few little matinée jackets that had been his sons'. He made me laugh too by saying how much he would miss me. He said, 'You've made yourself indispensable by constructing a completely unique filing system, which only you understand. But you always know exactly where to put your hand on anything I ask for.'

The last few weeks of work were hell on the tube. It was hot and airless. I often had to get off, take a few deep breaths, then get back on. Finally, after two and a bit months Peter came home. It was so good to see him again, but he slept in his sleeping bag on the floor – there wasn't room in the bed. His birthday was on 2 May, and I'd finished the cardigan, putting nice leather buttons on it. I think it was the only thing I ever knitted that came out perfectly. I left my job just after Peter got back and Mr Alton gave me thirty pounds as a leaving present – a small fortune to me – and made me promise to let him know when my baby arrived.

Then it was time to go to Swiss Cottage.

I wasn't sorry to leave the squalid room in Barkston Gardens, all those stairs, waiting for the bathroom and often needing to clean it before I could use it. But I was terrified, even with Peter at my side. I'd read a book on childbirth, but that was just facts, not how I'd cope emotionally. I was afraid the other girls would be nasty, and I expected the matron to be like Miss Hammick. I didn't want to leave Peter either. But as he'd said he'd never met anyone with so much courage, I didn't want to let him down.

We went on the tube, Peter carrying my case in one hand, my sewing machine in the other. It was a glorious sunny day, but even that couldn't lift my spirits. 'I'll come and visit you,' he said, as we walked to the house from the tube station. 'You'll soon make friends with the other girls. I expect you're a bit frightened, but it's the best place for you. Look how nice it is.'

He was right about it looking nice. The house in Swiss Cottage, called Oak Lodge, was lovely, with pretty, well-established gardens bright with flowers, and big semi-detached houses with wooden verandas at the front.

The door was opened by a heavily pregnant girl, who smiled cheerfully. 'Come in and I'll get Miss Mansell,' she said.

My first impression of my home for the next twelve weeks was a swathe of sunshine coming through a window on the wide stairs, a smell of furniture polish and someone playing a piano. A door opened into what I realized was the nursery, and I glimpsed a row of little canvas cots. A girl came out with a tray of used feeding bottles, nodded at me and disappeared down the stairs into the basement. As there was no crying, it seemed the babies had just been fed.

'Lesley?' a soft voice asked, and I got my first look at Miss Mansell, whom I would grow to admire, love and be inspired by. She was small, slim, had a lovely porcelain complexion and kind grey eyes. Although she had to have been in her fifties, judging by her grey hair, she looked much younger. 'You can leave your things there for now, but say goodbye to your friend and we'll go into my office for a chat,' she said. She turned away and I threw myself at Peter for one last hug.

'You'll be fine. I can see she's a good woman,' he whispered, against my neck. 'I'm going to miss you more than you'll miss me.'

I remembered touching his cheek as I looked into his dark eyes, noting as if for the first time that he had a crop of freckles on his nose and very straight white teeth. I wished it could be like it was in a work of fiction, that he'd tell me he loved me and wanted to marry me. But I knew deep down his feelings for me were like mine for him. We had become close friends, but that was all.

I stood in the open door onto the veranda to wave goodbye, biting back tears. Then I went to see Miss Mansell.

'Well, Lesley,' she said, with a smile, after she'd explained the rules, how the home worked and taken my maternity allowance book so she could cash the money each week to go towards my keep, 'by the time you leave here in approximately twelve weeks you'll feel as if you've been through an emotional washing-machine. You will see the luckier girls leaving with their parents and their baby. Many parents do change their minds once they see their grandchild. You'll also see girls leaving with their social worker, to hand their baby to adoptive parents.'

She paused, reached forward and took my hands in hers. 'Many people claim it's cruel not to take a baby away from its mother at birth. They say that to expect the mother to care for her baby for six weeks, then give it up, is barbaric. But it isn't. By feeding and caring for your baby for six weeks you have time to think everything through. To make the right decision for you and your baby. And I'll be here as a sounding board if you need me.'

There in that cosy little office I came to terms with what lay ahead. I would be with other girls in the same boat. I'd have the wonderful Miss Mansell close by, and it was early summer: nothing looks as bad when the sun is shining.

'I want to keep my baby,' I said.

'I've seen that on your notes,' she said, and half smiled. 'It is extremely difficult for girls without parental support or the baby's father to help them, but if that is what you want, Lesley, I'll try to help you with it.'

I left the office with a girl called Dorothy, who was asked to show me round. She was tall and classically beautiful, with her hair in two thick brown plaits. She was to become my best friend.

3

Oak Lodge soon became a very happy place for me to be. There were around sixteen pregnant girls, and twelve new mothers, but our two groups didn't meet up much except at mealtimes as the mums were busy feeding their babies and doing their chores. They tended to rest in the afternoons if they'd been up at night. We pregnant girls slept in a couple of dormitories on the first floor, the mums on the floor above. At night one mum slept in the nursery on a rota system so she could call the mum of a crying baby.

The pregnant girls had chores to do as well, washing floors, polishing them and cleaning bathrooms. It was considered good exercise. Many of the girls resented it, but I enjoyed it. After all, I was in a good place with no real worries. Dorothy and I volunteered for polishing the dormitory floors. We tied dusters to our feet and played at being ice-skaters, scooting up and down the room, polishing as we went and singing at the top of our lungs. In the afternoon we were allowed out for a couple of hours, and mostly we went to look in John Barnes on Finchley Road. Or we lay around in the garden in the sun.

Our babies were to be born at St Mary's maternity home on Hampstead Heath, and we had to walk up there each week for the antenatal clinic. I loved Hampstead village – there were so many pretty little shops but, of course, I was saving every penny. I think we got about ten shillings out of the maternity allowance as pocket money. I bought knitting wool for matinée jackets.

Dorothy had worked at the Foreign Office and I used to call her Dot of the FO because she used a lot of acronyms. We never talked about our babies' fathers, but I suspect hers, like mine, was a married man. She was not only stunningly beautiful but very intelligent. We would talk about books and put the world to rights, but she was naughty, too, like me and we both enjoyed bending the rules.

The high spot of the week was *Top of the Pops*, and the TV would be turned on just as we were finishing the evening meal. I can't really remember who we saw performing, other than Tom Jones and Herman's Hermits. But regardless of who was on, we'd all join in singing with them. A great many records from that time are stuck in my head and whenever I hear them I go straight back there. Chuck Berry's 'No Particular Place to Go' is one. It was a marvellously apt song for Dot and me to sing while polishing the floors. Then there was 'You're My World' by Cilla Black. We'd sing that together, using a hairbrush as a microphone. We thought we were brilliant, but no doubt we looked very funny with our maternity dresses tucked into our knickers for the polishing.

My claim to fame was knowing Millie of 'My Boy Lollipop' fame. I didn't really 'know' her as such, but my old friend and stand-in mum, Kathy, had returned to London and was living in Westbourne Grove next door to Millie and her family. I went to visit her about a month before I went to Oak Lodge, and saw Millie singing on a record stall in Portobello Road Market. Kathy reported that limousines came to her house to collect her and she had fabulous new clothes. There was something about Millie's rags-to-riches story that convinced me my life would turn out okay too.

Miss Mansell informed us one morning that there would be a little party for the members of the Moral Welfare Association one Friday evening. She was hoping it would be warm enough to hold it in the garden, and suggested that some of us might like to do a party piece.

Many of the girls were as imaginative as a rice pudding, but I thought of doing a little piece on germs. My plan was to write short rhyming couplets about where they were found, acted out by girls dressed as germs. We would sashay down the fire escape into the garden like models. Costumes would basically be a black stocking over our heads tied in a knot, and a dress suitable for the character of the germ.

My favourite, which I wrote for Dorothy, needed a special costume. Miss Mansell led us to a dressing-up box in the attic and there, among many interesting items, we found a very glamorous beaded maternity smock. My words for Dorothy to sashay down the fire escape to (hopefully) thunderous applause were: 'My name is Dorothy, the germ from the Hilton. I'm much too grand to be killed in Milton.'

I had virtually rags to wear as 'Lesley the desperate germ from the loo. She likes to live in pee and poo.' As my stepmother often said, I couldn't resist being vulgar.

It was warm that night, and our little show made all those do-gooders laugh. I heard one snooty woman say, in her braying voice, 'It's so nice that those Poor Unfortunate Girls have found ways to entertain us.' Dorothy and I managed to lift a bottle of cider and hid it in the sluice room to which we made frequent visits to glug it down.

Most of the girls hated church on Sundays, but to Dorothy and me it was an excuse to dig out our best dresses and a couple of hats we'd found in the attic. We had to sit in the back row of pews, of course, so as to not distress the local gentry. No doubt they sterilized our seats after we'd left. Having had such a religious childhood I would offer up prayers for a miracle in the shape of a job and a home for when my baby was born, and I fully believed it would happen. I think Dorothy just liked the peace in the church.

Then one night Dorothy went into labour. She came to my bed and shook me awake. I had to hand it to her, she knew how to dress stylishly, even for labour. She wore white high heels and a very smart dress. She'd even neatly plaited her hair. I went to rouse Miss Mansell and begged to be allowed to go with Dorothy. But it did no good. 'Dorothy is perfectly able to go alone,' she said firmly. 'Neither of you two is of a nervous disposition.'

I watched Dorothy go down the path and get into the ambulance alone, marvelling that she walked in those high heels like a model. If I hadn't timed her contractions before calling Miss Mansell and found them coming every two minutes I would have believed she wasn't in any pain at all. As she turned to wave to me and blow a kiss I vowed to myself that when my time came I'd be equally brave.

Dorothy's little girl was named Samantha. Years later my eldest daughter wanted to give that name to her new sister. It brought so much back. Dorothy's Samantha had a shock of dark hair and was a very pretty baby. My baby girl was lovely too and I did call her Samantha, thinking fondly of Dorothy.

While Dorothy did her ten-day stint in hospital I got to know a new girl called Linda. Some of the girls giggled about her because she read poetry. That just made me like her more. She was a florist, which appealed to me. I didn't know then that she would be my saviour in more ways than one. Or that some forty-five years later I would find her again on the other side of the world. Some bonds can never be broken.

But back to 1964, I was soon in hospital too, not in labour but because the doctor thought I had a dangerous complication. I didn't, as it turned out, but because I was under twenty-one they had to get my father's permission to give me a caesarean if necessary. It made me very nervous. I hadn't wanted my parents to know, and for them to hear it in this way was awful. I fully expected Dad and my stepmother to sweep in like avenging angels, but they didn't come or even write. Presumably because they didn't care.

The problem the doctors were concerned about involved taking me by ambulance to the London Hospital in Whitechapel where they gave my tummy a rather weird X-ray. I had to stand up with my back resting on something, drink water constantly and they X-rayed me as I peed. Talk about glamour!

As my baby showed no sign of coming of his own

accord, on 11 July they induced me. I remember that when the labour pains started Dusty Springfield was on the ward television singing 'I Just Don't Know What to Do with Myself'. Yet another song that would be tucked away in my memory bank as it was so appropriate for the moment. As the labour grew strong they moved me into a room on my own.

There can be nothing more terrifying than to be alone in labour for a first baby. It grew dark outside, but no one came to put on a light. I couldn't believe how bad the pain was and that no one cared enough to check on me.

Eventually a Polish midwife came, and she was very kind and calm. I had no pain relief, only gas and air right at the end, and made a point of not screaming. My baby was born at 3.20 a.m., a little boy weighing seven pounds thirteen ounces. As the midwife put him into my arms and I saw his little face I fell deeply in love with him. I told the midwife I wanted to keep him, and she looked doubtful. 'It will be so very hard for you both,' she said. 'When I first came to England and had my three children I had a big struggle. My husband left me, and we lived in two rooms. So I know what I am talking about.'

'I'll find a way,' I said confidently. In the afterglow of birth I believed anything was possible. I called my son Warren John.

Miss Hammick came to see me and advised me against trying to keep Warren. But I was convinced I could find a job and a home, and all would be well.

The saddest thing that happened at that time was Peter coming to see me to tell me he was returning to Australia with a bunch of young boys on the Big Brother scheme. It was a plan for good men like him to take young unaccompanied boys, and watch over them on the voyage. I did my best not to cry as I could see he was worried about me, but he held Warren, told me he was beautiful and that I'd be a great mother. As Peter walked away, the tears fell that I'd held back. He had been the best of friends just when I needed one, and I knew I'd never forget him.

After ten days I was back in Oak Lodge on a cloud of happiness and self-belief. I volunteered for laundry duty with Dorothy even though it meant starting up the boiler for the nappies even before the 6 a.m. feed. It was lovely weather that summer, and it was good to be out in the garden hanging up nappies so early: it meant I had a longer day with Warren. There was a veranda at the front of the home and we put the little cribs out there in good weather. Warren became lightly tanned and I joked he looked like a little surfer in his vest. I was applying for every appropriate job in the *Lady*, convinced that the equivalent of a fairy godmother would reply offering me a job and a home.

One by one I saw my friends leave, either collected by parents who'd decided they wanted to be grand-parents, or after handing over their babies. Dorothy was one of the latter and I'll never forget the courage of all those forced to give up their babies. Dorothy didn't come straight back from the adoption society as she was supposed to. She told me later she went to Hampstead Heath and walked for miles. I know she must have been howling, but she didn't admit it. I admired her stoic calm, but she didn't fool me into thinking she was fine: I could see the deep sorrow in her eyes.

I kept in touch with several of the girls I met at Oak Lodge for some years, Dorothy, Linda and a girl called Judy. I heard Dorothy became a doctor, and she sadly faded out of my life. Judy lived with me for a time, and we had many adventures together until she succumbed to mental-health problems. As for Linda, I'll come back to her.

I had several replies about a job and a home from the *Lady*. Some of them were weird, like a widowed shepherd in Nairn, in the far north of Scotland. He had six children and I imagined him in some grim little bothy. Then there was a man in Majorca, who sounded lovely. He was an English businessman, wanted a housekeeper and liked the idea of her having a child. He even sent pictures of his villa overlooking the sea. But Miss Mansell read the letter, looked at the pictures and warned me he sounded too good to be true. She said it would be better to find a place in England. Wiping tears from her eyes, she added that she wished she could keep Warren and me there to help at the home, but the committee wouldn't agree. As far as they were concerned I was a failure because I hadn't done the sensible thing and given up my son.

As time was running out I accepted a housekeeping job with an elderly Brigadier Pennyquick and his wife, in Heathfield, Sussex. It didn't sound wonderful, but at least I would be safe. On the day before I was due to go to Heathfield the man from Majorca telephoned the home. He was booked into the Savoy and had a gorgeous deep voice. He also sounded kind and genuine but I had to tell him I had agreed to work for someone else.

I have often regretted not taking a chance on him. As things turned out he might have been the answer to all my prayers. I doubt he'd have been as cruel as the Pennyquicks were.

The following day I was on the train to Haywards Heath, with Warren in my arms. Sadly it transpired that I had picked the absolute worst job possible.

The Pennyquicks were not just old and very grand but also cruel do-gooders. They thought taking in an 'unfortunate' was good for their souls. Mrs P would walk past Warren's carrycot on wheels, which she had loaned me the money to buy, look down on him and say, 'Poor unfortunate child, what will become of you?' She never once picked him up and even took my milk tokens to pay her milkman. I was breastfeeding Warren and really should have been drinking a pint every day but all I got was tea. She would make a small roast chicken last almost a week between the three of us and I was hungry all the time.

They were evil enough, but the house felt even more so. Dark, draughty, lots of rooms no one ever went into, cobwebs, years of neglect that would have taken an army to put right. Their one real priority was cleaning their vast collection of silver, which included, among other things, two huge pheasants. They made me sit in a poky, airless room in the evenings to polish it all, tureens, serving dishes, candlesticks, trinket boxes and endless heaps of cutlery. This treasure trove must have been worth a fortune, yet they lived like church mice. At night if I woke to feed Warren there was invariably a big spider crawling up the bedroom wall. I was frightened, hungry and I'd cuddle Warren tightly, wondering when the nightmare was going to end.

Their final act of cruelty was to accuse me of seeing a man in the village. Heathfield was two miles away and it was now October and growing cold. I was too exhausted to walk that far with Warren, let alone embark on an affair.

A few days later Mrs Pennyquick accused me of being a 'dirty whore' and told me to get out. It was pouring with rain that day, and I had a three-month-old baby. To make it even worse as they'd paid me two weeks in hand, they refused to give me that back because they'd lent me the money for the cheap little carrycot on wheels. I cried and pleaded with them, saying I had nowhere to go and no money, but they wouldn't relent. Yet they prided themselves on being Christians.

In desperation I went to the end of the lane and rang Linda, the poetry-reading friend I'd made at the home. She'd given up her baby girl for adoption, but something told me she would help. Bless her, she didn't hesitate for one second, and said she and her father would come to collect me. By the time they arrived, several hours later, I'd emptied rain off the storm apron on Warren's carrycot dozens of times. I'd got under a hedge to feed him, yet the rain still got through. I don't think I've ever felt such despair, before or since. Cold and wet, my teeth chattering, I even began to doubt Linda and her father would come to rescue me. And if they didn't, what would I do?

But they did come, and her father went up to the house and told Mrs Pennyquick what he thought of her. Then they drove me back to Linda's pretty one-bedroom flat in Princess Street, close to the Camden Town entrance of London Zoo. I don't know what I would have done without Linda's help and support.

I was full of gratitude for the roof over our heads, but I had no money to give Linda for rent. I couldn't get a job without childcare either. Later Social Services gave me only four pounds a week, because my name wasn't on Linda's lease. I could buy food with that, but nothing else.

During that time I met Paula Canning, a friend of Linda's, and she was great too. I recall she once babysat Warren without any experience of babies. She changed his nappy (in those days they were tow-elling) but when she picked him up it fell off. We have remained friends, despite a hiatus of many years before we were in touch again. Three years ago, she and her husband dog-sat for me while I went to Australia with my daughter to meet up with Brandon, my grandson, who was working there.

Even though Linda and Paula helped me in so many ways, I soon saw for myself that my situation was never going to improve. I couldn't get a home of my own without a job, and I couldn't get a job as there was no nursery place for Warren or ever a childminder.

Eventually I wrote to my father for help. It was two years since I'd seen him, and although I dropped the odd card to them with my address, there had been no response. I didn't expect him to take me home and stick up for me against Hilda but I thought he might help a bit with money so I could get a flat of my own. He came to see me and cradled Warren with tears in his eyes. 'My first grandchild and I can't tell anyone,' he said, in self-pity, not for one moment considering what I had been through and what lay ahead for me without help. There was no help with money either.

As an adult who has been through many awful times, and learned so much about human behaviour, I prefer to think Dad knew that if he took me home, Mum would make my life a misery. She would commandeer Warren, and I'd be the skivvy, ridiculed and abused when she felt like it. I have to remember that Dad must have gone through so much when my mother died and he had to make heartbreaking decisions about Michael and me. Maybe he felt adoption was the only answer. But that day I just wanted him to be my dad, to put his arms around me and tell me he cared. I knew I couldn't stay indefinitely with Linda, yet I was loath to apply for another live-in job after the way the last one turned out.

I had so many sleepless nights agonizing over what I should do. Then one morning I woke, looked over the end of the bunk bed I was in, and watched Warren sleeping in his little carrycot, beneath me. He was four months now, and outgrowing his clothes. I knew soon the carrycot would be too small and not safe once he sat up. I needed a proper cot, with space for it and everything else a fast-growing baby needs.

Then I realized that all those people who had told me it was virtually impossible to bring up a baby alone were right. I had nothing but four pounds a week and it was only a matter of time before Linda would say she needed help with the rent. Absolutely everything was stacked against me, and I knew I had to do the right thing for Warren, however much it hurt me.

Always one to act immediately once a decision has been made, I knew I had to do it that day, to start the ball rolling. After I'd fed, bathed and dressed Warren, I put him back in his carrycot, set it on the wheels, bumped him down the two flights of stairs and out into heavy rain. I knew exactly where the adoption society was, on the other side of Regent's Park. The rain was so heavy that the storm apron kept filling, and I had to lift it to drain it. By the time I got to the adoption society I was soaked to the skin. I walked in and said I wanted my baby adopted.

The women there looked at me as if I had two heads. 'We can't just take him,' one said in astonishment. 'We have to find the right new parents first.'

I burst into tears. I knew that, I said, but I felt I had to start the process.

They gave me a cup of tea and let me feed and change Warren, before taking down all my details. They reminded me that if I was completely serious about adoption, I should stop breastfeeding and get him onto a bottle as soon as possible. They said they would be in touch very soon.

I remember I got soaked again on the way home, and when I told Linda what I'd decided, tears ran down her cheeks and she silently hugged me. We both knew it was the right thing to do, and I was so glad that she didn't say it was inevitable.

It was just a week later when I had a letter from the adoption society, saying they had the perfect parents for Warren. I was given a date in early December. I often wonder if my impulsive action had made them move fast too.

The way I felt in the short time that was left with my darling baby must have been close to how people feel awaiting execution. So little time, and all the trappings of the festive season, lights, Christmas trees and decorated shop windows, heightened every emotion. Then there was the agony of stopping breastfeeding. Warren didn't like the bottle one bit, and banged his head on my chest in protest. My breasts were painfully engorged and leaking.

Linda and Paula were wonderful. They took Warren and tried to bottle-feed him away from me. Paula got me to sit in the bath and poured cold water over my swollen breasts. That didn't work, of course, but it was comforting that they tried to make everything better. I think it was Linda who finally succeeded in getting Warren to accept the bottle.

I made him a little red coat with brass buttons to go away in, and white knitted leggings. I nicknamed him Soldier Baby because he had such an upright back. Little did I know the couple I was handing him over to that day were army people.

Linda came with me. It must have been agonizing for her as she'd so recently given up her own baby. But she was insistent, and I loved her for it. Miss Hammick met us at the adoption society. In the waiting room there was a fish tank, and I was pointing out the tropical fish to Warren when a lady came in. She made a fuss of him, and when she held out her arms, I thought she only wanted to cuddle him. But she was out of the door so fast with my baby I couldn't believe he'd gone. I hadn't even kissed him goodbye.

I screamed, kicked and thumped on the door to get out, like a mad woman, but they'd locked it. Miss Hammick caught hold of me and said, 'Lesley, listen!'

I did listen. From somewhere upstairs I heard a peal of pure joyous laughter and delight.

'Your pain is that couple's joy,' Miss Hammick said. 'In time that will sustain you.'

I have accused that woman of being a tyrant, a dried-up old spinster and many other things in the past, but her wise words that day have stayed with me for all these years, and it was indeed just that which shone a beam of light on even the darkest days. She was right. Even now fifty-seven years later I can still feel his small body in my arms, recall the smell of him and see his wide smile. I've seen his face again in each of my three daughters, and my four grandchildren. Brandon the eldest, now twenty-four, has his birthday on 10 July, just two days before Warren's. When he arrived I felt I'd been given my boy back.

Each of my children gave me such joy, but there remained inside me a place nothing could fill. Sometimes when tickling their tummies or playing 'Round and round the garden' on their palms and they squealed with laughter, I would be transported back to hearing Warren's. I used to sing the Mary Wells song 'My Guy' to him all the time. It was in the charts in 1964, and whenever I hear it, tears well. Every 12 July I dedicate the day to him, looking at the photos, remembering and shedding tears.

I've tried to trace him. Back in the early days I left a paper trail of letters at the adoption society for when he was eighteen, but whether they were given to him, I don't know, and he has never put himself on any of the lists of people who wish to be found. I must respect that, and hope it's because he's been really happy with his adoptive parents.

In my third book, *Charity*, the heroine gave up her son for adoption. It was cathartic reliving the terrible loss, but I was also able to see I had made the right choice for Warren, even if not for me. I dedicated the book to all those many unmarried mothers in the fifties and sixties who didn't give up their babies willingly or easily.

Lately there have been stories in the press about the way young mothers were treated then, so many of them like my own, and far worse ones too. But what it did to our heads people rarely speak of. You can't see the scars and we've mostly managed to keep the loss internal. Having further children under happier circumstances brings joy, but we don't forget the missing child, not even when they are adult.

My friend Paula went on to have a son herself a

year after Warren's birth, but she was lucky enough to have the support of her parents and sister. Linda got married and had two more daughters, and though I lost track of these two wonderful women for many years, fate moved in mysterious ways and as you will read later, we were eventually reunited.

4

I didn't intend this book to be a misery memoir, but looking back at the last chapter, I'm afraid it reads like one. God forbid anyone would imagine I'm some poor soul lost in the sadness of her youth because I'm not. I was, and still am, a clown, a daredevil, a collector of people, and someone who values friendship above all else.

I read once that to become a writer, one has to have at least one of the following:

1. Irish blood
2. a screwed-up childhood
3. a Roman Catholic education

Well. I have all three – maybe two and a half as the Catholic part ended when I was six years old. However, there was a glut of Church of England thereafter.

Not that I ever thought of being a writer when I was young, but I've already said that I told stories. In wet playtimes I would spin a yarn to the other kids, which kept them enthralled. My elders called it lies. And I was always in trouble for it.

It was such a bleak time after Warren. I hastily sold his carrycot, and put his clothes and nappies into it for the people who bought it. I remember there was a little dent in the mattress where his head had been, and a tiny amount of fluffy blond hair on the flannel sheet. I kept that little sheet. I don't remember Christmas that year, but on New Year's Eve Linda said we must go to the Prince Albert pub opposite the flat. There was a handsome barman who paid me a lot of attention. He was called David Andrews.

Clearly I was hungry for love, and David sweet-talked me into going out with him. He was twenty-nine and hadn't long come back from Australia. He'd gone out as a Ten-Pound Pom, but there was so little work that he joined the army and had a very miserable time. He told me that after a year he couldn't stand it and went AWOL. He imagined if he was caught he'd be shot as a deserter, and hid away, working in a hospital mortuary. Eventually he couldn't stand the strain of looking over his shoulder all the time and handed himself in. To his astonishment, the senior officer gave him a discharge and told him to bugger off. He said they didn't really want Poms in Oz anyway. So David signed on as crew on a cargo ship bound for Marseille, jumped ship there and hitchhiked back to the UK.

All this might sound as if he was a bit of a lad, but

he was quite the opposite. A quiet, sensitive, responsible man, he had worked as a counter clerk at the Post Office until he had the idea of going to Australia. Even sadder for him, he fell in love with damaged me after one date and asked me to marry him.

Of all the dozens of men who have come and gone in my life, David is the only one I wish I could apologize to. He was kind and loving, a good man. I didn't deserve him.

Always impulsive, we got married on my twentieth birthday in February 1965 just seven weeks after we'd met. We found a couple of rooms in a nasty terraced house in Kentish Town (this was long before the area became fashionable). The sink and cooker were at the top of the stairs, the lavatory outside, and when we wanted a bath we had to go either to the council baths or to David's parents' flat.

His parents were just like Alf Garnett and his wife in *Till Death Us Do Part*. She was rather sweet but I thought he wasn't and I wondered how he could have produced a son as nice as David. He had worked at the Post Office sorting office all his life, right through the war, and his wife ran the canteen. Their home was on the ground floor of one of those forbidding council blocks built in the twenties and thirties. The council came round every few years and painted the interior cream gloss, which looked vile, especially with a brown imitation leather suite, and a central wartime Utility dining table. The only decoration was a vase with a dozen fake red roses given free with Surf washing powder.

Ada, my mother-in-law, realizing I was a bit 'arty', asked what she could do to make the flat nicer. I suggested a few pictures and books to which Alf responded, 'Don't talk to me about books. I bought the boys twenty-four encyclopedias, but they never read them.'

I had a job not to laugh out loud. Does anyone actually read an encyclopedia? You dip into one when you want an answer to a question.

So, imagine our wedding when my smartly dressed, intelligent and artistic father met my in-laws. To my consternation, the two men already knew one another. After twenty-five years in the Royal Marines, Dad was put in charge of the section of the sorting office that my father-in-law had worked in all his life. Alf hated him for that because Dad was a stickler for the job being done properly and had seen more of the world than Alf had. Dad was too polite to offer an opinion on Alf, but clearly despised a man who hadn't joined up to fight and disagreed with almost everything Dad believed in.

So Dad, already disappointed in me having had a

baby out of wedlock, was even more disappointed by the family I was marrying into. However it meant a great deal to me that Dad came when I invited him. I didn't think he would. But I was very glad my stepmother declined. I dare say she would have spoken out about Alf and the ghastly flat we were living in. Not to mention the amount of booze we had. One of David's friends gave us a cocktail bar. A fifties monstrosity, with mirrors and glittery black padding along the front, it was like the lights on Blackpool sea front when it was plugged in. I tried to pretend I liked it, but I cringed every time I looked at it.

The wedding was barely over when I realized I was pregnant again. I had harboured the idea of persuading David to help me get Warren back, but I knew that would be an awful thing to do to his new parents. I was overjoyed at the thought of a baby, but looking around at our flat and the street it was in, with dirty, rough, poverty stricken neighbours – like a setting from the hard-hitting sixties TV drama *Cathy Come Home*, which brought everyone's attention to the hardships of the poor in London – I knew I didn't want to bring him or her up in such a squalid place.

Then David was offered a job as a chauffeur for a doctor in Harley Street, and what was even better, it came with a little mews flat above the garage. David was perfect for such a job. He loved cars, knew

London like the back of his hand, always looked smart and could take orders. I often thought he'd have made a perfect butler too. It was good money, the flat was nice, if a bit dark, and there was no rent to pay. I couldn't believe I could proudly say we lived in Harley Street. I was asked if I would just pop into the big house each morning to make the doctor his breakfast. This consisted of two pieces of toast, and a two-and-a-half-minute boiled egg. The egg had to be exact. The doctor was very particular about many things. He refused to have his suits dry-cleaned and David said they stank when he pressed them. He also devised a route from Harley Street to the doctor's club, which avoided going through even one set of traffic lights. David drove him there in the rather splendid Bristol car.

The doctor's wife was a lovely, kind and very beautiful lady, and her car was a Mini Cooper. When she got David to drive her to friends, she'd say, 'Andrews, you can take your hat off now,' as soon as they were a mile or so away from home. He was also allowed to put his foot down, something the good doctor would never have approved of. David adored her, and I adored her, too, when she gave me some of her vast shoe collection, most of them Charles Jourdan. I kept them for years.

They had three daughters ranging from eighteen

to thirty, the elder two debutantes. The youngest was at a finishing school in Switzerland, and would do the Season after she left.

While I was in the house I snooped around and was blown away by five floors of splendour. There was even a room at the top of the house where all the evening dresses were kept, glorious ones that made me feel like Cinderella. And the furniture, gorgeous Chippendale chairs, highly polished tables made of woods I didn't recognize, chandeliers, wall-to-wall bookcases, fantastic paintings and ornaments to die for.

Now, I hasten to point out that I'd come from a nice home and Mum and Dad had brought back lots of interesting things from abroad. We had a baby grand piano, and Mum painted exquisite murals on some of the walls. But that house in Harley Street was like a film set. In today's terms it would be Downton Abbey. I almost expected to see Fred Astaire and Ginger Rogers flitting gracefully from room to room.

But, with my luck, happiness couldn't last. At six months pregnant I miscarried and was taken to the Middlesex Hospital. The doctor who employed us was very kind, sending along a top gynaecologist colleague, but no one on earth could have understood quite how tragic the loss was for me. Back then there were no counsellors to help. You just had to get on with it.

Apparently after I got home I'd go missing most afternoons and David would find me in the baby department of John Lewis in Oxford Street. I didn't know how weird I was being and now I really only remember the ball of misery inside me. Paula – my friend from when I was trying to keep Warren – had gone home to her parents in Seaford, Sussex, with Craig, her baby. She had a job in an estate agent's and she suggested that David and I might find a fresh start by the sea. I know David didn't want to leave his job, but he was so concerned about me that he agreed, and Paula found us a lovely new purpose-built ground-floor flat to move into.

The new start should have worked, but the misery came with me and I took to walking along the cliffs on Seaford Head for long hours with a dog called Boo-Boo. I used to volunteer to take Craig for walks too. After a while Paula suggested I get a job and I found one in the drawing office at Parker Pen in Newhaven. My job was to go around the factory replacing old technical drawings with the latest ones and to be a general lackey to everyone doing skilled jobs. There was a lovely tracer in the department called Freddie, who was no stranger to bad things happening to her. I have found that those who have suffered themselves tend to be the best amateur counsellors. On my twenty-first birthday I had a bad cold so hadn't gone to work. At lunchtime the door-bell rang, and there was the entire department bearing gifts and bringing cheer. Freddie gave me a little Pendelfin china rabbit, tucked up in bed. I still have it and would never part with it. A sweet memory of a kind, generous lady who understood me.

Meanwhile, poor David couldn't get a decent job down there and ended up driving a brick lorry. Being the stoic kind, on his first day he unloaded all the bricks without any gloves and his hands were torn to pieces. They did get better, but the job was awful. When I recognized how unhappy he was, and uncomplaining, I knew I should never have dragged him away from a job he loved in London. He couldn't go back to being the doctor's chauffeur, but he could apply to the Post Office to see if he could be a counter clerk again, as he'd been before he went to Australia.

They took him back, and for many weeks I stayed in Seaford working at Parker Pen while he was in London. I still walked miles with the dog along the cliffs at the weekend but I made friends with people at work, and I was on the mend.

Eventually I returned to London after rehoming Boo-Boo. David had found us a first-floor flat near Muswell Hill, but we couldn't take the dog there. I have always been good at talking myself into jobs, possibly because I can be a bit of a Pollyanna and employers take my enthusiasm for knowledge. That outwardly upbeat personality got me a job in a manufacturing furrier's on Oxford Street. Nowadays furs are not acceptable but in the mid-sixties rabbit coats and the famous embroidered Afghan, beloved of hippies, were all the rage. Of course, rich people bought fox, mink and mole.

The skins came into the basement of the building, and were sorted. The leathers, suedes and rabbit fur went off to a factory in Wales to be made into coats and jackets. The more exotic skins went to specialist furriers in the East End to be made into gorgeous luxury coats. I loved that job from the start for the people I worked with and the bustle of Oxford Street just outside the doors. The boss often called on me to model the coats for clients, which made me feel glamorous. But it was the staff who really made the job, including a handsome young man called Damien, who made me laugh.

On one occasion the boss sent Damien and me to stock-take in a cold-storage unit where wealthy clients stored their coats in the summer. You wouldn't believe the coats we saw in there, fabulous full-length minks and silver fox but the one that really knocked me out was a snow-white chinchilla, belonging to no less a woman than Elizabeth Taylor. For those who have never seen a chinchilla coat, the fur quivers in the most spectacular way and is as soft as cashmere. Of course I took off its cover, slipped it on and paraded up and down in that chilly place for Damien's benefit, feeling like a princess or a film star on a red carpet.

Damien was naughty, like me, and suggested we made love with me wearing nothing but the coat. I pretended to be outraged, until giggles overtook me. It never happened, but I've often wished it had. What a memory to store away!

I saw my first ever mini-skirt from the first-floor window of the office overlooking Oxford Street. The girl wore a black-and-white check one, with long, white, tight boots. That Friday on payday I bought my first mini, in the brand-new Miss Selfridge at the back of Selfridges. It was only about an inch above my knees, but within three or four weeks I'd shortened it dramatically. The extra weight I'd gained in pregnancy had finally disappeared, and I wore my shoulder-length hair in the popular style of that period called a flick-up, with a full fringe. Every film you ever see set in the early sixties the girls have their hair that way, along with Cleopatra eyeliner, pale face make-up and paler still lipstick.

That mini-skirt was partly responsible for me becoming disenchanted with married life. I'd had a miserable couple of years and suddenly Swinging London was getting started and I wanted to be in the thick of it. David might be the perfect husband, so tolerant, kind and loving, but all at once I felt suffocated and decided that the little wifey image wasn't really for me. I liked our little first-floor flat well enough, but it was off to his parents for Sunday lunch every weekend, and me cooking meat and two veg every night for us to eat in front of the TV.

Mothers often claimed that someone had led their child astray. My stepmother would snort in derision at this and say, 'Perhaps it was your child who did the leading.' I can't say who was responsible, but when I ran into Judy, my friend from Oak Lodge, astray began. I have to say that I always knew Judy was trouble. She'd once thrown a whole box of cutlery down the stairs to the basement kitchen because someone had said the wrong thing to her. She was a mod, she had no respect for authority, and there was no doubt when she arrived at Oak Lodge, a long time after me, she was taking speed. She arrived just a couple of weeks before I left, and as she was pregnant we weren't in the nursery together, but we became friends and she would come into the nursery and admire Warren. I suspect I was the only friend she made there. Her baby girl was given up for adoption long after I'd left.

Quite by coincidence our new flat was close to Judy's parents' café. I called in to say hello when we first moved there, but she was away somewhere. It turned out to be in prison, but Judy didn't tell me that for ages. To be fair to her, she was arrested with another girl who'd done some bad things. Judy hadn't joined in, and in court this was proved, so she was released. But she was wild, and when I finally met up with her, she appeared to be having the time of her life, out clubbing nightly in the East End. It sounded fabulous.

Dear, tolerant David encouraged me to go out with her, perhaps thinking a couple of outings would get the restlessness out of my system. But on the first night Judy took me into such a thrilling, dangerous world that it changed my view on life.

It began with just an East End pub, where Judy and I were treated like beauty queens by tough men in sharp mohair suits. Drink after drink was pushed into our hands and I was particularly admired for my posh voice. For a somewhat naive twenty-one-year-old it was heady stuff.

Later that evening we were taken on to a club called the Regency in Stoke Newington. It was run by the four Barry brothers, and was quite an amazing place, with a couple of bars, one with live music and dancing, a casino and a Chinese restaurant. Judy introduced me to many different men, and however naive I was, I soon cottoned on to the fact that they were, in the main, either wide boys or criminals. I met Tony Barry, one of the owners, and was immediately taken with him, partly because he was very like the pop star Adam Faith, my teenage heartthrob. Tony was also taken with me.

People have often asked me what 'a nice, well-brought-up girl' like me could possibly have had in common with the kind of people I met in that club. To be honest, I think the attraction lay in that they were so different. Maybe I even felt a bit superior to them. Add to that an element of danger, which is always thrilling.

That night I did nothing more than canoodle with Tony, but it was such heady stuff that I knew I couldn't stay married. To this day I'm still ashamed of my callous behaviour to David. I told him the next evening when I got in from work that I didn't want to be married any longer. It had lasted just eighteen months. Heaven only knows why he was so calm and fair with me, but he agreed I could stay in the flat and he'd go home to his parents. Maybe he had come to see what a damaged person I was and was glad to be out of it. I hope that was so, but I suspect I'm just trying to wriggle out of blame.

Anyway, he was hardly out of the door when Judy

and I arranged to have a party that weekend as my landlords downstairs had gone away for a week. The party started out okay, with friends of mine from work and Judy's friends who lived locally. But suddenly a host of gatecrashers turned up. I suspect Judy had spoken too openly about the party. They came in with crates of booze, and it got noisier and noisier. Judy and I cowered in my bedroom, and were really scared. These were rough, tough men and their equally tough, loud-mouthed women, and within half an hour people were banging on the front door, complaining about the noise.

Eventually the police came and chucked them all out, leaving me very shaky.

I remember standing in the sitting room the next morning, looking down at the lovely orange Kosset carpet, which David and I had saved up for and thought was so wonderful. It was soaked with beer, and cigarettes had been stubbed out on it. All day Sunday I scrubbed at that carpet, trying to clean it, without much success. Then my landlords came home, and gave me my marching orders. Neighbours reported that the partygoers were all louts, swearing, peeing in their front gardens and shouting abuse at anyone who tried to tackle them.

I had no valid excuses. When they discovered David had left, they said they were glad as he deserved better than me. They were right, of course. The following day I found a bedsit near Finsbury Park and moved out. I left the ruined carpet behind.

I have often come to crossroads in my life. Nowadays I weigh up the pros and cons, knowing the easy, seemingly more attractive road might lead to a quagmire waiting to suck me in. However, the bleak stony one could lead to even more inhospitable terrain. In the end you just have to trust your gut.

But with the disapproval of my landlords ringing in my ears and feeling bad about what I'd done to David, I chose the primrose path. I wanted to immerse myself in pleasure and adventure, and block out any kind of criticism and bad memories. It was early summer with the promise of so much fun ahead. I was young and free, and surely I'd had enough punishment in my life already.

There was a coffee bar in Finsbury Park, and I'd got to know some entertaining people there, including a madcap called Brian, who had an ancient Mercedes he'd painted blue. We all took speed, a drug I got to love as you could dance all night, walk home and still go to work the next day looking alert and bushy-tailed.

A gang of us went to Kew one night for a party in a lovely old apartment block close to the Thames with a communal garden. I didn't know the people who had thrown the party, but I think everyone behaved. Someone had brought the new record 'Out of Time' by Chris Farlowe and we played it constantly that night. I still love the song, and want it played at my funeral.

Early the next morning as the sun was rising, a group of us went down to the river. The Thames looked beautiful, as still as a millpond, with willows dipping down to it. Someone dared me to swim to the other side. Never one to back out of a dare, and all fear and common sense gone because of a couple of purple hearts (a form of speed), I stripped off my clothes, down to bra and pants, and jumped in. About two-thirds of the way across I was struggling. The Thames is much wider and the current stronger than it looks, and I realized I couldn't swim back. I managed to reach the bank and called to my friends to bring my clothes across Kew Bridge. But they thought it was funny to turn a deaf ear. So I was forced to walk across the bridge and the driver of every car that came along honked his horn at me. Cold and very wet, also barefoot and blushing, I made a mental note never to accept a dare again.

That memory still makes me smile. Even though I'm aware that having ingested a couple of purple hearts I might have drowned, I find it better not to dwell on such things.

I had a brief romance with Brian — he was fun, sexy and a kind man — but my sights were on Tony Barry, and before long Judy and I were back at the Regency. One night, after coming back to my bedsit, Tony revealed he was married, and if I wanted to see him I must come after midnight, as all the wives would have gone home by then. Wilson Pickett's song 'In the Midnight Hour' became Judy's and my anthem and we went to the club most Friday and Saturday nights.

Was I broken-hearted that he was married? No. An uncomplicated romance with someone exciting was all I wanted and I selfishly didn't think about his wife. Overheard conversations about 'jobs' Tony and his brothers had done made me aware he was a criminal, and he'd done time. Again with the stupidity of youth, that made him all the more attractive. But a handsome man who takes you to breakfast at the Savoy in a convertible Mercedes, then drops you at work can't be all bad, can he?

I was to find out that it wasn't Tony I had to watch out for, but jealous would-be top dogs, who could only get at him via me. One night Judy and I arrived at the Regency to be told by the doorman we couldn't go in. This suggested one or more of the other wives were there. A man came out whom Judy knew and said he'd walk us up to the main road to flag down a cab. But as we started to walk he said something derogatory about Tony, and I snapped back at him. With that he caught hold of me, punching and kicking me, like he was possessed. I remember Judy screaming and hitting him with her handbag, but by this time I was on the ground. He said something to the effect that Tony couldn't always protect me, which explained what this beating was about. He couldn't take out his grievance against Tony, who was too powerful in gangland terms, but beating up his girl was the next best thing.

I was badly hurt. Judy came home with me and tried to patch me up, but I should have gone to the hospital. I was afraid to in case the police were called.

I recovered quickly, as you do when you're young. I remember my boss quizzing me. He clearly didn't believe my cover story that I'd been in a car crash. Judy telephoned Tony, though, and it got back to us later that my assailant was hospitalized, which made me feel a bit better.

You often hear people say, 'He/she got in with a bad crowd.' Well, that was exactly what happened to me. Wanting to be with a man you can see only occasionally and late at night wasn't ideal, so I went back to the coffee bar looking for fun. On warm evenings we'd go to the swimming ponds on Hampstead Heath and get in after dark. It was gorgeous. No chlorine, just pure natural water, and so warm too. No wonder people rave about wild swimming these days.

One night after I'd taken purple hearts yet again, someone dared me to dive off the very high board there. Although I am a strong swimmer I could never dive, but I climbed up there anyway. Just as I was preparing to jump, terrified at the height, I suddenly remembered my swimming instructor saying, 'If you do a belly flop from up high you'll split yourself open.' I was too proud to climb down, so I made a conscious effort to stay straight. I must have achieved it as I was told I did a perfect dive. But it sobered me. I looked at that diving board a few days later and felt sick at what could have happened. That diving board was taken away eventually. I guess some other fool must have attempted to use it as stupidly as I did.

There were many wild experiences at that time, but none as dangerous as the diving, and I developed a reputation for being fearless and fun, which I went out of my way to maintain. I also befriended two unmarried mothers and often minded their babies. I didn't know then that they both thought of me as a sucker, someone who could be used.

Then one day I met a chap called Dougie in the coffee bar and fell for him, hook, line and sinker. He had brown eyes like a spaniel's and curly hair. I can't remember what he told me he did for a living – possibly, like so many of my new friends, nothing, or something villainous. I stopped seeing Tony and made myself available 24/7 to Dougie, which is always a mistake.

Meanwhile Sandra, one of the two unmarried mothers, was in difficulties as Joey, her baby boy, had been taken away by social workers and she had nowhere to live. She was not a good mum. I'd found Joey lying in not just a soggy nappy but a sodden pram. She fed him with junk, and he had bad nappy rash. On occasions when I'd babysit she often didn't return, leaving him with me overnight.

I'd just moved from one room to two rooms across the road. It was lovely on the top floor with a view across treetops to Alexandra Palace. I suppose I thought offering Sandra a home with me would make her more maternal, that she'd get a job and a decent flat so the social workers would let her have Joey back. After the problems I'd had with Warren, I think most people would understand why I did this.

At first it was good. Sandra seemed very happy and said she was going off to job interviews and trying to get a decent flat to bring her baby home to. I bought her some new clothes, and things for Joey, and taught her to cook simple meals, the sort she could mash up as baby food.

During all this I was crazy about Dougie, living for the times he could be with me. By then Christmas was approaching and I urged Sandra to ask the social workers if she could have Joey home for it. I decorated the entire flat, filled a stocking with things for Joey, and one each for Sandra and Dougie. Joey was allowed to come to us, so Sandra collected him on Christmas Eve. I had a small turkey to cook and all the trimmings, but Dougie never arrived.

I waited till two in the morning, and again all Christmas Day. I did my best to be jolly for Sandra and Joey's benefit, but I was so worried about Dougie. The only phone was in the hall and he'd never written down that number or given me a number to reach him. He didn't show up at all. Joey went back to his foster parents in the early evening, and Sandra didn't come back either. On Boxing Day neither of them turned up, and I was distraught.

Sandra returned on the twenty-seventh, saying she'd stayed at her mother's, but it was Dougie I was concerned about. He turned up a few days later and told me he'd been on some 'job', a jeweller's he and a couple of mates were tunnelling into. As the police were sitting outside, he'd had to stay in there, with no food or drink. I can't believe now that I swallowed such a pathetic story, and didn't immediately realize he was married and at home with his wife and children. But love makes fools of us all: I did believe it and was upset that he'd had no Christmas, that the job had had to be abandoned. I felt my miserable time was unimportant.

Tony Barry had a phrase I've never forgotten: 'Don't get involved with mugs.' I did get involved with them and I was certainly one myself at that time.

5

I cringe a great deal when I remember that period of my life in Finsbury Park, mostly because I was ridiculously gullible and trusting. I didn't go to the Regency any more as I was in love with Dougie and lived for the times he came to see me. He always made excuses for why he didn't make prior arrangements. With hindsight, I should have recognized that as suspicious.

But I can be a terrible ostrich when I don't want to face up to something, and rather than sticking my head in the sand, I was intent on encouraging Sandra to get her act together. She was making no attempt to get a job, or a flat of her own, and without them she had no chance of getting her little boy back. I even began to suspect she didn't want him, but to me that was too appalling for words.

I think it was in February close to my twenty-second birthday when I felt ill at work and came home early. I walked into my bedroom and found Dougie in bed with Sandra. I was so shocked I ran to the bathroom where I was violently sick. When I eventually came out, the pair of them had gone. That night was the longest and most wretched ever. I couldn't get warm, I kept being sick, and I was heart-broken at the betrayal. What hurt most was that Sandra could do such a thing to me. Where was the loyalty? I'd been keeping her for several months and she knew I was in love with Dougie.

I might have been an ostrich, gullible and far too trusting, but I wasn't a pushover, and I have never backed down from a fight. Revenge is a dish best served cold, and I knew if I waited to get mine Sandra, being somewhat thick, would assume I was afraid of her and think she'd won.

It was two weeks later when I decided to act. Needless to say, Dougie hadn't called round even to try to apologize. I was sitting in the hairdresser's, and as I was wearing a pale suede coat and having my hair put up, I knew that I would give no advance warning that I was on the warpath.

Guessing Sandra was with her mother, who had thought I was her daughter's saviour, when my hair was finished I put on some lippy and marched round there. Her mother answered the door and greeted me cheerfully. I think she hoped I'd come to ask Sandra back to my flat – the way she called her daughter certainly suggested good news was imminent.

Sandra appeared and, seeing me smiling, came

right up to me. She was dumb enough to imagine I'd forgiven her. I grabbed her shoulder with my left hand and punched her as hard as I possibly could on the nose. I had the satisfaction of seeing blood spurt out, like a fountain, and knew I'd broken it. I casually wiped my fist on her dress, slapped her face a couple of times and told her if she ever came near me again I'd kill her.

Her mother was screaming and I told her if she didn't shut up I'd hit her too.

As I walked away I saw I had blood on my suede coat, but it was a small price to pay.

Unbelievably Dougie had the cheek to come round to my place the following day. Did he really imagine I was going to give him a rapturous welcome?

'You made a right mess of Sandra's face,' he said. 'You broke her nose. I never thought you were capable of something like that.'

'You have no idea what I'm capable of,' I replied, tempted to break his nose too. But he put on a wheedling voice and claimed Sandra had come on to him and he'd never wanted to do it. I almost laughed, because the scales had fallen from my eyes and I could see what a maggot he really was. I ordered him to get out and never come back.

I went once more to the coffee bar in Finsbury Park, and one of Sandra's friends kindly informed me Dougie was married and that was why he hadn't come at Christmas.

It didn't come as much of a surprise. Neither did her putting Chris Andrews's record, 'I'm Her Yesterday Man', on the jukebox. She was another nasty piece of work, like Sandra, so I walked out with my nose in the air.

I had come to my senses, though. I had to get off the self-destruct path I'd been on since I'd given up Warren. I'd lost a kind and decent husband, but it wasn't too late to get my life back on track.

I found a flat in Archway with three girls who were music students and had three pianos in the vast messy living room. I knew I wouldn't have anything in common with them — they were seriously worthy types whom the sixties seemed to have bypassed. But I needed time to lick my wounds in the company of normal, hard-working people and think what to do next.

I took as much of my stuff from the flat as I could manage on the Saturday with the intention of going back on Monday for the rest. I got back on Monday to find every single box had gone. Someone must have seen me taking stuff out and had forced the door. Alternatively, it might have been instigated by Sandra or even Dougie. There was nothing I could do about it but cry. The only things of any real value to me were a hand-crocheted bedspread my great-aunt had made, and a white kid coat, a present from the furriers. I was very sad to lose them. Thankfully I'd taken my sewing machine and a needlework cabinet made for me by my father. If I'd lost them, I think I'd have gone spare.

I rang Tony Barry, looking for sympathy, but quite predictably he said, 'I told you not to hang out with mugs.' But he took me out then, and kept in touch for a long time until he got into serious trouble. I'll explain that later, but when it occurred, I didn't tell him off for mixing with mugs!

The move to the musicians' flat turned out to be serendipitous. Just a few weeks later one of my flatmates said she'd been invited to a little party in Baker Street by a rather odd but interesting posh chap called Richard. She was keen to go but the other girls weren't, so I went with her.

She was right, Richard was odd, as was the mansion block the flat was in. But however odd Richard was, I liked him on sight, and his other friends who were there. Nearly all were at City University, and mostly a year or two younger than me. Their flat was in the kind of squalid mess four or five young men are prone to make, but there was a lovely sense of fun in all of them. I felt I'd found my real tribe.

Among them was a chap called George, in his

second year at City University. He came from Wood-stock. He was clever, enthusiastic, fun and instantly smitten with me, which was lovely after the miserable times I'd had recently. He also had a Lambretta scooter, and would have whisked me home on it later, but I had to think of my flatmate, who'd sat poker-faced all evening. Clearly out of her depth.

George and I became lovers, and as he was living in university halls, and I was sharing a room with one of the pianists it was difficult. But Richard soon became a really good friend and suggested I move in with him and the other boys. The room was tiny, but that didn't bother me, and I was in my element cleaning the place and behaving like a mother hen. It was also just a walk to work and George could stay.

Richard had very florid speech. 'I think we'll have a social event this evening' was one he trotted out often. He had windmill arms, and as he talked he waved them about. It was very weird, but sort of endearing. He didn't have a nasty bone in his body. He famously made a trifle in a plastic bucket for one such event and said it was the only thing large enough. Needless to say no one fancied eating it. I'd used the bucket just the day before to wash the kitchen floor. I also remember going to a Vicar and Tarts party with him on the tube. He was wearing a dress and fishnet tights, and to my horror as I sat opposite I

Lesley, age seven, with crooked teeth and pudding basin hair cut.

Hilda Cant in her early nursing days. Possibly late 1920s.

My real mum, in about 1938.

My real mum, Michael and me, 1945.

Michael and me on the Dymchurch to Dungeness miniature railway, 1949.

Mum, Dad, Selina and Michael, with me in the middle, 1951.

Hilda, me (age nine), my adopted brother Paul and Mary, a foster child.

Michael, Selina and me, plus Malcolm, a foster child.

Camping coach holiday – Michael and Paul at the back, me (age fourteen), Hilda to the right. Auntie Celia, her sister, to the left.

Dad, Michael, Paul and me at Blackheath boating ponds. I'm fourteen.

Linda holding Warren in
Oak Lodge.

Warren (age four months) just days before I had
to give him up.

inda with my first husband, David, 1966.

My friend Jo as she was when
I first met her in Aberdeen
in 1968.

Bill and Toots in Trafalgar
Square, Spring 1968.

John and Lucy at Borough Green, Kent, 1971.

John with Lucy, taking her first steps, early 1971.

Lucy and little friend.

Me with Lucy, 1972.

saw he had no pants on under the tights, and his tackle was revealed in glorious horribleness.

Clive, one of the other guys, was the heir to a famous brewery and frightfully public school too, of course. He never put his clothes away, just dumped them on his unmade bed, and at night got in under them all, or fell onto the pile. One day Richard took all his clothes and dumped them in the bathtub. Clive came home drunk that night, got into the bathtub on top of his heaped-up clothes and slept there all night. One could only suppose his clothes smelt to him like his bed.

We had such a lot of fun as summer arrived. I whizzed around London on the pillion of George's scooter, wearing a fourteen-inch mini-skirt, going to concerts in parks, street markets and to dances at the Students' Union. We also had rowdy parties at the flat. It was the kind of innocent fun I should have been enjoying in the previous year instead of fraternizing with thugs and gangsters.

I suppose it was inevitable that we would be asked to leave that flat. All the other tenants were sober middle-aged people and we were far too noisy. I came up with the idea of renting a house and found a semi-detached on Sinclair Road, Golders Green, backing onto the North Circular. The area was called Brent, but Brent Cross Shopping Centre hadn't been built back then. Later I was to claim we put the Sin in Sinclair Road. Our landlord was a rabbi, living in Gateshead, but on his rare visits he seemed to like me and tolerated more than five people living there.

One guy from Richard's flat, Bob Battershill, came with me. He was a very odd fish who always wore a bow tie, but he was dependable. Richard went to Crouch End and set up a similar house but we remained firm friends, and I advertised in the *Evening News* for other people to share the house. George was back in Woodstock, and although he often hitch-hiked at weekends to be with me, I couldn't count on him for rent.

It was almost unheard of then for both sexes to share a house or flat, but I decided to have boys as they were less treacherous, and I'd rather clear up after men than girls. As you might expect I picked the boys for their looks, intelligence and being party people. To this day I can boast I chose wisely. They were students at City University, mostly in their first year, and right away they became 'my boys'.

Pete Holt was a tall, blond, blue-eyed dreamboat studying civil engineering, Alan Jones from Cambridge wanted to be an airline pilot (I have no idea if he made it) and Tim Manley was doing English and later became the editor and owner of *Knave*, a top-shelf magazine. These three and Bob were the mainstays and I made five. Other people came for a while. One we called Noj, that was John spelled backwards as there were several other Johns around. He worked for a jukebox firm and got us an old one, complete with hundreds of records. We had it blasting out all the time. We rarely watched TV, except for *The Prisoner*, which we were addicted to. In the show all the characters had a number, the hero being Number Six. I gave all my boys and visiting friends numbers and, of course, I was Number One.

Aside from their rent, I took one pound fifty – or thirty bob (shillings), as it was then, from each of them. For that they had an evening meal (such as shepherd's pie) and other essentials like bread, breakfast cereals, milk, cleaning stuff and toilet rolls. I cooked and they washed up on a rota.

We were weekend 'flower children', going out to clubs with our faces painted. The Middle Earth in Covent Garden, when it was still a fruit-and-veg market was a favourite. I remember the first time we went there we saw the Crazy World of Arthur Brown. He had a record out called 'Fire' and set fire to himself on stage. We weren't really into drinking: dropping LSD, smoking cannabis and taking the odd tab of speed was more fun. We were burning the candle at both ends, but my motherly skills kept us reasonably sensible. Once a week we'd go to the launderette nearby, and nip into the pub while the machine did the washing. We'd have dinner parties at our or Richard's house, and somehow the boys still studied for their degrees.

I had recently got a new job as a telesales girl with the first edition of *Yellow Pages*. We didn't know when we phoned for interviews that we were being vetted for our voices. Lord Thomson dreamed up and owned *Yellow Pages*, and it was innovative: before that there had just been the boring *Business Directory*. Our job was to persuade businesses to take out snazzy adverts. It was a brilliant idea, and most companies wanted to be in on it. We girls were given good training. To this day I could sit down and ring someone with the same snappy sales pitch and probably get them hooked.

So imagine a tall modern office block in Ealing, with thirty or so young extroverts all with interesting voices! We had to work hard, but we'd flick onto one another's phone lines and chat when the boss was busy. At lunchtime we'd gather together for more socializing, but when I told them I shared a house with four gorgeous men, I could see they didn't believe me. But my twenty-third birthday was coming up in February. The boys and I had planned to have a party, so I invited the girls. I couldn't wait to see their reaction.

The girl I remember best was Elizabeth, known as Toots. She was five years younger than me, and had come down from Aberdeen intending to marry her boyfriend, Billy. I suppose I felt maternal towards her – she was small and pretty and I loved her on sight. It became a friendship that lasted for ever.

A great many of the girls from work couldn't come to the party, mostly because of the distance, but Toots did and after that night she couldn't come often enough. It was a fabulous party, and my boys had all clubbed together to buy me a silver bracelet with all their different zodiac signs on it. I was very into astrology in 1968, and there was also a charm that spun round and said 'We love you'. I treasured that bracelet for years, and it was only recently I found it had gone missing. But the love and friendship the boys gave me have stayed with me. We went our separate ways eventually, but my affection for them never faded and I know they brought out the best in me, not to mention enough material to fill several books.

One night the police raided the Middle Earth club. The sexes were segregated, boys to one side, girls to the other. It was a fabulously weird place with light shows, and scaffolding platforms instead of proper seating. But when the police turned the main lights on it looked pretty seedy. Anyone who had drugs they hadn't yet taken dropped them on the floor. Toots and I were as high as kites and we were horrified when policewomen wanted us to strip to our underwear to be searched. They were convinced Toots was under-age, and when I insisted she was eighteen, they turned on me too. They held us back for further questioning. When we finally got out, Covent Garden was packed with people, including our friends, and they bellowed out a huge cheer. Word had got around we'd been arrested. Thank goodness we weren't – I doubt we could've kept it together.

I left *Yellow Pages* after about four months because it was such a horrible long journey round the North Circular to work. I wanted to start my own business making clothes and I could do that in my bedroom at Sinclair Road. I had quite a big order from a new boutique in Golders Green to make waistcoats and matching mini-skirts of my own design in needlecord, but the lining and the five covered buttons on the waistcoats proved very fiddly. I think I was working for what would now be about twenty pence an hour. I did some private dressmaking too.

Eventually I decided that dressmaking was not a get-rich-quick occupation, and I turned to promotions work. Back in the sixties all you needed to get plum jobs were good legs, the ability to sell and a willingness to be on your feet all day. I promoted miraculous oven cleaners, every kitchen gadget known to man, including a melon baller, stuff to mend holes in tights (it didn't really work) and umpteen different perfumes and face creams.

I also did stints at the Ideal Home Exhibition, one day selling a cleaning gadget for venetian blinds, the next a brush to remove dog hairs from upholstery (I was given a pot of hair, which I suspect came from a barber's, to sprinkle on!). I liked that job and sold out of the brushes. Then there was the Motor Show, draping myself over the bonnet of a car, offering would-be buyers cigarettes and drinks. Obviously we girls weren't expected to sell the cars. Back then it was always men. Just as well in my case as I knew nothing about cars. But I liked men.

Several things happened that summer. My old boyfriend Tony, the nightclub owner, was arrested and charged with murdering Jack 'The Hat' McVitie, alongside the Krays. He had been paying them protection money, and when they told him to get them a gun, he did, as it wasn't advisable to say no. Tony's defence when it came to trial was that he had known the gun's firing pin was broken, and he wasn't present when Reggie stabbed McVitie instead. Having once met Jack at a party I couldn't manage to squeeze out one tear for him. But I was concerned about Tony. He wasn't a bad lot like the Krays.

Later that year Tony got bail and invited me out for the evening with his brother. I took Toots along and we thought it very exciting as detectives followed us from club to club around Soho. I think that shows just how silly we were. A little after that I was called into a police station to be questioned about Tony. I genuinely didn't know anything about his life – men like him didn't divulge anything to their women. He did once laughingly tell me that his team had stolen a lorry load of Marmite, which turned out to be for the Chinese market and all the labels were in Chinese. Obviously they couldn't sell them.

I found it rather lovely that he never boasted, and that the one story he did tell me concerned a disaster. He was certainly a real gentleman to me. However, the policeman who interviewed me said if he was my father he'd lock me up so I had no contact with such men.

It was that remark that made me realize I hadn't heard from my father since my brother Michael's wedding in 1966, two years earlier. Both he and my stepmother had blanked me there. They got a lift to the registry office with Michael's about-to-be in-laws, and they left me on the platform of Bristol's Temple Meads Station. I spent the whole wedding feeling like an outcast and wishing I'd stayed in London. I expected that by now he'd forgotten he even had a daughter.

Around that time, I got a job as a Bunny at the Playboy Club. I had no real desire to work there, but it was good money, twice as much as I'd be earning in an office. It turned out to be far less fun than promotions work. Long hours in a smoky environment, the other girls were very plastic, and the high heels were a killer. All the girls I got to know thought it was a stepping stone to finding a seriously rich man. But in fact the days of famous film stars frequenting the club were over. The clientele were mostly forty-year-old northern businessmen in London on a jolly. All I got out of that job was a slightly enhanced view of my self-worth, and later it led to better promotions jobs. In the main it was tedious and I wasn't there very long. In truth I've had more fun at a bus stop or in a greengrocer's than I had in a place where some people imagine dreams come true.

Meanwhile, George was doing his finals. We were at a party one night when I got chatting to Brett, an American probation officer in England on holiday. George must have told him he was doing an exam the following day because almost as soon as he had left our house the next morning, Brett appeared. He was gorgeous and produced some hash cookies. Of course, me being me, I took one eagerly. I was something of a rarity at that time because I didn't smoke, (I learned later) so when people were smoking joints

I just coughed a lot and never really got stoned. But having the cannabis in a cake is a whole different ball-game. I began to laugh, as Brett did, and soon we were rolling around on the floor being very silly. It was a hot day, and we decided to go to Hyde Park – we thought it would be fun to take out a dinghy on the Serpentine.

We sailed to the middle of the lake all right, but after one brief lap any wind vanished, and we were becalmed. Brett had sailed before, so had I, and we both knew the theory of tacking back and forward to chase any breeze, but the sails remained sullenly limp. Without any idea of how to get around this problem, we lay in the bottom of the boat howling with laughter.

I have no idea how long we were out on the lake, we were too stoned to care, but eventually we heard the boatman ordering us to come in. All we could do was shout that we were becalmed, though other people in dinghies seemed to be moving, albeit slowly. Finally a man came out in a rowing boat to bring us in.

On the tube ride home I remembered George. I knew he'd be hurt that I wasn't home to ask about his exam. He also wouldn't be too pleased to find I'd been out with Brett all day and got stoned. I said goodbye to Brett at Hampstead and went on alone. It was only as I walked up Sinclair Road from the tube that I realized how spaced out I was. And it reminded me of my fifteen-year-old self when I'd got drunk on vodka. I'd forced myself to act normally when I got home, and luckily I managed it.

But George was observant. He'd already noticed two used coffee mugs on the kitchen table, which made him remember the American from the night before, and the interest he had shown in me.

Had I been unfaithful to George, I would have gushed over him, and bent over backwards to convince him I'd have had a much better day if I'd been with him, but I hadn't even kissed Brett and I can't stand jealous people. So when George started the Spanish Inquisition I flounced off into the garden after telling him not to be so boring.

I think I realized that day that our relationship was doomed. I'd met his widowed mother, who clearly didn't approve of me, and George would be back in Woodstock for at least a year after the summer break, which meant he'd want me to go with him. Woodstock is a lovely town but I knew no one there, except the dreaded mother.

As it turned out, I didn't have to make any decisions then. They were made for me, when Toots, my friend from *Yellow Pages*, moved into a flat in Chiswick and asked me to join her.

I have always believed in 'problem-solving by

inactivity' and when I kissed George goodbye on his return to Woodstock, I didn't promise anything. I hoped he'd look up his previous girlfriend and think how much more suitable she was for a chap who'd just got a first and had a dazzling career ahead of him in electronics.

Meanwhile I found another new job, this time in the computer department at the Egg Marketing Board. Back then computers were as big as a house, even though the scope of what they could do was very limited and ordinary people like me were not allowed anywhere near them.

I was in charge of the machines that printed the cheques for the egg producers, tucked them into addressed envelopes and franked them. Very space age. My training for overseeing the machines and the girls who worked them amounted to about five minutes. I was selected for the job because I had potential leadership capability, so the boss told me. Perhaps the lack of training for me, or for anyone who worked elsewhere in the company, was why the Egg Marketing Board was disbanded. All that anyone ever remembered about it was the slogan 'Go to Work on an Egg'.

6

The best thing about the Egg Marketing Board job was that it was in Oxford Street. Very handy for shopping. Second was that the computer was always breaking down, or other companies wanted to use it, and during those times we girls either sat in the staff room or went out to the shops.

Mr Haslam, the manager, was a skinny little man who used to call me into his office on almost any pretext, possibly because my skirt was so short and legs so long. I have to admit I played up to this, especially when he was complaining about the girls' timekeeping. He made us sign a book, and we had to put not just the time when we arrived but the reason we were late. Everyone was very inventive with the reason. One I loved was 'I was guarding my plates.' That came from a girl who had a flatmate leaving: she was convinced she would steal the plates, so she didn't go to work until the flatmate had gone out.

My excuse was 'You know how it is.' Well, we all do, don't we? Why bother with something more descriptive.

Mr Haslam said I was 'subversive'. I liked that. Preferable to lazy, rude, stupid or gormless. Was I? I suppose so. I delighted in letting him think we were well behind with sending out the egg cheques to watch his stress levels rise. I was also quick to support any of the girls who were threatened with the sack.

During this time I was keeping in touch with George by letter, which seemed kinder than just blanking him. I was, after all, very fond of him. And we still had a couple of engagements we'd agreed to go to together, including the wedding of one of his closest friends.

Then I met Myles. He was rather shy but blond and handsome, and lived a little further down Chiswick High Road than me. He played cricket, had never taken a drug in his life, and perhaps this was why, when I invited him round to the flat where I lived with Toots, she took a totally unreasonable dislike to him. It was mutual, but she found pleasure in putting on the Beatles' 'Nowhere Man' every time he came through the door. I suspect she was just afraid I'd ride off into the sunset with him.

I didn't want to do that, but Myles was a superb lover, even if somewhat uncommunicative. But there was always aggravation between him and Toots and he sulked when my old boys came over to see me. Jealous, I suppose. When he invited me to his home in Brighton, in late August 1968, I was very happy to go.

It was a blissful time. The weather was hot and so was he. The moment his mum had gone to work he'd jump into bed with me. I forgot about everything that week, and it was only on the day before I had to go home that I began to panic. You see, the wedding George and I had been invited to months earlier was the next day. I couldn't back out at the last minute. I had hoped that I'd given George enough hints that the wedding was the end of the line for us. I felt he was smart enough to have accepted I'd moved on.

But was that the case? I have learned from past experience that men will often decide I'm the love of their life when I'm halfway out of the door. Quite a few have said I didn't explain myself. My excuse for that is that I thought it was a kind let-down. So, I went back to London alone, hoping for the best. George arrived in Chiswick soon after me, and he was hardly through the door when he pulled out a ruby engagement ring and asked me to marry him.

Not for one moment had I expected that! I had imagined he might grill me about where I'd been since he last saw me, or that he'd be cold and distant because he knew it was over. But not a marriage proposal. I was stuck in a horrible situation, wanting to spare his feelings so we could get through the day amicably, but I couldn't pretend to be thrilled when I wasn't.

In the end I went for the 'Get out of jail free' card. I said it was a total surprise, and a lovely one at that, but I needed time to consider whether or not I was ready for marriage again, the first one having been a complete failure. He had the look of a spaniel that had been pushed off your lap. But I ignored that and busied myself getting dolled up for the wedding.

Soon after George's arrival, Roneen, Toots's step-mother, arrived from Aberdeen to stay for a few days. I hadn't met her before, but despite being in her forties, I had been told she was great fun. She was also motherly and intuitive, a heaven-sent distraction from being questioned by George.

Then we heard on the news that a big storm was coming.

No one in London ever takes any notice of weather warnings, and George and I were no exception. But by the time we got to Croydon the rain was so heavy it was tempting to go back on the train. But we ploughed on to the church by taxi, only to find the aisle was already wet, and they were putting down planks for the bride and groom. By the time the ceremony started, those planks had water lapping over them.

It was a disaster. I felt so sorry for the bride and groom and their families when they'd waited so long for this happy day. The vicar hurried along the service, then advised us to forget about the reception and all to go home, especially those who had a long way to travel.

Someone offered me a lift back to the station, but George was chatting to his uni friends, and I assumed he'd either stay with one or go back to Woodstock.

Soon after I got to Chiswick I heard that parts of London were flooded and the tubes shut down. A glance out of the window at Chiswick High Road told me that it was already a shallow river, and I feared the Thames would break its banks.

Then Myles arrived, also unexpectedly. He'd caught an early train back when he heard about the storm, and come straight to me, assuming the wedding would have been called off. He was desperate to see me. He was hardly through the door before a few other friends turned up. They'd been on their way somewhere when they were turned off tubes and buses. Our top floor flat was quite big, but it was beginning to look like an evacuation zone and stank of wet clothes.

The doorbell rang again and there, to my horror, was George. He was soaked – I think he'd walked miles. All trains home had been cancelled but in truth he'd come back to be with me.

The remains of that day and the evening were a

nightmare I can never erase from my memory: too many people milling around, rain hammering down and stopping anyone leaving, not enough food for everyone, Myles and George silently eyeing each other balefully.

Roneen was our saviour. She took it upon herself to mediate. Myles was totally aware of my situation with George as I'd told him what was going on before we'd gone to Brighton together. Thankfully he was understanding.

But George, usually so easy-going, highly intelligent and balanced, kept crying. As day turned to night it got more fraught. Someone had to share my bed and in the end I chose Myles. We lay there like two pokers, both feeling miserable. There was an old couch in the hall we called the Heffalump. George lay on that and Roneen stayed with him, counsellor, mother figure and comforter.

I think at the time Roneen saw me as a siren, luring men by casting spells over them, possibly because she'd been a bit like that herself. She'd been a bit wild and had been married twice. She stayed for a week after the flood, I think, and Toots and I would come home from work to a cooked meal, ironing and cleaning done. Then when we'd eaten she'd say, 'Right girls, where are we off to tonight?' And she was game for everything.

So out of that awful night and cooked meals on tap, we became close friends and stayed so right up until she died in her seventies. I could tell her anything, and used to write to her regularly. I think of her and my stepmother Hilda as the two most formative influences in my life, for polar opposite reasons. Roneen's daughter, my dearest friend Jo Prosser, whom I hadn't yet met at that time in Chiswick, shares so many of her mother's wonderful traits.

Back to the morning after the flood, to our relief the floodwaters had abated! George had disappeared with the ruby ring in his pocket, and I felt terrible that, after all the good times we'd had the previous summer, it had to end in such a bad way.

Not long afterwards I managed to break Myles's heart too. We both lost our respective jobs, for different reasons, and he moved to Kilburn. I began to think Toots had been right to call him 'Nowhere Man'. He seemed to be on a self-destruct mission, drinking, betting and bitter towards me because he wasn't the centre of my world. I can't remember what happened to split us up, but I think the cruncher was that Toots and I hatched an idea to go to America.

It was the time of the hippie trail to India, taking in Marrakesh, Afghanistan and ending in Kabul. Every person with a hint of hippieness wanted to go, but most, including me, didn't make it. Billy, Toots's boyfriend, had gone with a group of mates. They spent their last night in England at our flat, smoking so much dope it was a wonder they even set off, and made us pea green with envy that we weren't going too. They got no further than Marrakesh.

The Chiswick flat didn't look so good as autumn set in. We were freezing in that huge draughty attic, so much so we even slept in one bed to keep warm. Toots had lived in a bedsitter in Fulham Road, Chelsea, before she'd found the Chiswick flat, so when she heard a couple of rooms were going, we decided to move. The American idea was still in our heads.

I loved it right away at 138 Fulham Road, even the shabby, grubby, tiny rooms and the filthy toilets: I set to work on them with spirits of salts, and brought them back to showroom splendour. The eight or so bedsits were above an antiques shop, and to this day it's still the scruffiest house in the area, or it was the last time I saw it. Next door was the Baghdad House, on the crossroads of Drayton Gardens and Beaufort Street, a thrillingly exotic restaurant where Toots's cousin Val worked. At that time the most exotic thing I'd eaten was spaghetti bolognese. Not that I was welcome in the Baghdad House: the Arab owner, Val's lover, thought I was Jewish with my dark hair and eyes. Val and Toots had gorgeous red hair, which the Arabs in the restaurant were prone to twisting round their fingers and saying, 'So pretty.' I only went in there when Val was alone.

The ABC cinema was on the other side of Drayton Gardens. Directly opposite 138 and the corner of Beaufort Street there was a furniture shop called Tulley's. All the sofas in the large windows were covered with plain calico. I used to gaze out at them in puzzlement. It was years before it dawned on me that you didn't have them like that in your home: once you'd chosen your sofa the shop would upholster it in your choice of fabric. How dumb was I to think plain calico was some kind of Chelsea trend! Another plus about that address: the Household Cavalry rode by early every morning. Always one for a man in uniform, I often had my nose pressed against the window to watch them.

I was back doing promotions work by day, and by night we burned the candle at both ends. All our bedsits were tiny, just a single bed, a gas ring and a tiny wardrobe. We used to bang on the pipes to wake each other up. I painted my little room yellow and white, and made huge brightly coloured paper flowers. It became known as 'The Nursery' and, despite the room's small size, it was amazing just how many people I could squeeze in there after the pubs had shut.

One evening Toots and I went to Finch's further

down Fulham Road, a lovely traditional Victorian pub. There at the bar was the most gorgeous man I'd ever seen, blue-black hair, sparkling blue eyes and an Irish accent. Toots lit up – she knew him well – but before I could get the SP on him, all I knew was that he was called Aidan, he'd seen us and said, in that gorgeous Irish brogue, 'What'll you girls be having?' I've never been known to be stuck for words, but I was then and must have stammered out, 'I don't know,' or something like that. To which he responded, 'If I'm going to fuck you tonight you'll need an anaesthetic.'

If it had come from a less fanciable man, it would have sounded crude and crass. But from him it was hilarious. In the weeks ahead he was to make me laugh many, many times, but I was far too scared to attempt to get off with him. Great philanderer that he was, he was also very kind. I was in agony with an abscess under a tooth and he drove me to the all-night chemist, then took me home and tucked me into bed with a hot-water bottle. He was a bit of a rogue, but far too charming for anyone to be offended.

Aidan died quite young, and to immortalize him I wrote him into my book *Camellia*, giving him a three-in-the-bed scene, which I know he would have loved. He had a sidekick, a man called Steve who was not in the same league in looks, intelligence or sense of humour. We used him shamelessly to buy drinks, taxi us around, or anything else we could think of. I remember he always wore denim. The film *Midnight Cowboy* was on at the cinema during that time. We called Steve 'The Daylight Cowboy'.

Donkey's years later I was giving a talk at the Du Maurier Festival in Fowey and a woman, several years older, collared me when I'd finished speaking and asked me how I knew Aidan and Steve. Such a blast from the distant past was mysterious and exciting so I immediately asked her to have dinner with me at my hotel. I think her name was Rhona and she was still living in Chelsea. She was one of the set who drank in Finch's back in the sixties although I didn't recall ever meeting her.

She had recently run into Steve. For old times' sake she'd invited him to dinner at her flat to find out about the other people she used to hang around with. It was during the dinner that Steve asked her if she knew Lesley Pearse, the writer. He was indignant as someone he knew had read *Camellia* and was amazed to hear about Aidan and Finch's in it. Rhona couldn't recall me at all, but back then I was Lesley Andrews. When she learned Lesley Andrews was now Lesley Pearse and was appearing in Fowey at the festival, she decided to come and meet me.

Rhona said she and Steve had no sooner finished

the meal than he got up from the table and walked towards her bedroom. She asked him where he thought he was going.

'To bed. Come on,' he said.

To which she replied, 'What makes you think I'd want to go to bed with you?'

'Well, I brought two bottles of wine,' he responded.

I laughed so much at that story. We were the generation who used the mantra 'If you can't be with the one you love, love the one you're with,' but did he really believe she'd be up for it after just a bottle of wine?

Also he was still wearing a denim jacket! Possibly the one I remembered.

However much fun Toots and I were having in Chelsea, the idea of going to America was still firmly in our heads. As my brother was then working at a university in New York, I applied for a visitor's visa. In my naivety I didn't do any research and furthermore told the truth about myself: that I would be giving up my job and home to go as a visitor to the States.

I was turned down 'as likely to become a public charge'. But at least it informed other friends that you had to establish you had a home in England and a job to come back to. I didn't brood on it for long. Lots of new fun friends, out every night and, in my case, lots of male attention. I had odd times when I'd listen to Leonard Cohen's sad songs and identify with him. 'The Stranger Song' was one – God knows I'd met enough of those! – and 'Hey, That's No Way to Say Goodbye' another. The first reminded me of all the mugs I'd been involved with, however briefly, the second of good relationships, which for some reason I'd run out on.

Yet at the bottom of all this introspection was the pain of losing Warren. Sometimes it was so acute I'm not sure how I got through the night. I used to wonder if it would ever go away. I can say now it never does. There have been long periods, especially when my other three children were born that I was able to bury it. But in the words of another song's title 'There's Always Something There to Remind Me'.

However, back to the sex and drugs and rock and roll in my Chelsea period: it was wild. Every day seemed to bring something exciting, whether that was a new club to go to, a new man, fun friends at work, or outrageous clothes to buy. I know now it was just another way of hiding my sorrow. I was reckless. I didn't plan for anything to last. I was already tainted with the belief that nothing good ever does.

We girls were very keen on Biba. At first it was quite a small shop in Kensington Church Street, but the clothes were glorious. I remember for Christmas buying wide-legged red culottes and a diaphanous black chiffon shirt, my boobs only partially concealed by breast pockets.

Over the Christmas period we went to a party somewhere in Chelsea. Billy, Toots's boyfriend, was with us. He was working on digging the Victoria Line, I think, with the intention of going to uni the following year. I loved Billy as he had such wit and a great sense of fun. Anyway, I got absolutely legless at that Christmas party and I was on a sofa in the large kitchen, and some strange man was trying to kiss me. Billy was always protective towards me, the Scottish male thing, and he picked up a Christmas pudding and lobbed it at this chap, ordering him to unhand me.

It smashed against the wall and pieces of it showered all over me and the amorous chap. Billy said loudly in his defence, 'It added a seasonal note to the festivities.' Something that still makes me snigger.

I don't know whether or not he was the same person as the man with a van who offered to drive me, Billy and Toots home. I assume so, as Billy claimed he was trying to grope me on the way. Suddenly Billy leaped forward and stuck his fingers up the man's nostrils, jerking his head backwards. I think Toots and I must have screamed. Next thing we knew Billy had this chap out on the pavement, whacking him.

I woke up the next day at 138 fully dressed, apart from my boots. As I got out of bed and started to undress, pieces of Christmas pudding, which had been trapped in my bra and blouse, showered onto the floor.

Later, when we went down the road towards Finch's, we saw a considerable amount of blood on the pavement, and I remember Toots saying such scenes were commonplace in Aberdeen at the week-end, but she'd hoped London would modify Billy's behaviour. I don't think it ever did.

In the few days between Christmas and New Year, Toots and Billy were homesick for Scotland and Hogmanay. I was seeing a fun guy called Tony, and I came up with the idea of the four of us going up to Aberdeen. None of us had enough money, but that wasn't going to deter me. I had a chequebook left behind by a girlfriend in the Chiswick flat, and as she'd reported it lost, I thought I'd use it.

In those days there was no such thing as bank cards for identification. You could produce a letter addressed to you, a library card, almost anything. The chequebook owner had left behind a couple of pieces of ID too, so I could pose as Catherine Clark from Chiswick.

I didn't really think of it as a criminal act, only a jolly wheeze, and I said if we presented ourselves at the air terminal in Brompton Road before the banks opened, we could buy four tickets and be in Aberdeen in an hour.

So that was what we did. It was foolproof, and I was the hero of the hour. I didn't get return tickets as there was a chance the airline would find out and stop us on the way back. I planned to go home by rail.

We had a wonderful time in Aberdeen, though I regretted dressing for glamour with a teeny miniskirt, boots more suited to the dance floor than trudging through snow, and no thick woollies. The temperature was well below freezing.

It was there in Toots's dad's house that I finally met Jo, Roneen's daughter, the stepsister Toots was mean to. Jo was seven years younger than me and extraordinarily pretty with long blonde hair like silk, a porcelain complexion and big blue eyes. I loved her on sight. I'd have given anything to have such a lovely little sister, but perhaps Toots's problem with her was plain jealousy because Ian, her dad, liked Jo, and so did everyone else. We went into town one day on the bus and I remember Jo practically tucking herself under my arm for protection from her stepsister. I didn't understand it: my adoptive sister Selina was cleverer, smaller and prettier than me, but I had always loved her.

Ian had borrowed a little house for us four to stay in. I don't think it had any heating, and it was so cold all of us slept in one double bed to keep warm. But alcohol warmed us during the day, and after we'd drunk the New Year in, and kissed half the population of the city, we went first footing, taking Roneen, Toots's stepmother with us. I'd never heard of first footing. Tony and I were amazed that us Sassenachs were treated so well. Every house we went to, family friends and relatives of Billy and Toots had laid on a buffet, and they were all so welcoming, plying us with drink and food. Buses ran all night long through the snow, which was just as well as we appeared to be right on the edge of the city.

The partying didn't stop after one night: two days later we were still visiting people and the buffets remained, sandwiches curling, but the weather was too cold for anything to go off. I've only got to hear Marc Bolan singing 'Ride A White Swan', which I believe I heard for the first time in Aberdeen, and I'm back in a snowy street there.

7

We travelled back to London by train, and what a nightmare it was. Toots, Tony and I were crippled with mammoth hangovers – Billy had stayed behind with his family – and most of the other people crowded onto the train were either drunk or feeling as poorly as we were. Twelve hours of hell.

Toots was wearing tartan trousers and an old man lurched into our compartment to call her 'Tartan Breeks'. To this day I always call them tartan breeks and try to do the Scottish accent.

On the final leg of the journey, the bus back to Chelsea, I remember stating I was going nowhere and drinking nothing for the foreseeable future. I meant it too. In fact the only place I can remember going to in the next few days was the Hungry Horse, a fantastic pie shop on Fulham Road. To this day I've never eaten a pie to equal theirs.

I was sticking to my plan, just going to work and coming home, but one evening Toots burst in full of excitement. She'd run into a guy who had been a lodger in her father's house in Aberdeen. He was known as Speedy and played bass guitar in a soul band called Trifle. He was playing that night at the Scotch of St James club, and urged Toots to come.

I didn't need much persuasion. It was something different, and sounded rather grand. I was also bored with my own company. The Scotch was a good place, still going now, in fact, and the band Trifle sounded just up my street as I love soul music. Speedy came to talk to us in a break from playing, and asked me if I fancied anyone in the band. I said the trumpet player, but Speedy said he stuttered, so I lost interest. That turned out to be untrue. It was the sax player who stuttered.

Anyway, Toots arranged to meet Speedy again the following night, and I stayed at home. But in the early hours she came into my room, shook me and said I'd got to get up. It seemed Speedy had another man at his flat, and Toots didn't want to be alone with two men. I obediently got dressed and went with her. When we got to Speedy's, the other man turned out to be the trumpet player. Toots promptly disappeared with Speedy into another room, and John (I hadn't actually learned his name then) was rolling a joint.

There was something very special about him. He was around thirty, with soulful dark eyes, an olive complexion and short, brown, curlyish hair. Like most musicians he was very slender and later he told me he chose to play the trumpet rather than a heavy instrument as he had arms like bean sprouts. I was soon to find he had a great sense of humour and keen intelligence.

We talked and talked. I learned he came from Becontree, near Dagenham, and his granny had a dustman boyfriend who had got him a bugle off the cart when he was seven. He'd played it constantly until he joined a youth club with a band, and they lent him a trumpet. His granny said if he saved up his paper-round money she'd give him two pounds for each pound he saved so he could buy his own.

He'd been playing professionally since he was fourteen, when he knocked off school to play with George Melly and his jazz band. He told me so many funny stories, but always in a hilarious self-deprecating manner.

I was getting sleepy by that time as the joints came at regular intervals. I told him I'd just seen the Jane Fonda film *Barbarella*, and there is a very sensual bit in it when the angel builds her a nest. All at once John instantly made one with all the many cushions in the flat, and got into it with me.

I'll do the Victorian novelist thing and close the door and curtains to avoid telling the next part.

It seemed to me it was only a blink of an eye that Toots came in, drew the curtains back and said it was time to go or we'd be late for work. I was astounded by the daylight: I'd thought it was still the middle of the night. Two songs by the Doors will always remind me of that night: 'Hello, I Love You (Won't You Tell Me Your Name)' because I only found out his name was John Pritchard afterwards. (What a floozy I was sleeping with a man whose name I didn't know!) The other was 'Love Street' and we called Fulham Road 'Love Street' from then on.

It is absolutely true that love can come along like a bolt out of the blue, changing your life completely. I had looked into John's dark, Omar Sharif eyes and fallen hook, line and sinker. He was charismatic, funny and so interesting. Although jazz was his first love, he'd moved over to pop when he played with Lulu and Dusty Springfield. He was five when his father came back at the end of the war, but then walked out soon after, and John was brought up by his Jewish grandmother, his mother and, to some extent, his older sister. No strong male to compete with and win over! He basically educated himself by knocking off school constantly and spending days in museums. That had worked: he seemed to know everything.

Nothing was the same after that night. I went to work in a daze, and arrived home to find he'd got into my bedsitter and filled it with hundreds of daffodils.

A funny thing happened just after meeting John, when he was away up north at a gig. I'd popped next door to Val's flat at the Baghdad House with Toots, because Roneen was there with her daughter Jo.

Now Val had been taught to do belly dancing, and she often did it in the restaurant. That night there were lots of people in Val's flat and someone asked her to dance for us. She refused point blank. It was her night off. But sometime later I saw a hand come round the door and put a record on the record player. It was the belly dancing music! The door opens wide and in sashays Roneen in the full regalia, except beneath the gauzy top she has a sensible middle-aged woman's big bra. She actually did the dance very well, but I looked across to young Jo to see absolute horror on her face. It was the 'How could you humiliate me like this mother?' face. The rest of us were laughing and clapping, and Roneen's finale was an attempted splits.

That evening was a bright spot in an otherwise bleak time for me as John was away many nights touring with Trifle, and it was agony waiting to see him again. It actually hurt, I loved him so much. All the previous men in my life faded to insignificance next to him.

Ironically Toots also met the man who was to

change her life around the same time. But it wasn't Speedy. Three Americans turned up at 138, who were friends of a Canadian we knew. We went out with them that night and I watched Toots fall in love with a man named Mark. A rocky road lay ahead, which in itself could be another book, but that's her story, not mine. As for Billy, he married a Dutch girl, but he and Toots are still in touch, as I am too with Billy.

If Toots and I had known the heartache and problems that were to come with loving these two amazing, complicated men, who basically took us on the ride of our lives, would we have asked to get off at the first stop?

Having John staying at 138 was difficult with just a single bed. I would go to bed early when he was out at a gig and wake up when he came in during the early hours. He slept when I went to work. It wasn't sustainable and I couldn't stay awake at work. I had to find us another flat, first a place in Earl's Court, then a cheaper and bigger, but nastier, place in Wandsworth. We had to share a bathroom with the landlord, a somewhat seedy character, and go through his flat to reach it.

The view from the bedroom window was of the chimneys of Battersea Power Station, belching steam 24/7. We used to lie in bed imagining the poor devils working in such a grim place. These days, any flat in

Wandsworth would cost a fortune, and the power station is now a fantastic shopping and leisure mall. I believe you can even go up the chimneys.

In February John had to go on a three-week tour of Spain and Portugal. I was bereft at just the thought of being without him. Yet, as luck would have it, my promotions agency sent me on a training course to a carpet manufacturer in Brighouse, Yorkshire, which took my mind off him somewhat. I was one of a group of girls being trained as colour consultants to work in carpet showrooms around the country. This involved learning every last thing about how carpets were made. At that time the carpet mills were quite terrifying places, stinking of dyed wet wool, and the machinery was deafening and dangerous. It was also terribly cold, but at least we were staying in a small hotel, which was quite cosy. One night we all went to see *Doctor Zhivago* at the local cinema. I cried the whole way through it because Omar Sharif made me think of John.

Towards the end of the course, the management threw a party in the mill's reception area for us girls and various department managers from carpet stores. I was told off immediately as my dress was too short, and informed I was to wear a knee-length skirt on all occasions while working for Firth's carpets. That would prove difficult when all of the skirts and dresses I owned barely covered my bottom. But I was also given the prestigious stores in London and on the south coast, including, among others, Harrods, Whiteleys in Bayswater and Beales in Bournemouth.

All us girls got plastered that night, and I was vaguely aware of a young blond man among the droves of middle-aged ones, eyeing me up. It was snowing hard when we went back to the hotel, and when I got into my room I found, to my amusement, that the blond chap had found a ladder and was attempting to climb it to get into my room. I opened the window to tell him to go away, and when he wouldn't, I pushed the ladder. The last thing I remember was seeing him lying on his back on the ground. I must have fallen onto my bed and passed out. I woke much later, freezing cold, to see a pile of snow on the carpet. It had come through the open window. When I looked out, he had gone. I had to shovel the snow out of the window with a tumbler before I could shut it.

With the mother and father of hangovers, my last day in the mill was torture. To this day I can still smell the dye, wet wool, oil, and hear the loud clacks of the looms. Most of us girls were in the same state, and we all wanted to die. But that song 'I've Got My Love to Keep Me Warm' had never been more appropriate. I was jubilant that I'd managed to get through two weeks without John, and had trained for a well-paid job that would go on for several weeks. I would be staying in hotels from Monday to Friday, which meant I wouldn't see much of him, but at least I wouldn't have to be in the horrible Wandsworth flat, and when I had to be there, he would be too.

When I took the train home from Yorkshire, the thought of a whole week alone in that flat was awful as I had no promotions job to fill it and no television to pass the time. Ever resourceful, I went to the ABC cinema in Fulham Road and became an usherette for a week. I saw *Finian's Rainbow* with Fred Astaire and Petula Clark so many times during that period that I knew all the songs by heart and most of the dialogue too.

I spent the day before John was due to arrive back at Southampton with Toots at 138. I must have driven her half mad as I was counting the hours till I'd see him. But she was as bad – she couldn't talk about anything other than Mark.

I was due to start work at Beales in Bournemouth on Monday at ten and I had a train ticket to get there and a room in a hotel booked for me. But during early Sunday evening I came up with the idea of hitchhiking to Southampton to meet John at the docks at 6 a.m., and then I'd catch the local train to Bournemouth.

All I knew about Southampton was that it was on the south coast. But my old friend Judy, from Oak Lodge and north London days, had a car, and she was generally very savvy about maps and roads, so I rang her and pleaded with her to take me to the appropriate road. These days it would be the M3. She picked me up in Wandsworth as I'd had to go back there and pack some clothes. Bless her, she did exactly as asked, although she gave me an uncharacteristic motherly lecture on the dangers of hitchhiking alone on a rainy, cold night.

I struck lucky: the first truck that came along was going to Southampton. The driver told me I was a silly girl hitchhiking when it was dark but I think he thought it romantic that I was going to meet my man.

'Has he got long hair?' he asked. This was proof he disapproved of hippies and, of course, musicians came under the banner of people to fear or despise.

'No, it's short and curly,' I said in relief.

'And is he going to marry you?' the truck driver asked.

'It's a bit soon to think about that,' was my response. 'I've only known him about six weeks.'

Since that night I've hitchhiked many more times and find it odd that some people who give you a lift feel they have the right to order your life and ask very personal questions. I've met religious people who try to save or convert me. I've had a marriage proposal, been offered a tenner to get into the back of a coal van, and my favourite weirdo's whole dashboard was covered with 'Jesus Saves'. He said he was on his way to church, and his little boy was sitting in the back of the car, and yet he reached out to touch my boobs. Needless to say I made him pull over and leaped out, shouting, 'A fine Christian you are! You'll burn in hell!'

Fortunately nothing like that happened on the way to Southampton and the driver who was a sweetie insisted on taking me to where the ferries from Bilbao came in. I had completely misjudged how long it took to get to Southampton, and when we arrived it was only one in the morning so I was in for a long wait. It was freezing in the waiting room, which was like a big bus shelter, draughty with no heat. But that didn't curb my excitement. I was wearing my black and white rabbit coat, and my long red boots, which had cost almost a week's wages. But I wished, instead of going for glamour, I'd put on a pair of warm socks and a thick jumper. I also regretted not bringing a book.

The wait seemed endless, and there was nothing to distract me, not even anyone to talk to. The clock hands moved so slowly I began to think someone was playing a trick on me. It also gave me time to consider that perhaps I had been a tad hasty. I had no way of contacting John so I couldn't be sure he'd actually caught the ferry. I wasn't even certain the hotel would let him stay with me. Then, of course, he might need to go back to London with the band – for all I knew they might have gigs arranged. And having travelled through the night without any sleep, how was I going to cope at work? My well-intentioned romantic race from London was now looking decidedly foolhardy.

Finally there was an announcement: the ferry was coming in and, although it was still pitch dark, I could see lights in the distance. The waiting area was busy now, and I overheard someone say there had been an earthquake in Lisbon, and storms in the Bay of Biscay.

A couple of uniformed ferry staff took up positions at desks, presumably to check passports as the ferry was coming into dock.

I had moved to the barrier through to the docks, twitching with excitement. But when I saw the ferry had been secured and a companionway put in place I couldn't contain myself any longer. I ducked under the barrier and legged it down to the ferry.

I could hear men shouting for me to come back, but I ignored them. My little suitcase was banging on my legs, but I kept going. Then I saw John at the top of the companionway, and he came hurtling down with obvious delight. The long cold wait was forgotten as we hugged and kissed.

It transpired he had been in the earthquake. He described how he'd woken to find the wardrobe bouncing on the floor and only realized the cause when he looked out of the window and saw locals in the street in nightclothes. He claimed it was two days later when the band reached Bilbao that he realized he had his underpants on back to front. But that was John. He could always make me laugh. He'd also been very seasick in the Bay of Biscay as had almost every passenger.

He'd bought me an oval Seiko wristwatch, which I wore for years, and even when it finally broke and couldn't be repaired, I kept it.

We caught the train to Bournemouth and the hotel let him stay. We were lucky the room was ready, and aside from some canoodling, we fell asleep for a couple of hours. He walked me to Beales for ten o'clock, promising to be there at four to meet me.

I don't even want to remember how dull it was to work in a carpet department. I was so tired I said to one chap, the youngest there, that I was tempted to lie on the pile of rugs and have a sleep. His response was odd: 'I wouldn't do that. You'll find your dress covered in carpet fluff.' I wondered if he had ever dared to lie down on the rugs.

Finally as I swayed with tiredness, not daring to sit down in case I dropped off to sleep and fell off the chair, it was four, and home time. My memory of John meeting me at the store's front door and the icy windswept seafront as we walked back to the hotel is still as clear now as it was then. I remember, too, thinking that I couldn't bear to stay in Bournemouth without him. I even considered ringing the promotions agency to tell them I'd broken my leg or something, anything, just to be with John. But he was the voice of reason. He pointed out that he'd be away from home too, and I needed to keep my job so we could get a better flat. And, besides, we had that night together, if I could stay awake.

I learned the true meaning of the line from Kahlil Gibran's *The Prophet* that night: 'The pain of too much tenderness.' I knew then that John was The One.

It was strangely ironic that I picked up the *Telegraph* after breakfast the next day and there on the front page was my old boyfriend Tony with the headline 'All I could do was pray.' He'd been acquitted at the Kray trial at the Old Bailey. I believe he was the only person who was. He looked even more like Adam Faith in the picture.

My life had been up and down for what seemed like for ever, and the Krays' capture and the upcoming trial had been going on for a lot of it. I'd stopped following it as it was all so nasty. But Tony had been one of the good guys, at least to me, and he'd flitted through my mind often. I'd hoped he'd be okay, but I'd expected him to get some sort of sentence. But that morning I was so happy, and his news made me happier still. He'd been kind and generous to me, and I thought he'd be glad I was no longer hanging around with mugs. Though he'd probably say a penniless musician was just as bad.

When I got back to John in London on Friday night he had good news. Trifle were going to record the Beatles song 'All Together Now', and on the B side, 'I've Got My Thing', a number they'd written themselves.

Suddenly a vision of fame and fortune hung before us. Few people believe this, but back in those days a band like theirs might get only a hundred pounds or so for driving to somewhere like Manchester, and after petrol was deducted and digs for the night, there was precious little left for each of the band members. They did better at London venues, of course, but it certainly wasn't a get-rich-quick career. The managers and promoters made the money, not the musicians. But back then they philosophically called it 'paying your dues'. Even stars like Tom Jones and Engelbert Humperdinck, with fantastic voices, had spent years playing in working men's clubs. But perhaps the reason men like Tom Jones are still going is that they learned their craft the hard way.

For John and me it was a very exciting time. The record was made, Trifle were booked into London clubs for easier publicity, and they had a big following, so all the signs looked good. One day I bought John a second-hand brown leather bomber jacket from Kensington Market, the go-to place for trendy outfits. John was one of those men who took no interest in clothes, but I had persuaded him he had to look like a rock star if he was to become one. He put the jacket on, and as we walked down Kensington High Street he looked at his reflection in a shop window and turned to me. 'Do I look like a rock star?' he asked. He did. But I doubt he ever believed it.

I was in hospital the day they were to be on television – I can't remember why, clearly something very minor, but I was in a cubicle off the main ward, and through a window I spotted the band on TV. I sped into the main ward, despite admonishment from nurses, and turned the sound up. I was so excited it was a wonder I didn't have a heart attack.

John and I were living on hope and love. I missed him so much while I was in Bournemouth, then in Brighton, that I almost jacked in the job, but then I was sent to Harrods.

Up north people wanted big patterns. The most

famous one Firth's made was called Autumn Leaves, and featured huge orange and yellow leaves. You still see it occasionally in hotels. I was told by the girls who worked in Birmingham, Leeds and Manchester that people would come in with a swatch of multi-coloured curtain material and a picture of their three-piece suite, which was perhaps striped. When the girls suggested a plain twist, they were met with horror. They wanted the world to know they had a new carpet, the louder the better.

Down in Bournemouth I had sold a few discreetly patterned carpets, but in Harrods it was all plain. Furthermore they didn't want some upstart of a girl offering suggestions of colour or quality. The only outlet I had for my creativity was to try to sell customers the most expensive carpets, fawning over those who carried handbags that had probably cost more than I earned in a year.

Those customers were all such snobs too. I'm good at selling, and in all my previous jobs I'd always made it a fun experience for my customers. So much so they would often stay chatting to me long after the sale was done. But not in Harrods: women with gorgeous clothes, steely eyes and lips that never cracked into a smile enjoyed making me feel small and stupid. How I hated it there!

I got through the dullness of the carpet job by

daydreaming of how life would be when Trifle hit the big time. I went to almost all the gigs in London and I could see how much people loved the band. I met Geno Washington one night. He said I was the 'grooviest chick in the place'. I saw Family, Jimi Hendrix and so many other bands that were huge then but have since either died, like Jimi, or retired. But there was a problem with Trifle that I didn't dare voice: the lead singer, George Bean (he'd once had a band called George Bean and the Runners).

George was the nicest man. He knew the music world inside out and had many starry friends, such as the model Chrissie Shrimpton and Cat Stevens, but he wasn't a great singer. No one ever admitted it because it was his band, but I remember one night at the Bag o' Nails club in Kingly Street, a guy in the audience asked to sing with them. That man was Chris Farlowe, who'd had the smash hit with 'Out of Time', written by the Rolling Stones, that I'd danced to all night in Kew. I think George must have known who he was as he invited him up. The band played their usual soul stuff, but with Chris singing it was an electric performance. He might not have been pretty and lovely like George but, my God, he could sing.

All the band were totally loyal to George, but John saw the light that night – after all, he'd been playing professionally since he was fourteen, and with the likes of Lulu and Dusty Springfield. He said he wished Chris Farlowe would ask him to play in his band.

George died in 1972, of leukaemia, and it was only then I think that many people who knew him well realized his languid manner and lack of energy were perhaps due to his illness.

Despite all our dreams and hopes, 'All Together Now' didn't hit the heights, much to the band's disappointment.

I can't remember when or why John left Trifle. He liked all the guys, but maybe it was when he auditioned for Samson. I remember how excited he was about joining a jazz rock band. He described them as being like Chicago, only better.

The leader, Ian, played French horn and wrote all the arrangements. He was small with a helmet of curly hair – to me he looked like Napoleon. But I've got an overactive imagination. He certainly was very talented. I think he'd been at some prestigious school of music. There were two Leslies, bass and lead guitar, an organist called Norman, and Rod the drummer. They all came from Wythenshawe, near Manchester.

It was this band I wrote into my first book, *Georgia*. I used their looks and personalities because I grew fond of them all and I wanted to reveal the hardships that young, talented musicians faced back then, and the unscrupulous people who fed on their talent and naivety.

I think it was around the same time that John and I got a decent flat, just a modern studio with kitchen, bathroom and parquet flooring, which I loved. What neither of us liked, though, was that the kitchen window at the back opened onto railway tracks, the main London to Scotland line. At the front a busy road went from Swiss Cottage to Kilburn. It was okay when it was cold and the windows were closed, but on hot evenings it was terribly noisy. However, we were thrilled to have a decent place to live. I was doing pretty well with promotions work, and Samson looked as if they were going to be a huge success: they had a famous manager, who had handled the Small Faces and made them the huge stars they became, plus many other well-known bands.

At first it was all great: they were headlining at places like the Marquee club, getting rave reviews in music papers and building up a big following. The other boys were all in their early twenties and had grown up together near Manchester, but John in his thirties was a Londoner and clued up about the music business. The others were all living in a flat out in the sticks, and the first time I met their manager I felt a cold chill. Max – that wasn't his real name, but that's what I'll call him in case he sends someone round to kneecap me – had made the big-time in the 1950s with American stars, like Brenda Lee and Gene Vincent, and latterly the Small Faces. He was a handsome, big bull of a man, and right away I sensed he didn't like John being with me. Not because there was anything wrong with me, but because he wanted the whole band in one place, dependent on him. John was not only older and wiser than the others, but he had me to look after him and a decent place to live.

John didn't agree, not then. He thought I was being paranoid, but as I listened to him saying how the manager was buying them smarter stage clothes, new instruments and having them professionally photo-graphed, I realized the man was clocking up all this expense and would take it back the moment they began earning big-time.

John had known Steve Marriott of the Small Faces for a very long time. They had been on the same cinema tours and hung around together, so when he bumped into Steve sometime later, he heard straight from the horse's mouth that heavies had been sent round to make Steve toe the line. They never earned more than fifty pounds a week when the Small Faces were going out for thousands of pounds. Only then did John begin to see that my premonition about the management might be right.

Soon various things happened that made the boys question whether their management had any real belief in the band. They were sent to Germany as a backing band for a couple of pathetic brothers who happened to have a famous mother. Max had convinced her that her sons were great singers. They weren't but Samson did their best to cover up this shortcoming, because they didn't want to be seen as a rubbish band.

Next Samson spent a weekend in a studio making a record, which they knew was brilliant, and should have been a chart-topper, only for Max to sell the song to someone else, including the backing track that the boys had laid down. I could go on and on listing the mean, cruel and dishonest things that that man did to the band, but it would make tedious reading, and all the time the golden carrot of fame and fortune was still being dangled in front of their faces.

On 12 July that same year, '69, I was on my own as John had gone to a gig. It was Warren's birthday and always a tough day for me to get through. But it had been exceptionally hot, and I was doing a promotion in the kitchen department of Whiteleys in Bayswater. I could barely manage to speak, let alone talk customers into buying the miraculous oven cleaner I was demonstrating. By the time I got home I was exhausted but the flat was so hot I doubted I would ever get to sleep, especially with the sound of trains on one side, cars and lorries on the other.

John had got some sleeping pills for me because he felt bad about waking me when he came home from gigs in the small hours. Until that night I hadn't tried one, but this time I took one as I was desperate to sleep.

John arrived home about five in the morning with the roadie, Noj, my old friend from the Sinclair Road house. That morning he'd come in to say hello to me for old times' sake. Much later I learned that they realized immediately something was badly wrong. I didn't wake as I always did when John came in, and as he came over to the bed he saw that the sleeping-pills bottle was empty.

I certainly hadn't intended to end it all. I can only assume that I partly woke, saw the bottle and took the rest. They couldn't wake me and rang the doctor, who very callously told them he wasn't coming and the hospital had real emergencies to deal with. He told them to make me drink salt water until I vomited, then walk me round the room to keep me awake. Apparently they had a job to get my mouth open enough for me to drink, but they did eventually and I vomited. Between John and Noj they walked me round and round, and when I finally opened my eyes they made me try to read the titles of books on the shelves.

I couldn't put a sentence together, but I was aware of what was going on around me. I felt like an eyeball stuck in cement. My limbs didn't want to move, and I couldn't hold a cup. Then the doorbell rang. Noj went and called back to John that it was David. John thought it was Max's son David, who handled day-to-day band stuff so he said to come in.

But it wasn't that David. It was my ex-husband, and suddenly he was in the room while I was wearing a nightdress, vomit in my hair, being supported by two men. Later when I thought of how that must have looked I was mortified. If I'd been David I might have felt I'd got my comeuppance, but as I said before, he was a kind, lovely man, and to this day I wish I could apologize for all I put him through.

I remember he sat on the bed and wiped my face, neck and hair with a wet flannel. 'It's his birthday, isn't it?' he whispered to me, perhaps thinking John didn't know about Warren. 'One day soon you'll have another baby and everything will be all right again.'

It turned out he'd come to get me to sign our divorce papers. He could have posted them but he was working in Swiss Cottage and thought he'd call as he had to walk past my flat. I didn't ask but

I guessed he had someone else and wanted to get married. I only said, 'I hope she's kinder to you than I was.'

After that morning, I never saw him again. I hope he lived happily ever after as he deserved to. It took me a few days to recover, and I often wondered what would have happened if John hadn't come home when he did.

Soon after that I found a new job, managing a fabric shop in Chiswick. I had always loved sewing and I was good at it so the job was perfect for me. After the near-death situation we felt it was advisable to move again and Chiswick was the perfect place. We found an attic room with a kitchen in a cupboard. The road was leafy and attractive, just a short walk across Turnham Green to the tube and to my job. John liked the proximity to the M4. I got my mojo back and painted the room white, slotted the old-fashioned bedstead into the window recess and painted that white too. I made Tiffany-style lamp-shades in orange and white polka dots, rewiring the overhead light so it came down low in an alcove, and bought a jolly orange rug to cover the landlord's worn-out carpet. We were thrilled at how trendy and cosy it looked.

I loved my new job. My boss had been in the rag trade and had connections that enabled him to buy fabric remnants cheaply. I would put them on a table outside the shop, usually three-yard lengths, just enough for a dress. They sold like hot cakes. But many women who bought them didn't know how to use a pattern. I used to pin the pattern to the material and cut it out for them. Often I'd be showing them how to set sleeves or put a collar on too.

I met some lovely people while I was there, including Erin Pizzey, who opened a refuge for abused women. I often cut things out for her, in fact I'd have made the whole dress because I liked her so much. She was in her way a great influence on me. When I write about abused women, it's often stuff she told me about. Oddly enough she became a novelist too.

Our first Christmas was a very happy one. John made a little felt stocking for me, which he sewed on my machine while I was at work (and broke it) and I was thrilled at all the decoration he'd put on it, not to mention the imaginative little presents inside. We were very wrapped up in each other and I rarely saw any of my old friends.

In February 1970 Samson were sent to play at the Star-Club in Hamburg, once again giving the band a boost of confidence as the Beatles had been playing there when they were first noticed. I can't remember how I engineered it to go too – maybe I paid my own fare. But I suspect it was kismet. We were horrified by the seedy hotel we stayed in and John developed a stye on his eyelid and wore dark glasses the whole time. It was bitterly cold and we had no money to go anywhere, just hung around waiting for the evening performance. On Valentine's Day we stayed in bed, and I know with utter certainty that that was when our baby Lucy was conceived.

It's funny how one good thing can cancel out all the bad. I came back to England in a bubble of happiness, convinced that all our other dreams would come true too. They certainly seemed to do so for quite a while.

Samson were to be part of a big cinema tour. Steve Marriott's new group, Humble Pie, would be heading the show, with someone called David Bowie at the bottom of the bill. For John it would be good to be reunited with Steve and, hopefully, Samson would reap rewards in being noticed countrywide.

There was also a famous stage designer – I think his name was Sean Kenny. He employed two men, Dick and Mick. They created a huge polystyrene elephant for a fantastic light show. John dubbed them 'Dick and Mick the Elephant Men', and the three became close friends. One came with us to see *Gone with the Wind*, and afterwards took us back to his flat in Ladbroke Grove where he kept very smelly ferrets. I liked the man too.

During rehearsals John brought David Bowie home with him. He was blown away by this guy who was playing acoustic guitar on the show and had some very wild ideas on everything. I'd made a shepherd's pie and he stayed to have some with us. I'd recently bought an old wicker baby crib and painted it white. The paint wouldn't dry, possibly because I hadn't cleaned the crib first, so I was making a loose cover to go over it. He laughed, and during the course of a very jolly evening he wrote some words down on a cigarette packet. I remember 'A little crib and the paint won't dry', 'A lovers' story' and something about a trumpet to blow and a book of rules. But I didn't think much about it at the time.

After that I saw him a couple more times. Once he brought me a pair of pineapples, which I had a craving for. He came in with them inside a pink sweater, like breasts, and John and he became quite close when the tour started. John had a little blue ex-Post Office van, and David often travelled in it with him – I suppose the official transport was either a bit frantic or uncomfortable.

John told me a story set in Liverpool. He, David, Steve and one of the Elephant Men met some very strait-laced young ladies in the theatre, from the Liverpool Philharmonic Orchestra, I think it was. They got themselves invited back to wherever the girls were staying. The boys were all smoking cannabis, and they asked the girls to play for them. Reading between the lines, I suspect the boys behaved badly, but who did what with whom I never got to the bottom of, but one of the girls had sex on three dining-room chairs pushed together with one of the boys while the other girl carried on playing her cello. It seemed that even strait-laced girls could behave like groupies at a whiff of stardom.

John and the rest of the band were so happy throughout that cinema tour. David's first record, 'Space Oddity', reached number thirteen in the charts, which was thrilling, and he was moved up the pecking order on the programme. John said it was the happiest, most rewarding tour of his career, but that happiness ended on the last night.

The last event was at the Festival Hall on the South Bank in London. For John as a Londoner it meant everything to play at such an important venue in his home town. For the rest of the band it was as if they had finally arrived.

I had gone with him to watch the show, and we arrived to find Samson had been pulled off. It was heartbreaking, and unfair. Some bigwig had insisted he had no option but to pull one of the acts as the show was too long, but surely they could have got each act to shelve one of their numbers. Rod Stewart was there that night and gave John a bottle of champagne as a consolation gift. Nice thought but nothing could console him.

Max, the band's manager, was lurking in the shadows, and I know in my heart it was his doing. A deal done with someone else. Who knows? But what I didn't know then was that it would start something in John that could never be put right.

8

The change in John wasn't perceptible to others, not even his mother, but it was to me. I tried to tell myself it was silly anxiety because I was pregnant. But try as I might to throw myself into the joy of having a baby and sewing for her (we called her Lucy from conception), I couldn't ignore the troubling signs in him. I saw several old friends at that time when John was off at a gig, but I didn't share my worries with any of them. I just hoped it would blow over.

It manifested in anger at his manager, but he was unable to speak to him and air his views so I took the brunt of it. Each time he saw the man there was more stuff to get upset about. He would rant, but when I tried to get him to discuss it with me in a rational way, he claimed I was too stupid to understand. I stopped trying and hoped for the best.

As spring came in, another girlfriend of mine, Lizzie Brook, told me that a room and a kitchen next to her bedsitter were available. Our attic, though cosy, was very small and at the top of the house. We'd been to Lizzie's place in Shepherd's Bush several times and it was a light, bright house, with the two landlords living in the basement. They were pleasant chaps and weren't put off by me being pregnant. The rooms were on the first floor, and we only had to share the bathroom with Lizzie. The street wasn't great, like the whole of Shepherd's Bush at that time, but as John pointed out, trying to get a pram up the stairs in Chiswick would be a nightmare. I liked the idea of living next to Lizzie, even though, like Toots, she was planning to go to America before long.

We moved and, as always, I painted the room and some of the furniture, and made it very homely. We hadn't been living there very long when John had his first real meltdown. Once again it was about Max, but it was far worse than usual. He was purple in the face with fury, and the more I tried to calm him down, the angrier he got, accusing me of not understanding what had been done to him. I had made a pot of tea before this started, and as he went on and on, I picked up the pot and hit him on the head with it. Lizzie came through the door just as I'd done it, and she froze in the doorway to see John with tea and tea leaves running down his face. The teapot was on the floor unbroken. Fortunately the tea wasn't hot enough to scald. Lizzie burst into laughter, quickly followed by me. John stormed out.

He saw the funny side later, and after he'd cleaned

himself up, he apologized. He said he would have to leave Samson as he couldn't cope with all the disappointments, being treated like an idiot and still not earning a living wage.

I had to agree it was the only solution. We know now from Steve Marriott that Max had done worse to him, even though the Small Faces were about the most popular group of that era. Their success was despite the management, not because of it.

I remember hearing, though it could be an urban myth, that the Beatles had gone to Max with a view to his managing them, but he'd kept them waiting in the hall of his apartment for so long that they'd got up and left. If it is true, thank heavens they left or their astounding talent might have been whittled away by the man's arrogance and greed.

John left the band, and I didn't see any of the boys in Samson again. We heard they'd split up. The two guys called Les joined the Ivy League, Ian Kewley went to Paul Young and Rod the drummer was with Juicy Lucy. But as my long-awaited pregnancy continued, while I held down a full-time job and started a little business too, my days of nightclubs and following bands were over.

John got some gigs with various bands, did a bit of session work, but nothing with any permanence turned up. That, of course, didn't help his mental state. I left the fabric shop, fully expecting to get state maternity benefit for eighteen weeks. But my employers hadn't been paying my National Insurance stamp. They must have been in financial difficulties as they closed the shop when I left.

I came up with what I thought was a brilliant idea: I'd take a stall in an indoor market. I wanted to be in Kensington Market but there were no stalls vacant. However, the manager said I could have one in Charing Cross Road market. When I found it was for stamps and coins I should have made a run for it. But, ever an optimist, I thought I had the power to make my stall so bright and vibrant that the world would flock to it. After all, it was so close to Trafalgar Square, with all those thousands of tourists, how could it fail?

I certainly created a very jolly stall. I made children's lampshades, which were like hot-air balloons with a little basket beneath for a small teddy bear to ride in. I made frogs that were like bean bags, a colourful print on top, toning corduroy beneath and bulging eyes. They were great as, filled with beans, they could be posed, thrown around, stacked up or whatever. I found some pigeon feed, small hard beans, to stuff them with, and made twenty or thirty a night. I cut out and sewed them, John would turn them right side out and fill them with the beans.

Then I just had to hand sew the hole and put on the eyes.

I also advertised for people to bring me their handicrafts and I would sell them, taking 20 per cent of the selling price. I had droves of people offering me their work – paintings, mobiles, batik scarves and children's dresses. There were paper flowers, hand-decorated boxes and tins, knitted baby jackets, bootees and bonnets, leather cases for glasses, wallets and dog collars, too. I was astounded at how many crafts people there were.

But I have to say, my humble bean frogs were the biggest seller. They were seven shillings and sixpence, about forty pence in today's money.

I wasn't making a fortune by any means, but we were getting by. Then, just a couple of weeks before Lucy was due, our landlords dropped a bombshell: the council had bought the house to make a hostel for the homeless. Who in their right minds would make a couple homeless when they were expecting their first child, then let another homeless person have their place? Our landlords were very apologetic, but it seemed they had no choice. Lizzie found a room somewhere near, and the other tenants all seemed sorted. It was just John and I who had nowhere to go.

John minded the stall while I did the rounds of

flat-letting agencies. I thought with my big bump I'd get the sympathy vote. I had, of course, gone first to the council, but although they got me to fill in forms to be put on the register, they made it quite clear that one imminent birth didn't give you any extra points, not when there were people on the housing list with three or four children. Some agencies were sympathetic, many more rude, but whether kind or not, they all said they had nothing for us.

We gave up the stall, getting the crafts people to collect their stuff, and the rest we took home. With a new baby and no home, I certainly couldn't run a market stall and make items to sell. Then, just the weekend before I was due, I heard of an agency further up Charing Cross Road that handled flats in purpose-built blocks. I went to look at the cards in their window, fully expecting they would all be the expensive mansion-type blocks that I knew in Earl's Court, Kensington and Victoria, but to my surprise they had far more ordinary places that were affordable.

Over that weekend I was in a state of blind panic, but to keep John on an even keel I managed to hide it. I told myself and him that the worst-case scenario was that we'd have to take a bedsitter as a temporary measure. There were plenty of those available in Shepherd's Bush. Although it was not where anyone would want to be with a new baby it would be a roof over our heads.

I made John put on a suit and tie on the Monday morning. And I wore a flowery maternity dress that made me appear even bigger than I was. I felt we had to look totally respectable to gain sympathy. We had a reference from our landlords stating what great tenants we'd been and why we were forced to look for a new home.

We caught the bus to Charing Cross, and as we approached the agency I told John that I would do the talking, and even if I sounded totally unreasonable he was to back me up.

The woman on the reception desk said immediately they had nothing for us. She didn't even ask what area we wanted, or what rent we could afford. I don't think she liked the look of us. But I wasn't going to accept that. I pointed out there were several flats advertised for rent in the window and we were going to sit right down and wait to be offered the keys to one of them. This we did, and after about half an hour a man came over to us and said we couldn't possibly sit there and wait: we'd already been told they had no flat for us.

'We have to wait here,' I said, managing to squeeze out a tear or two, and embarking on an Oscar-winning performance. 'We can't go anywhere else. My baby is due tomorrow, and we must have a flat.' I gave that man the reference and pointed out it was not our fault that we were being made homeless.

I had made some sandwiches that morning and a flask of milky coffee. At one, we got them out, ate them, and drank the coffee. People came and went, some enquiring about flats, a few tenants with a complaint about plumbing or windows that didn't shut properly. One man came in shouting at the receptionist because he'd been threatened with eviction for subletting. He was promptly ushered into a room at the back, and emerged sometime later looking much less sure of himself.

I could feel tension in the air about us two calmly sitting there. The staff had whispered conversations between themselves, always looking over at us.

'We're still here,' I called, at one point.

It occurred to me they might ask the police to evict us. And I certainly didn't know what we'd do then. John whispered to me that we'd better go. I called him lily-livered, and said I wasn't going anywhere.

It was around four in the afternoon when a tall, dark haired man, who turned out to be the manager, came over and asked us to come to his office. I asked if I could go to the loo first. I'd been bursting for ages, but didn't want to leave my post. John had nipped out earlier, but I was the one who had to be seen as rock like.

Once in the small back office the man said they didn't normally give in to blackmail, but due to my obvious advanced pregnancy, they had decided to give us a flat in Sydenham. 'It's unfurnished with two bedrooms and it's on the ground floor,' he said.

I felt like hugging him. We filled in a form, paid a deposit in cash, and suddenly the keys were on the table. It was ours.

We caught a bus to see the flat, and I remember John patting my tummy, saying, 'It's okay to come tomorrow, Lucy. We've got a home for you.'

We were over the moon with delight when we saw the flat. It was clean and bright, recently painted, at the front of the four-storey block, probably built during the forties. It was slightly below the level of the road. From the windows we could look at people waiting for the bus.

I wasn't fazed by the lack of furniture – I knew the landlords in Shepherd's Bush would let us have any-thing we wanted. When we asked, they said they'd take John and the furniture over to the flat as soon as we liked. That night I scooted round all of the now empty rooms picking stuff out. They even gave us a carpet.

The very next morning, 20 November, I felt the first contractions. I would have to rely on John to arrange the furniture. Lizzie turned up that morning, reliable as ever. She'd known the due date and had come to see if it had begun.

By midday my contractions were coming every two minutes and we got a taxi to Queen Charlotte's Maternity Hospital. Lucy was born at 3.20 p.m., weighing seven pounds thirteen ounces, with a mass of dark, curly hair. Quite the most beautiful baby I'd ever seen.

I was disturbed by the speed at which the sister wheeled her away from me, saying only that she needed to see the paediatrician. John had left a few moments before, as he and Lizzie were going to make the first trip to Sydenham.

I was taken to a ward, and left, no further explanation. By six and visiting hour, I was crying so hard it was a wonder there wasn't a mini lake around the bed. And still John didn't arrive. I thought Lucy must have died, and no one wanted to tell me. Not even John. But then he came bursting into the ward, grinning from ear to ear. It seemed he'd been greeted as he arrived and told that Lucy had swallowed some of the gubbins during her birth. They'd got it out of her now and she was fine. He said she was lying there in her cot in the special-care unit, looking like a champion among all the tiny premature babies.

It was only then that I felt able to breathe, dry my eyes and wait for the nurse to bring Lucy to us.

I cannot find words to describe the joy I felt as she was put into my arms. Another child can never be a substitute for one you've lost, but Lucy was never a reminder or a replacement, just beautiful Lucy, and she was ours. I felt blessed. I didn't care then that we had no money, that my father and stepmother would probably never acknowledge her birth, much less want to see her. I wasn't concerned about what lay ahead of us. As long as I had John and my baby all would be well.

9

Lucy might have brought complete joy with her, but the government conspired to make us all as miserable as possible in early 1971.

First there was decimalization, and all the shops rounded up their prices assuming we wouldn't notice. The weather was terrible. We even had snow on Boxing Day of 1970 and the freezing conditions continued. Then came the power cuts, with the electricity cut off for a couple of hours every afternoon. Our flat was all electric, so I used to take Lucy into my bed and stay there until the power cut was over.

Lizzie came to see me because she was leaving for America. She'd bought me the album *All Things Must Pass* by George Harrison. The title seemed prophetic, but she had always been the kind to sense undercurrents, and maybe sorting out the flat with John had made her aware that he was a little unbalanced.

A few years later when I played the album *Abbey Road*, by the Beatles, I saw it as the soundtrack to our love affair. We played it constantly. 'Here Comes The

Sun' was my pregnancy number and John was my Sun King. Eighteen months later he was becoming 'Mr Mustard Seed'.

But when Lucy was just a few weeks old I hadn't even considered Mr Mustard Seed, and I still believed a job would turn up that would make everything all right. As no music jobs were coming John's way he signed on the dole. Unfortunately the postmen were on strike and the dole office was so packed with striking men he couldn't speak to anyone. He came home in disgust, and that meant no money.

I did what I always did in a tight spot: I made things and sold them. Before Christmas I'd resorted to going to Leather Lane market with my remaining hundred or so bean frogs in a suitcase. John stayed in the car with Lucy while I stood in the cold shouting, 'Bean frogs, ideal Christmas present, only seven and six.'

They all sold too, and I never wanted to see another frog, ever. But I resorted to sticking a postcard in a shop window, offering curtain making. It kept the wolf from the door, but it was a tedious job.

Then, out of the blue, I got a call from a promotions agency I'd worked for in the past. They wanted me to sell Mr Kraus tights in Selfridges. Hot pants were the latest fashion. They had a bib and straps but were very bottom-revealing, so Mr Kraus made sheer tights that were perfect to wear with hot pants. They'd asked me because they had it on record that I had great legs, very flattering. I didn't point out I was carrying a lot of baby weight still.

A childminder was needed fast as John looked horrified at taking care of Lucy alone, and the prospect of expressing milk for her was daunting too. But we needed money so there was no choice.

I arrived on the day to find Barbara Windsor and a former beauty queen were there to add more kudos to the products. Barbara had her own tailored brown leather hot pants. The beauty queen, who was prancing around on a podium, had red velvet ones. I had to wear the Mr Kraus pair, which were synthetic suede and badly fitting.

Despite my reservations, especially about leaving Lucy with a stranger, even if she was approved by the health visitor, it turned out to be a fun job. Barbara made funny quips, like 'Ooh, me tits' whenever she bent over. And the beauty queen attracted crowds to our stand, while I did the actual selling. Barbara Windsor was so kind, immediately realizing I hadn't wanted to leave Lucy, and she encouraged me to ring the childminder to reassure myself she wasn't screaming the place down. She wasn't. The childminder said she'd never had such an easy baby, lying quietly in her carrycot when she wasn't asleep.

But returning to work showed me that I'd missed working, and as it didn't look like John was going to find another band and keep us, I'd have to do it.

I loved John so much. If it had been possible, I'd have liked to be with him all day every day. To me he was everything, yet I wasn't blind to his faults. He tended to blame others for anything that went wrong. Most of this stemmed from his upbringing. I had become fond of Lillian, his mother, but she was weak and couldn't say no to her son about anything. She'd had a hard time during the war, working for the telephone company, shinning up telegraph poles to fix the wires when bombs knocked them out. Gloria, John's sister, was a few years older, and their granny lived with them too, so John was very much the little prince, protected and spoiled in the all-female house. He didn't even have his hair cut till he was five and had to go to school. I saw a picture of him in which his curly hair was right down to his shoulders and he looked like Shirley Temple. His father appeared briefly after the war, and immediately left again, never keeping in touch with his wife or children. Lillian never divorced him. When Lucy was five or six, Lillian found out her husband had died, and claimed the life-insurance money. Unbelievably she'd kept paying it for nearly thirty years. I thought that was quite astute of her!

So there I was, worshipping a man who had no real grasp on everyday life for ordinary people. Had he been able to join a band with a permanent residency in a club or hotel, he could have been happy. His idea of heaven was the big bands of the swing era, Joe Loss, Duke Ellington, where the musicians put on their band suits, played their hearts out for several hours, then went home. I couldn't blame him – that scenario sounded pretty blissful to me too. But it seemed to me the music world of the seventies was a jungle, full of men in sharp suits preying on the young and idealistic musicians.

John did try to get ordinary work, but the jobs rarely lasted more than a few days. He just didn't have the skills needed. Then one day he came home to tell me he'd been offered the job of running a newsagent by Bromley South railway station. If he was a suitable manager, he could have the two-bedroom flat above the shop. Free.

For three or four days he went to work at six in the morning to learn about marking up the newspapers for the paper-boys and -girls to deliver. At nine o'clock the day staff would come in, so John would be in the background, ordering stock and suchlike, until it was time to cash up at the end of the day.

I prayed very hard that John would take to the job, but the first day he was left alone to do the newspapers by himself, he almost walked out. Perhaps it was foolish of me, doing what his mother had always done to appease him, but I said I'd go with him the next day, with Lucy in the carrycot.

Even I was daunted by the huge stacks of *The Times*, the *Daily Telegraph* and other papers dumped outside the shop. They had to be hauled in and, from the moment the shop door opened, people flocked in to buy them before catching the train. I did the selling and taking the money, while John marked up the papers. He had finished before the first paperboy arrived – there were thirteen rounds! But I couldn't imagine how he would do that job while constantly being interrupted to serve cigarettes, sweets and papers.

So that was it. I went with him every day. Within a fortnight the management said we could have the flat. The thought of moving again was horrendous, the packing and unpacking, all with a baby too. But I was pragmatic. I liked the flat, which had character. The large sitting room across the front of the shop, had wonky walls and a low ceiling, but it was at least a hundred years old and it was all painted white. It had two bedrooms, while the kitchen and bathroom were down behind the shop. But the big attraction was that I would be there, no packing Lucy into a carrycot each morning. I had no doubt I'd do the lion's share of the work, but I could cope with that. Besides, with no rent or bills to pay we could save up for a small house of our own.

I talked one of the newspaper delivery men into helping us with the move. I can remember thinking as we packed up our stuff one evening, ready to be collected the next day, how I'd imagined when I had a baby I'd have time to play with her, to take her for walks, to cook and sew, all those motherly tasks I like doing. Yet mostly I felt as if I was a lone mother, organizing, planning and absolutely everything else. I was also concerned now that we might have jumped out of the frying pan into the fire.

As it turned out I was right to worry. In no time at all John wasn't getting up to open the shop. I had to do it. Selling was my thing so I wasn't fazed by the number of people rushing in every morning to get papers and cigarettes, and I got marking up the papers off to a fine art, and even found time to speak to each of the paper-boys and -girls as I put their papers into the bags. But Lucy was awake upstairs, waiting to be fed, and though she rarely screamed for attention, my boobs would start leaking, and I suppose, along with extreme tiredness, I was becoming resentful.

The two women who arrived for work at nine must have realized what was going on when John wasn't around, but I lied, saying he was out doing a paper round as a boy hadn't turned up, or that he'd taken some paperwork upstairs. Those two women were lovely, kind, helpful and so interested in Lucy. Now I'm older and wiser, I know they must have felt sorry for me.

A dancer friend of John's came to stay for most of the summer. His name was Brian, and John had met him when they were both in Beirut performing at the casino there. This was long before my time. Brian had been with the Royal Ballet, and he'd let John share his apartment in Beirut. John's stories about his friend were amazing. He had played the beggar on a magic carpet that flew over the saloon in the casino, but when he stood up on the carpet and began to dance, his rags fell away and a prince in fabulous costume remained. I was half in love with Brian before he even arrived, and he was a true prince, making my life better. He called himself Lucy's fairy godmother and he would rehearse in the mornings with her in his arms. She'd giggle with glee, and sometimes I wonder if that's why she still loves dancing. As she got bigger and I had to work in the shop, I'd put her baby chair on one of the ice-cream freezers and almost everyone who came in made a fuss of her.

All that summer Brian loved taking her out in her pram, and insisted I dress her in frilly clothes so he could show her off. Some days he was at rehearsals for shows in London, but he always said he missed Lucy when he was away.

Meanwhile John was doing less and less. He'd go into London supposedly to put himself about and find out about auditions. I could see from Brian's facial expressions that he thought his old friend was just out getting stoned. Once I heard him tell John he'd found a diamond in me, but if he didn't pull his socks up, he'd lose me. I didn't think that was possible – I loved him too much – but I did start to think of other ways to live in which the money I rang up in the till went to us, not to a company that owned a string of newsagents all over London.

Then I saw an advertisement for a general store in Borough Green in Kent, with a little house next door. The rent was incredibly low, and I talked John into going to see it.

The old lady who had the shop had clearly lost all her trade because she couldn't cope. Just a glance round, and I saw cobwebs, a bacon slicer full of rancid fat, a cold counter with black mould. The floor didn't look as if it had been cleaned for years. The little house, which you entered through a door at the side of the shop, was much the same. But my mind was buzzing with ideas.

Get rid of the food that no one would buy, keep

sweets and cigarettes, then make it a pretty gift shop. I could do the same as I had at the Charing Cross market and advertise to sell craft works on commission. It wasn't in a shopping street but on a short road that led from the station down to the main Maidstone Road at the bottom, a bit of a rat-run, but at least people would see it. We needed advance rent, money for the legal stuff, and some for stock. John couldn't see how we'd get that together. But I had a cunning plan. While I was at the fabric shop in Chiswick I'd got to know my bank manager quite well. I'd even made him a bean frog in Barclay's colours. I was sure I could persuade him.

I *did* persuade him. In fact, he said he couldn't see how I could fail with such a low rent and my ability to sell. He went out of his office for a few minutes and I quickly turned round his papers to see he'd written: 'Mrs Pritchard is a force to be reckoned with, but the business will have to be in her hands. Her husband is weak.' I would have liked to take the manager to task and tell him he had no idea how talented my husband was, but common sense told me not to say a word.

He lent us enough money for the rent and some stock, and I left jubilant.

John painted a shop sign, 'A Little Something'. While I scraped the Pink Shield Stamp stickers off the windows. For those who don't remember them you got stamps each time you bought something and when you'd filled a book with them you could swap them for something like a carpet sweeper.

We advertised all the shop equipment, cold counter, bacon slicer and freezer, for sale at a hundred pounds and a man came who, I sensed, was dodgy. He got his men to load the stuff onto a truck, and I was right as he then refused to pay me. John was out somewhere and Lucy was in her cot upstairs. But I locked the shop door, with him inside, put the key down my blouse, and asked him if he really wanted to be the kind of man who would cheat a mother and child out of what he owed.

He threatened me. At one point I thought he would attack me and wrench the key from my blouse. It was stalemate for quite some time. He prowled around the shop, clearly hoping to find another way out, and I kept up a litany of how low he was sinking to rob me and my child.

Eventually, he got out a wad of notes and flung the money at me.

John and I sweated blood cleaning and painting the shop. We found a company who sold pretty enamel teapots, kettles and mugs, along with glassware and fantastic rugs or wall hangings. We also bought sweets and cigarettes to sell too. We took out an advertisement in the local paper to announce our grand reopening. I had a giraffe nibbling a tree, and a caption 'Browsers Welcome' with 10 per cent off on opening day. The night before, it began to snow. I stayed in the shop putting the finishing touches to everything. John went to bed. I felt sick seeing the snow: it meant no one would come to the grand opening. But I carried on regardless. It was a good thing I did, because suddenly a young woman knocked on the shop door. She'd lost her way driving in the snow, and needed to make a phone call.

I let her stay the night on the sofa. You wouldn't have put a cat out on a night like that. She left the next morning, and it was only much later I found she'd left fifty pounds in an envelope, behind a cushion, thanking me for my kindness. I put that money into the till, convinced it would create more money. It did, not a lot, but people in the village came in despite the snow and thought the shop was wonderful.

I wish I could say that John put his back into helping me with the shop and Lucy, but he didn't. He would disappear up to London to look for work, a euphemism for going to bars that musicians frequented. And always there was twenty pounds or so gone from the till. But as I felt he was trying to pull his career back together I didn't begrudge the money. But between those trips to London he would often just lie on the sofa doing nothing.

One day a woman came into the shop. She was different from the usual people who called in. She had a tanned face as if she worked outside and her clothes were a bit shabby but interesting.

She stood in the shop for what seemed like ages, then turned towards the reeded glass door that led into the house. 'You have someone in there who is suffering,' she said eventually.

I wanted to bark at her, 'What about me?'

But I didn't. Instead I let her tell me that she had Romany blood, and had a smallholding nearby. She said her son had worked as a graphic designer, and that she sensed he was about to have a breakdown, so she'd brought him home and put him into a caravan in a field on her property. She said he was there for several months, but he got better in the peace and quiet. 'Your man is going the same way, always worse for artistic people,' she insisted, even though I hadn't told her he was a musician. 'This house and shop have some kind of black vibe. Misfortune, curse, I'm not sure, but I feel it.'

I think she was right. There was some kind of black vibe on that place. The old lady who sold it to me told me how her aunt had died suddenly there. And sometime later I was to find out that everyone who had owned it in the past had had a tragedy there. But, of course, I didn't believe in such things then.

I bought Easter eggs and did a wonderful Easter and spring arrangement in the window, only to find a dead mouse in full view among it. Plus the most expensive eggs in the storeroom had been nibbled. John was getting worse, often raging at me, and I begged him to go to the doctor. He did eventually but came back in disgust as the doctor had lectured him but refused to give him any drugs.

Friends came down on the train from London, and although they didn't say much about my situation, I knew they were anxious for me.

Then one day John was in the shop while I fed Lucy in the house and he came to me to say two old ladies were asking for me. To my shock they were Hilda, my stepmother, and her sister Celia. Over the years I had always informed Hilda and Dad when I moved, not that they ever responded. I hadn't had so much as a birthday or Christmas card from them since I'd left home. I had seen Dad fleetingly, of course, after Warren was born, and I went once into the offices where he worked as a security officer on the Strand, early on in my pregnancy with Lucy. He was very scathing about me looking like a hippie. I was wearing an embroidered cheesecloth dress, plus a beaded band around my head. But so was practically everyone under thirty in London. So I was astounded Hilda had turned up.

They came into the house for a cup of tea. It transpired Celia had passed her driving test at seventy or so, and they'd thought they would explore Kent. Mum must have been very disappointed to find I had a clean, healthy and adorable baby, plus a pretty shop, which actually had customers in it. Of course her eagle eyes picked up that John wasn't quite the ticket. She said nothing then, but a few years later she referred to him as 'a broken reed'. Celia was a retired children's officer and was as nice as she always had been. Mum said very little. They departed within half an hour much to my relief.

The visit was upsetting. No explanation was offered as to why Mum and Dad had ignored me for so long. Neither was I given any hope that that might change. I realized, too, that the reason I never heard from Michael or Selina was that Mum still worked on the principle of Divide and Rule. She hadn't passed on news of me to them, or my new addresses. It was to be years later that I managed to contact them. Awful, really, that she purposely discouraged siblings from having contact with one another.

At least Mum and Celia turned up on a day when I didn't have to hide anything, because soon after big cracks in John's and my life together began to appear. He became a Jekyll and Hyde, one moment calm, happy and good-natured, making me laugh and being closely involved with Lucy, but at the next that could change suddenly for no obvious reason. With hindsight I came to see he didn't like having to be responsible for anything or anyone, Lucy being the only exception. He would happily take her to the swings or on long walks and read her books, though changing a nappy was a step too far. He liked to be smoking cannabis, and if he had none, drink or pills might give him a buzz. He called it 'altered consciousness'.

He had begun smoking cannabis as a fourteen-year-old knocking off school to play in a jazz band with men old enough to be his father. I'm not going to paint myself lily white – I, too, liked being out of my head from time to time for fun. But being a parent and running a business meant I had to stay sober and straight, at least until Lucy was in bed. I had learned from an early age that there were no safety nets in life. I could never call home and ask for a loan. I couldn't go back there if I had nowhere to live. I had to be responsible for myself, and now Lucy. But I hadn't expected to be responsible for John as well.

The situation quickly accelerated. One evening I heard a kind of howl from upstairs and I went up to find John sitting on the floor in Lucy's room crying, his trumpet in his hands all mangled. He wasn't coherent, but I understood he'd crushed it with his bare hands because he felt he'd been given the talent to play it, but Fate and the crooked manager were preventing him from using it. I was mostly shocked that he'd had the strength to wreck the instrument. Trumpets are solid, and his was a 'Con', as I understand it the Rolls-Royce of trumpets. But I tried to soothe him, saying it was just a bad patch, things would improve, someone would need a trumpet player soon.

Then he cut me to the quick by saying I'd turned him into a shopkeeper. That was so unfair. I'd used my wits to make a living for the three of us. I did 90 per cent of the work and had 100 per cent of the worry.

Just a few days after the trumpet incident, John jumped out of the front bedroom window without any trousers on and ran through the village. I wasn't aware he'd done this, until I had a phone call from the woman who had rescued him. She'd been driving through the village, and she recognized he was mentally ill because she'd been through something similar. She took him home and gave him one of her tranquillizers, then rang me to come and get him before her husband got home.

I couldn't drive, I hadn't had so much as one lesson, but somehow I managed to get to her house in first gear in the car without having an accident. John didn't seem aware of who I was.

I went to the doctor the next day and begged for his help. As I'd half expected he was useless. He suggested sectioning John, but he didn't think his behaviour warranted that. He just prescribed Valium.

I won't go into details, but things grew steadily worse. John began ranting to me, some of which made sense but more didn't, and put jazz records on at full volume. It had got to the stage that Lucy ran to me when he started and buried her head in my lap. By then she was eighteen months and no small child should witness that. One night he began thrashing about downstairs after I'd gone to bed. He was pulling pictures out of art books, and ranting again. When I went down and tried to calm him he threatened me. That was it. I went back upstairs and spent the night in Lucy's room.

At seven the next morning I went down to find absolute carnage. Hundreds of torn-out pages from art books were stuck to the walls, mostly Michelangelo's work, records had been broken and cushions torn open. Feathers lay like snow over everything. Drawers had been tipped out. It looked like the work of a burglar who was trying to make a point. I could just see that point: he was highlighting that many wonderful artists and musicians had not been appreciated in their own lifetime. But I was scared and I'd had enough. I fed Lucy, got her dressed, put everything on her pushchair and went off to catch a train to Maidstone to try to get some help from Social Services.

They were worse than useless. A cold-eyed woman looked me up and down, as if not approving of what she was seeing. 'We can take the child into care,' she said, 'but we can't do anything for you.'

I was appalled that she didn't even use Lucy's name, just spoke of her as 'the child'. I left, struggling not to cry.

I went then to Ashford to see Aunt Sybil and Uncle Jim. Sybil had wanted to adopt me when our mother died, and I'd spent many holidays in Ashford with her. In truth I always wished she was my mother. But she was useless too. 'Go back,' she insisted. 'He might set the shop alight.'

I arrived home to find the police there. They'd been called by our neighbour that morning because of the noise in the night, and then, not seeing Lucy or me, they thought the worst had happened. Meanwhile John had taken the whole bottle of Valium, yet he was still standing, though not making much sense. One policeman had been left there. He had listened patiently to endless rants from John, with his despair that I had left. The poor man was sympathetic, but more concerned about Lucy and me.

With his help I put John to bed and reassured him

I wasn't leaving him. But I knew he needed real help, and I would have to fight to get it for him.

John was taken into Warley Hospital in Essex. When the ambulance came he was so keen to get in that he didn't turn back to me and Lucy or show any concern for us.

I found it almost impossible to visit him as the journey from Kent to Essex was so complicated, especially with the shop and Lucy. I hitchhiked once, but John showed very little interest and I think I knew then it was the beginning of the end. The shop was failing too, mainly because John had seen the takings as his personal moneybox. I struggled on, unable to get any help from Social Services as I had a business. My landlord offered to sell the property to me for a ridiculously low figure, which I think was two thousand pounds. This was at a time when house prices were rising. I suggested to my bank that they lend me the money to buy it so that I could sell it as a going concern with the freehold and make a handsome profit. They said that was unnecessary, that when I found a buyer for the business, they could deal with the sale of the property at the same time. I suggested that an unscrupulous buyer could go behind my back, buy the property directly from the present owner, then wait and starve me out.

Predictably the bank said I was being paranoid.

But that was just what happened. The buyer was a singer at the Stork Club, and I imagined him in the cabaret singing songs of love, then plotting to get one over on me. Funnily enough, it turned out that the woman who had said the house had a dark vibe was right. And Mr Stork Club had been living in the house for a couple of months, with the shop rented out, when he fell down the stairs and broke his neck. Needless to say I didn't send him any flowers.

10

I won't bore you with how I wound up the shop. Let's just say it was extremely distressing. With John in Warley, and a new unscrupulous landlord, who was determined to starve me out, I ended up with barely enough money to put down a rental deposit for a house in a tiny village near Battle. It was a lovely place, owned by the lady of the manor, the first bit of luck I'd had in ages.

The weirdest and most hurtful thing was that once John became better some three months later he showed no interest in coming back to me. He was discharged from Warley in the late summer of 1972 with a clean bill of health. Without ringing or writing to me, he went straight home to his mother's house in Dagenham. It appeared he bore me no animosity, but it was as if he didn't recall what had put him into Warley, not to mention what he'd put Lucy and me through.

I tried to be calm and find reasons for his behaviour. Was it the property in Borough Green that had spooked him? Or was he ashamed that he'd perhaps never be able to hold a job down and provide for Lucy and me? If it was the latter, I'd supported him since we first met, and I'd told him a million times it didn't matter who earned the money.

I had been forced to sell his car while he was in hospital, but he had approved that, and I can't think of anything else I did or didn't do that would make him choose his mum over me. It wasn't as if she even wanted him there: her brother had moved in with her and she was enjoying a nice peaceful life. We both knew John would upset that apple cart.

I was fond of Lillian and I'd kept in touch with her during all the difficult times, but I was worried that if John started playing up, she wouldn't be able to cope. She was weak and easily frightened, and John had always been disdainful of her. But I came to think it was for the best. She was his mother, after all, and I didn't want Lucy witnessing any more scenes. Also, I was at a low ebb. John never took on board that I'd struggled to keep body and soul together for months, dealt with solicitors, social workers, the unscrupulous new landlord, and backbiting in the village about us. I was stupid to imagine that when he was well again he'd understand what I'd been through and even fight for Lucy and me.

I admit I'd drawn up my own agenda, though I never got a chance to show it to him. There were to be no more rantings or expecting me to find money for benders in London. In return I'd support him while he went to auditions. I'd even find the money to buy a new trumpet. And I wanted a happy, harmonious life. Now I was starting to understand that the last item would never happen.

Out of the blue my old friend Judy from my raver days in London suggested she could come and share the house in Battle. It wasn't just the prospect of splitting the rent that appealed. I hoped it might be fun. There had been very little fun for a long time.

It was autumn when we moved. As we drove away from Borough Green, Paul McCartney with his new band Wings was on the radio singing 'Heart of the Country'. We took it as a good omen. I was soon healing and enjoying just being with Lucy, showing her cows and sheep, deer in the woods, and not wanting anything more.

Judy had found a job selling humorous books to shops, and had a car with the job, so at weekends we could go out and explore the villages around us. I remember finding Bateman's, Rudyard Kipling's home – he had been my hero as I'd loved his books so much. I wondered then what it must be like to become a famous author and live in such a picturesque house. I often read 'If' and wondered how anyone could write such a remarkable, thought-provoking poem.

John wrote the occasional loving letter to me, and I came to the conclusion that he'd opted out of being a partner and father because he'd discovered in Warley he just couldn't do normality. As time ticked by I even saw a kind of nobility in this, and as he still wanted to be part of my life, and watch his daughter grow, I found that was enough for me and I began to look forward again.

To my surprise my father came to see me around the time of Lucy's second birthday in November 1972. I suppose it was instigated by Hilda having turned up at the shop a year earlier, and that perhaps when I sent the new address I hadn't put John's name on the letter. But Dad didn't question me about what had gone wrong, and admired some heavy curtains I was making for someone in Battle. He said he'd always been impressed by my skill in needlework.

It was a funny sort of day. He enjoyed taking Lucy for a walk with me, and sat her on his lap to read her a book. Mum had always said he was the strong, silent type, and I assume that meant she'd discovered he couldn't talk about feelings or show emotion – not that she could do either of those things! – but he gave me a hug as he left. The only disapproving thing he said was 'When are you going to stay in one place for longer than three months?'

I thought about that remark while I was writing

this, and I was shocked at just how many different addresses I'd had. I'd made each of them real homes, however humble they were. The interior designer in me had to pretty them up, on a shoestring, of course, yet something would happen and I'd leave, usually without a backward glance. Sadder to me now is the number of friends I'd made over the years, friends I really loved, who, for one reason or another, had disappeared as I moved about.

But back to the house in Battle. Judy got the sack from her job shortly after Dad's visit and had to give the car back. She admitted she'd often sat in lay-bys instead of calling on the shops she was supposed to visit. She said she found it impossible to psych herself up to go in and try to sell. I didn't know then that she had mental-health problems – back then no one admitted to such things. But I wished she'd told me she was struggling as I'd have gone with her to work and helped. I have often thought since that that job would have been perfect for me, if only I'd been able to drive. I liked the products, and I'd have given my all to sell them.

As a result Judy said she wanted to go back to London, and suggested I go with her. I was tempted in as much as I couldn't afford the rent on the house alone. But I didn't think London was right for Lucy, and I wanted to be alone with her somewhere beautiful and peaceful until I could work out what I was going to do next. I was now twenty-seven, I'd had countless new starts, made so many mistakes and I couldn't afford to make any more.

I put an advert in a newspaper saying I wanted a flat or small house for my daughter and me. I called myself a quiet, responsible tenant, which wasn't exactly true, but I got a response from someone near Hythe in Kent. They had a flat above their home, and had two daughters just a little older than Lucy.

I hotfooted off to see it and was blown away by how nice it was: the top floor of a detached house with no neighbours. In truth it was easier to get to Paris from this village, than to Hythe – there was a small airport just along the road, and only a few buses a day into Hythe. The house overlooked marshland, with the sea in the distance. The view from the sitting-room window was wonderful. With two bedrooms, and two reception rooms, plus kitchen and bathroom, it was big, the small amount of furniture was very nice, and there were carpets everywhere.

I got someone to help me move my stuff to the flat, and for the first three months I led an exemplary life, being a good mother, decorating the dining room and bathroom. I even went to church. And I made a few curtains for people.

Having said I couldn't afford to make any more

mistakes, I suppose it was loneliness that made me engage with a pair of obvious deadbeats on the bus coming home one afternoon. They made me laugh, brightening what had been a long sad winter. In fact, Lucy and I spent Christmas entirely alone. Watching the New Year celebrations on TV, I offered up a silent prayer that 1973 would be better than 1972 had been.

But deadbeats or not, that couple introduced me to alternative Folkestone. The old high street running down to the harbour was Kent's answer to Haight-Ashbury, albeit nearly six years after the Summer of Love in San Francisco. Hippiness was alive and well in that narrow, winding road. There was a big shop selling way-out clothes, which was owned by a man called Archie. It had previously been his Greek family's coffee bar. And various other tiny shops sold all kinds of hippie paraphernalia. The British Legion club had been taken over by the freaks, and the first time I went there Jimi Hendrix's album *Electric Ladyland* was blaring out through the open windows, and a long-haired guy wearing purple velvet flares and an embroidered jacket was sitting on the sill, legs dangling. I felt I'd found my tribe.

Before you could say, 'Pass the spliff,' I became part of all this. A journalist called Nick had come to the flat to interview me about my interest in astrology a month or so before, and some people who had read the article called me the 'semi-straight astrol-oger on the hill'. I got the 'semi-straight' moniker because my flat was always clean and tidy. Back then it was unusual for ravers to buy washing-up liquid and bleach.

It was around the same time that I met Beatrice, who is still a dear friend to this day. She was living in a squat in Hythe, and when I visited she was trying to wash her hair in a washing-up bowl. She said she wanted a bath, so I said, 'Come home with me and you can have one.' Our fate was sealed by hot water and bubble bath. I also christened her Bee.

She moved in with me a couple of days later. She'd been training as a nurse, and something had gone wrong, but Bee's mother was a real lady, a wonderful woman, so Bee hadn't been dragged up, any more than I had. I guess we were twin souls, and as a bonus, she loved Lucy on sight.

But we were wild. I can think of dozens of slightly shocking but funny times with her, such as when we decided to become strawberry pickers. We were col-lected in Hythe on a lorry and taken out onto the marshes. The other pickers were itinerant workers with their kids. Lucy loved it. We knew we wouldn't last a day without some chemical help, and Bee would wake me with a cup of tea and a purple heart. When we got to the fields, we stripped down to bikinis as it was very hot. And we attacked those strawberry bushes like a couple of well-oiled machines. We had a dozen punnets to fill on a tray and were paid so much a tray. But the speed we picked at astounded the farmer: most of the other pickers were less than a quarter of the way down their row, and we were back at the start, stacking our fruit and setting off for the second.

We got fantastic tans, and as the speed stopped us wanting to eat we also got very thin. By late afternoon we no longer knew whether to kneel to pick, lie down or bend over. We ached in places we didn't even know we had. But the following day we did it all over again. I went down to nine stone and while I was in the bath I could feel every bone in my spine. Worse still when I looked into the mirror I saw Cruella de Vil looking back at me. It was a good job the strawberry season was a short one.

We were burning the candle at both ends, and in the middle too. My flat became Party Central, and with no buses people had to doss on the floor because they couldn't get home. I've always loved Joe Cocker: I can remember getting up in the morning, stepping over sleeping friends to put on one of his albums and saying, 'Morning, Joe.' Bee introduced me to Joni Mitchell, and we'd lie on the floor in the evenings with a shared spliff revelling in the beauty of her work. There was Pink Floyd too, and, of course, David Bowie, and on his *Hunky Dory* album I found the words he had written on a cigarette packet before Lucy was born. They were now in 'Kooks'. I read recently it is thought to be about his son, but I doubt that: David would never have bought a second-hand crib and painted it so badly it never dried. And it was John who played the trumpet, not David.

Ironically the first song Lucy sang was 'Starman', only she sang 'Tar Man'.

Bee and I painted our eyelids like rainbows, we had denim dungarees and platform shoes, and Bee cut her fair hair short on top in what she called the chrysanthemum cut. Mine was a shoulder-length black bob with a full fringe. Archie, who had the boutique in Folkestone's old high street, was a regular visitor, but my landlord didn't like him. When he offered me a job in his shop I was delighted to accept, and for a while Bee looked after Lucy until I was able to get her into a Montessori nursery school in Folkestone.

It may sound as if Lucy was not properly cared for during this period, but I assure you I never forgot about her for one moment, and she was always with me. On top of that, all the friends I had in those days loved her. Known to all as Lucy Pooce, she was a star. Bee was responsible for getting her to eat better.

With me she only liked yogurt, oranges and soft-boiled eggs, but Bee, who was vegetarian, introduced her to brown rice and veggies. One of the great things about the hippie era was that to have children was cool. They were included in everything.

I liked working for Archie, and it was good to be back in the mainstream of life. John visited occasionally, and said he was doing some gigs with old friends from his jazz days. I fully accepted 'we' were over. He never spoke about the past. In fact, it was as if he'd forgotten it all. Meanwhile I was enjoying my life: I had a few beaus, and Bee was such a good, supportive friend. We had more fun than was good for us.

We used to make cakes with cannabis – Lebanese was best for it – and Bee, who loved cooking, excelled at producing cakes that looked fab and made us as high as kites. One evening two policemen called at the door. They were following up on a guy I'd had a very brief fling with. He had left taking my chequebook, and was using it all over the place. The two men were young and attractive, and they settled down in my pretty sitting room, with the lovely view towards France, clearly not anxious to leave.

Now, very little crime happens in that neck of the woods, and in those days most policemen knew very little about cannabis. It didn't stink a warning as the present-day stuff loaded with chemicals does. Even rolled into joints it smelt a little like joss sticks, which we burned all the time.

So I was chatting away to them, glad of some male company, and Bee came in with a tray of tea and cake. We exchanged glances about the cake, and her cheeky expression made me laugh. She offered the guys a slice. They took it and ate it. About half an hour later they had taken off their jackets and were lying back on the sofa, laughing their heads off at everything we said. I put a Pink Floyd album on and they listened, clearly loving it. Finally one asked, 'Who is that?'

When we said Pink Floyd they looked astounded. 'We always thought that was a terrible noise, but it's lovely.'

Later we had to chase them out – neither of us was into seducing married policemen, especially such naive ones. Bee and I hoped they would go home and give their wives the night of their lives. Cannabis, especially in a cake, can help . . .

Unfortunately we had to get cross with them when they kept returning. On the last occasion we told them they were never to come back. My landlord was in his front garden when they arrived, and instead of behaving as if they were on official business, they hid behind the police car. That made them seem far more suspicious, and doubtless confirmed my landlord's suspicions that Bee and I were a couple of criminals.

In the middle of summer I came up with the idea of having an Australian Christmas party. I dug out the tree, the decorations, even found old cards to stick up, and invited all my friends for Christmas lunch, with instructions to dress and talk like Australians – 'How's it going, cobber?' All very silly and great fun. It was also a baking hot day, so after the turkey lunch we jumped into a Transit van and headed for Hythe beach.

I must point out that Hythe is full of retirees, and as we ran down the beach, pulling off our clothes to swim, they were horrified. We read a couple of days later in the local press that a group of Australians had invaded the beach, swimming naked and making a great deal of noise. I believe the police were called, but we'd had the sense to clear off before they arrived.

As the summer faded, my landlord downstairs had had enough and gave me notice. It was just as well. We'd had the best of times, larking about with equally silly people, but we knew we were on a slippery slope and it was time to rethink our future.

Bee and I loved the book *Cold Comfort Farm* and its unforgettable characters. During our time around Hythe we'd spotted many people who were similar types. A herd of cows was put in the field behind our house, back in spring, and when a bull arrived one day, we named him Big Business after the one at Cold Comfort Farm. Sometime later just about every cow in the field had a little replica of BB, which we found very amusing.

The main character in the book is Flora Poste. Following the death of her parents, and with no means of supporting herself, she hits on the idea of writing to each of her relatives, with a view to moving in with them. Bee and I saw this as a splendid idea, especially if you could find a niche where you weren't expected to work. Sadly, I knew none of my relatives were either interesting enough to bother with or living in the kind of splendour I dreamed about. But Bee had some cousins near Castle Douglas in Scotland, who, she believed, lived in a castle and ran a children's home there.

Our madcap idea turned out to be perfect for Bee: it transpired they had a school and a children's home, with the Rudolf Steiner ethic. These were mostly damaged children, but Pop, as Mr Bardsley was called, soon healed, taught and loved them. The Bardsleys liked Bee and took her on as help in the school. It turned out to be the perfect job and life for her.

I will add as a postscript that Bee has since devoted her whole life to such children, and to the Steiner ethic. Unable to have children herself she became a

Universal Aunt. She was and is multi-talented, first at making me laugh and being a wonderful, inspirational friend, but latterly she started a choir, plays several instruments and has gone on to give so many children and adults love and friendship. Now as old ladies we can still giggle about our youthful exploits. But thank heaven *Cold Comfort Farm* put us both back on the right track. I am proud to call Bee my friend.

So, Bee disappeared up to Scotland, and as I had no interesting well-heeled relatives, I resorted to advertising myself in the *Lady*, prepared to be a housekeeper or nanny in return for a home for myself and my little girl.

I had dozens of replies, some unbelievably bizarre. A farmer in Ayr would give me a cottage in return for milking his cows. A man alone with his five children needed help. I went to see him as he was in Kent, and his home was the dirtiest and untidiest I've ever seen. I'm not surprised his wife left him. He was a terrible slob. Finally I had a letter from a man who ran an office on the Fylde in Lancashire who wanted a housekeeper. His wife had died and he had a little girl a few months younger than Lucy, called Polly.

Deep down, even before I caught the train to meet him, I knew it was a bad idea.

As my new employer Ernest Langridge drove me home from Kirkham station with his sweet little girl, Polly, chatting happily to Lucy in the back seat, I felt reassured about being his housekeeper. He was well-mannered, seemingly caring, but it was Polly I was most taken with. My heart had gone out to her when I was told she'd lost her mother to cancer when she was only nine months old. Apparently her relatives back in Nigeria took no interest in her. She had her father's family close by, but they were old, no young children anywhere, and she hadn't been attending a playgroup or nursery. I was relieved she seemed able to respond normally to Lucy.

However, I wasn't impressed by the Fylde, with its boringly flat terrain, and I was a bit alarmed at how far we seemed to be going from any shop, bus stop or other form of civilization.

I was expecting an interesting house, but no! It was a big, totally boring detached oblong box. Not one attractive feature. Not even a pretty garden. Once inside my heart sank further. It was perfectly nice, if you like brown and beige, but so, so dull. Even Polly's bedroom, which she would share with Lucy, had no jolly pictures, mobiles or anything other than an array of toys.

Even more alarming, from the sitting-room windows I could see a concrete pit, with a few inches of stagnant water at the bottom. Ernest said he'd had it dug as a swimming pool but it was never finished. 'Isn't it a bit of a death trap for Polly and Lucy?' I asked tentatively. I had already noted that most of the plants in the garden appeared to be dead.

'I've told Polly to keep away from the edge,' he said. As if a not yet three-year-old would take that on board.

I wasn't much of a gardener then, but I knew dead plants when I saw them. I asked if he'd forgotten to water them.

'No, I watered them, but this is clay soil. Apparently rhododendrons don't like it.'

I could see there were at least thirty. Why would anyone fill a garden with a plant that's a one-trick pony, blooming for just a month each year, and not find out if it would even flourish in the soil?

I was beginning to think Ernest might be a bit thick.

He also owned two fierce Rhodesian Ridgebacks, Rex and Duke, which were shut in his office and rarely, if ever, taken for walks. It was scary, with two small kids in the house, and I like dogs.

But I bonded with Polly quickly and easily. She delighted in stories and cuddles. She had the worst collection of books I'd ever seen, and when I told Ernest so he said, 'A book is a book.' So there's absolutely no difference between *The Tale of Peter Rabbit* and a cheap, grotty book from a bargain shop? Well, at least I had Lucy's with me to read to them both.

Three days in, he wheeled his chair closer to mine as we were watching TV and asked me to marry him. Fleetingly I thought Lesley Langridge had a nice ring to it. But it was only the briefest of thoughts. Very gently I said I'd been married enough times and reminded him I was a housekeeper. I said he ought to find a girlfriend: I would cook them dinners and look after the girls when he went out.

A week or so later I was beginning to feel trapped. I couldn't get away from the house or take the girls on a bus or train, and Ernest didn't even want me to take them out for walks. He used the excuse there was nowhere to go and no pavements in the country-side. I said there must be footpaths, and nature walks were great. Around that time I discovered from a cousin of his who called round one day that Polly had never had her inoculations, and as far as I could tell, she'd not even seen a health visitor. That worried me. A child on her own with a lone parent should be checked from time to time. He certainly wasn't incapable, but until I arrived Polly had been with his ageing mother when he was at work.

One day he drove the four of us to the Lake District, and before we got out of the car at a pub for lunch, he said if anyone should remark on Polly's colour, we should say we adopted her. I was horrified and said I would do no such thing.

Then when Rex bit Polly's cheek I exploded. Ernest had let the dog out, and before he could shoo him into the garden, Polly had come forward to pet him. I was on my way down the stairs, and wasn't quick enough to sweep Polly away. Of course I didn't expect Rex to bite her. Luckily I was quick enough to prevent a really bad bite, but it was on her cheek and, of course, terrifying for her and me.

Ernest took Rex out and chained him up in an old caravan in the garden. He barked constantly for about four hours, then went quiet. Much later Ernest went down there and found Rex had hanged himself on the chain.

That stupid, stupid man wanted the two girls to come and watch him bury the dog. I told him what I thought of that idea in no uncertain terms. He still took Polly, even though I said she had had enough of a trauma with the bite without having to see a dog buried.

That was it for me. That night I told him he'd have to find another housekeeper. I said I'd stay until after Polly's third birthday, which was only a few weeks away in July, and make a lovely party for her, but after that I'd leave.

He sulked big-time, refused to eat the meals I'd cooked and then, once I'd gone to bed, I'd hear him opening cans. By now it was hard to be in the same house as him. But I felt I had to for Polly and, of course, I had to find somewhere else to live. I couldn't afford to go back down south, but while he was at work I arranged on the phone to rent a tiny flat in Lytham St Annes. I couldn't go to see it, but the estate agent described it quite well, including the size of the place, and I had to trust him. I arranged for a man with a van to come and collect my stuff a few days after the party.

The party was successful, with beautiful weather, and I pulled out all the stops making cakes and party food. His relatives all came, but there were no other children, which was sad. I felt like crying because Polly was being deprived of a normal childhood. It was going to be hard for her once she went to school, possibly the only black child there, but if he'd allowed me to get her into a playgroup she'd have had other children at her party and ready-made friends when she went to infant school.

I confided in the same cousin who'd told me about Polly's lack of inoculations that I was leaving and she told me I was just one of a string of women and girls who had come and gone. She clearly didn't blame me. She also said his wife had had a twelve-year-old daughter when they married. When her mother died she ran away and Ernest didn't report it for a couple of weeks. She was found in Blackpool sleeping rough. Ernest immediately said she was to be sent home to relatives in Nigeria. My heart ached to think of a twelve-year-old grieving for her mum, so terribly unhappy that she ran away.

Lucy and I left Ernest's house in the early hours before he woke. We walked down the country lane, in the dark, to catch a bus, or hitch a lift to Lytham. I couldn't go during the day or I'd have had to leave Polly alone. I didn't want to look at that man's face ever again, not even to say goodbye.

The time I spent in Lytham St Annes was, in the main, utterly miserable. I made the tiny one-room flat with kitchen and bathroom quite nice and, for some time, I thought the landlord was kind. He was Irish, with a great sense of humour, and when he saw how I'd painted the flat, he bought me a rug he'd got at an auction to hide the shabby carpet. Soon after, I made three big mistakes. The first was being too grateful and enthusiastic about the rug, the second was accepting his offer to take us to the fun fair in Blackpool, but the third was the most serious: I agreed to a trip on his boat up the canal to Lancaster. I had no idea how far that was, or how long it would take. It was a beautiful late September day, with lovely scenery, and Lucy and I were happy.

But as we got to Lancaster he said we'd have to stay the night as it was too late then to go back. As I recall it was about four in the afternoon, and it wouldn't get dark till about eight. I said no, we had to go back, and he accused me of leading him on. He was a married man, of at least fifty, and while he was good fun, I couldn't have fancied him even on a flaming skewer. I've always had many male friends who were just friends. I had thought he understood that.

I tried to let him down gently, the usual stuff, 'I like you, but not like that. Besides, there's Lucy to think of,' but his face darkened and I was scared. Even if I had fancied him, any man who looks like that when you've said no is someone to run from. But how could I run? I didn't even know how far it was back to Lytham, or how to get there.

So, I had to say I was sorry he'd got the wrong idea, and with a sullen face, he turned the boat around and we set off home in silence. I thought that was it, that he'd leave me alone after that, but I reckoned without his spite. A few days later I found an eviction notice posted through my door. I wrote back to him and said he couldn't make me leave: I'd always paid the rent on time, I wasn't a nuisance to the other tenants, et cetera.

When I heard nothing more, I assumed he'd thought better of it. Meanwhile autumn had arrived with a vengeance, and it was very cold. On the day he had said I was to leave two men arrived at the door, pushed their way in and hauled out the gas fire and the cooker. Again it was the spite that hurt most. I was distraught, but I ran to the police station, as I had no phone, and reported it. The police said they would look into it. Meanwhile I must go home and lock the door. It was grim. I couldn't cook anything and it was icy cold.

Lucy and I snuggled up in bed to keep warm. Later we got some fish and chips from the shop and the next day two different men arrived with the cooker and gas fire to reinstall them. The police had insisted this was to be done and that he couldn't evict me.

That year my friend Bee came and spent Christmas with us, and as I'd managed to find a babysitter we went out to a club in Blackpool. It was a fancy-dress night, and we went as fairies. Bee was the good one, in a white costume made from net curtains found in a charity shop, and I was the bad one: I dyed more net curtains black. We decorated them with tinsel, Bee in silver, me in red, and we even sewed it on our knickers. Needless to say the skirts only just covered our bottoms. The song that reminds me of that fun night was 'When Will I See You Again'. We both got off with a couple of chaps. The one I picked, Will, turned out to be quite sweet, and I was glad of his company during the cold winter months. He became very fond of Lucy.

My thirtieth birthday was in late February, and I awoke to a banging on my door. There was John, with some presents for me. He'd come by coach overnight with no warning and hadn't even sent a card at Christmas. He was cold, hungry and, as it turned out, penniless. I'd have to pay his fare back. I had enough problems without that. I was living a hand-to-mouth existence, so I was quite short with him. I fed him, gave him a fiver, which would have lasted me till the next dole day, and said he must go. I realized at long last that that door was firmly shut. Even if he was taken on by a world-famous band and earned a fortune, he'd still be unreliable, and I'd never know when the next bomb would drop.

The woman upstairs shouted abuse down at me. Her favourite insult was 'London whore'. I knew I couldn't stay in Lytham much longer. The money I got from Social Services was so little that, by Sunday afternoon, I had only a quarter of a pound of mince to make spaghetti bolognese and nothing for the gas and electricity meters once they ran out. So, I used to bundle Lucy up and take her for a long walk. It wore us both out, and once we'd had our tea we'd get into bed, watching TV until the meter gave up.

I made Lucy's clothes in those days and was an amazingly frugal cook too. I didn't waste anything. I had an evening job in a cocktail bar at a posh hotel on the seafront, but I had to pay the babysitter so it was hardly worth it, except that Lucy liked her and it gave me a chance to speak to adults. But once there were faint signs of spring I felt I had to move south and did what I'd done before. I put an ad in a paper asking for a job and a home.

A reply came from a map company in Bristol. They wanted a rep for their products and said if I was suitable they could help me find a flat as they had good contacts.

The only time I'd been to Bristol was to my brother Michael's wedding to Jean in 1967, and though I'd seen no more of the city than Quakers Friars where the register office was, and a bit of Clifton for the reception, I'd liked it, even though events at the wedding were upsetting. As I said earlier, my father and stepmother blanked me. I don't think I'll ever forget the humiliation of that day. Michael and Jean were marrying because he was taking up a post at Rutgers University in New York. He'd be gone for three years.

On the journey home, Dad and Mum had got in another carriage with Paul, my younger brother. However, later Paul came down the train to find me, gave me a big hug and said he was sorry. Yet despite the miserable memories I still wanted to go to Bristol.

I talked it over with my good friend Will, and he said he thought a new start in a place I liked where I could get a nursery place for Lucy until she went to school would be ideal. He said he would take care of Lucy while I went for the interview, and even paid for my return train ticket.

The night before I went to Bristol I found the address of Joan, an old friend from Folkestone, and amazingly she was living in Clifton.

I said earlier I had a knack of always being accepted for jobs, and this firm, Constables, were the same. They asked if I could drive, and I stupidly said yes, having some wild idea of doing a crash course and passing my test. I even came up with a ridiculous idea of getting one of those three-wheelers you could drive on a motorbike licence.

When I got out of the office, I looked at Joan's address and asked someone where Princess Victoria Street was. They pointed across the road to The Mall, and said it was at the bottom, five minutes away.

I knocked on the scruffy door next to the pub, and Joan opened it. It was so good to see her again – we used to call her Joan the Bone from Folkestone, because she was thin. She looked very like Twiggy back in the day. We went straight into the pub next door and, over several drinks, I found her daughter Lucy (thereafter known as Little Lucy) was a year younger than mine, and Kim was eleven. She went to the Steiner school in Bristol. Joan laughed at my plan for the job but said I must come to Bristol and I could work at the nursery Little Lucy was at. My Lucy would be starting school in September.

I went home later on the train half-cut, wild with excitement at going to Bristol. I even drafted an advert to put in a Bristol paper asking for a flat. Joan said I could stay with her, but I knew that wasn't ideal. Amazingly I had a response to my advert very quickly. The man had a two-room studio-style flat coming available. The rent was low and it was in Cotham, not far from Clifton where Joan lived. When I rang her at the pub next door to tell her the news she said there was an excellent school there too.

Only problem was that I had no money for a train ticket. Will had lost interest in me now I was leaving, and anyway, I hadn't been able to pay him back for the previous train fare. But that wasn't going to deter me. I would hitchhike. Having written back to the landlord in Bristol to say I'd be down to view the flat on such and such a date, I was committed. I'd hitched to Scotland with Lucy when Bee first moved there, so I'd do it again.

It was a warm, sunny day in mid-May when I set off and I got a lift as far as Strensham services just outside Birmingham. The helpful lorry driver pointed out a big red lorry parked up. 'He's going to Bristol, ask him,' he said.

As I walked to the red lorry holding Lucy's hand, I saw that the driver sitting in the cab was not just young but handsome, with a tanned bare chest and shoulder-length black curly hair.

I walked round to his open window. 'Can I beg a lift to Bristol?' I asked, putting on my most winning smile.

'By all means,' he said, and actually got out of the cab to help us in. He told me later he'd noticed the other driver pointing him out while he was eating his sandwiches, and guessing what was coming: he ate the last one quickly so he wouldn't have to share it.

That man made me laugh all the way to Bristol. I had the oddest feeling that the bad times were now behind me, the sun was shining, the flat would be nice, and Lucy and I would be happy ever after. And we were, well, mostly, for twenty years.

12

As we were approaching Bristol, having laughed and chatted the whole way, Minnie Riperton's song 'Lovin' You' came on the radio. There is birdsong on the track and my driver said, 'Is that birds I hear?'

There was almost childlike innocence in that remark and it touched me. I remember a line in the song, 'Stay with me while we grow old.' And I wanted that.

It was far too soon to make any judgement about the man. I knew he was called Nigel, was twenty-eight, and had recently been in the Royal Navy. I liked his straight-off-the-fairground look, though in truth nowadays fairground men don't look like a young John Travolta. I really liked him and as we drove through Westbury-on-Trym towards Clifton in Bristol the roads were lined with blossom trees and it all seemed quite magical. I felt I was about to move into far happier times.

As he dropped me at the end of Princess Victoria Street he scribbled his phone number on a scrap of paper and said, 'If you're bored in Bristol, give me a ring.'

I decided I would wait a week before I called. I didn't want to look too keen. I had stuff to occupy me anyway. I'd seen the flat in Cotham and it was far from perfect. It needed serious sprucing up and I would have to share a loo with someone else on the ground floor. But on the plus side, it had a shower, even if it looked ropy. The kitchen, which was mucky with no fridge, was behind a screen in the living room, but the huge bay windows overlooked Cotham church, a beautiful old grey stone building. The road was quiet, and a big lilac tree was coming into flower in the garden. I had lived in much worse places and made them lovely.

When I went to see if I could get my benefits transferred to Bristol, I discovered I'd been dramatically underpaid all the time in Lytham. That was why I'd found it so hard to manage. To my amazement and delight they said this would be repaid to me and I could claim for help with moving costs.

Meanwhile, staying with Joan, I was enjoying life again, meeting new fun people, and the nursery Joan's Lucy attended wanted me to start work with them for the new term in September. But at the back of my mind was Nigel. When I finally rang him from a telephone box, his mother answered, and I was surprised to hear such a well-bred voice, I don't know why.

She was pleasant, but I guess he'd told her how he'd met me and she was thinking, Hitchhiking with a child! I don't want someone like that for my precious son! But she did offer to take a message.

I said I'd ring Nigel back and I did, and the upshot of that was he asked me if I'd like to come out on Saturday night.

He did tell me his mother had said, 'Well, at least she's well spoken.'

Our first date wasn't the most successful. He took me to a club called the Dug Out, the music was so loud we couldn't hear each other speak and at one point, after a few drinks, I kissed him on the cheek. He floored me by saying in my ear, 'Don't ever kiss me in public.' If I'd thought he could hear me I would've retorted, 'Don't worry, sunshine, I'll never kiss you again ever.'

He had a rally car, and instead of taking me home he took me up on the Downs. It was tipping down with rain, and the roll bars made it impossible to get comfortable. But he did ask for my address in Lytham and volunteered to collect me and my stuff when I moved to Bristol. I didn't think that was likely to happen.

Blow me down, I got back to Lytham two days

later and there was a letter from him. It was on a pretty notelet, probably one of his mum's, but he said how much he liked me and was sorry he'd been such an animal. He also repeated his promise to help me move.

Moving day arrived, I was all packed up, the entire flat cleaned, and was waiting for Nigel to appear, when a friend's husband called round. Having no phone of my own, I'd given Nigel my friend's for any emergency. It seemed there was a problem: he'd got as far as Birmingham when the truck had broken down. He'd gone back to Bristol to get another.

I assumed this explanation was a lie, and he was letting me down. I had a job not to burst into frantic tears as I knew my landlord had a tenant coming in at lunchtime the next day and I'd never be able to get someone else to move me at such short notice. However, my friend's husband said he thought Nigel was genuine and I was to come round to their house for some food. This I did, only returning in the evening after Nigel had called again to say he'd be there by eleven that night.

He arrived at five to eleven. But there was no way we could go then. I remember he'd brought with him a bottle of mead. I often wondered why, it was an odd sort of drink, but perhaps he thought I was odd enough to like it. I slept with Lucy in one bed, Nigel

Bee and Lucy, 1972.

Bee, Lucy and me posing, 1973.

New Year 1973, all dressed up
and nowhere to go!

Me in a long skirt, 1973.

Mum and Dad shortly before Dad died, 1979.

Bee with the kids, 1981.

Lucy, Sammy and new born Jo, 1980.

Miss Teleng promoting and selling one of the very first computer games, 1981.

My first electric typewriter, about 1986.

'A Little Something' in Clifton, Bristol, on opening day, 1985.

The shop in Borough Green.

Georgia (age nineteen), the inspiration for my first book *Georgia*. This picture was taken when she first came to work in my gift shop in 1985.

The Promise launch party in Bath, 2003.

My seventieth birthday treat with Jo Prosser, 2015.

Martin and me at the book launch for *Betrayal*, 2023.

Fifty-five years later with Jo, still my dear friend, and with me at Claridge's to celebrate thirty years in publishing.

in the other; all the bedding was packed but we had a blanket each.

We left the next morning with the insult 'London whore' roared out of the first-floor window, with that woman's nasty voice ringing in my ears. I was so glad to be leaving there.

We got as far as Preston when Lucy remembered she'd left Big Bear, her beloved teddy, which I'd made before she was born, back at my friend's house. I fully expected Nigel to say, 'Too bad,' but he didn't. He just turned round and went back to get it.

He was gaining more and more Brownie points with me and it seems he wasn't the callow guy I'd taken him for on our first date.

When we arrived at the flat in Cotham, the landlord wasn't there to let me in. Nigel climbed in through the window, but climbed out again equally quickly. 'You can't stay there! Squatters have been in. Come home to my house,' he said, looking very anxious.

That was a kind offer, but not one I could take him up on. I got him to go in again and open the front door so I could inspect the flat. I've seen plenty of squalor in my time, but Nigel's view of it was more evidence that he'd been carefully brought up. It was a horrible mess, but nothing some rubber gloves, a few bin bags, disinfectant and wide-open windows couldn't sort out in a couple of hours. Thankfully the bedroom was clean and we had our own beds.

As Nigel carried in boxes, he was impressed to see I had an electric drill, and enough cleaning products to swab the decks of the *Queen Mary*. The landlord had left the keys on the hall table. I never did discover if one of the other tenants had used them to throw a party in my flat. Or whether it was a random squatter. It didn't matter. After Nigel had gone I soon had the cleaning under way.

Nigel turned out to be very sweet, though he would have hated anyone using that adjective. He dropped by most early evenings, I assume because he was worried about me. He was somewhat surprised to see me mixing concrete to bed in the wobbly shower, and one evening found me completely stoned after I had been fixing laminated panels. I didn't know about glue sniffing in those days, and that was what I'd been inadvertently doing as I squeezed glue-covered panels behind the shower fitting in an enclosed space with no ventilation. Fortunately, Nigel turned up before I passed out.

I wondered in later years when glue sniffing became all the rage what the attraction was. It was a black sort of buzz, no fun in it. Even music sounded like a dirge. But then I suppose my generation had done the speed, the LSD, the cannabis cakes, and nothing could top those for pure fun.

Nigel went on holiday with 'the lads' to Cornwall that year, and I think lost his position as leader of the pack when he was seen buying me perfume and writing a letter to me. But by then I was pretty stuck on him too, and we had a lot of fun when he did car rallies. If he'd been sponsored by someone I think he might have made a real name for himself as he was fearless, charismatic and a first-class driver. I remember once at Cheltenham he had a fire in his car while racing. He didn't stop or even slow down, just threw the burning carpet out of the window.

But it wasn't his driving skills that won my heart. It was the way he saw Lucy and me as a complete package. He included her in everything we did, and his friends were just as lovely to her. We had days out at Weymouth, and he often took us down to Devon and Cornwall in his truck. Sometimes he pitched an ancient tent for us to sleep in if it was too late to go home.

It was a lovely summer that year, a forerunner to the amazing one of 1976. Lucy and I sometimes took the train and a picnic down to Severn Beach and the open-air swimming pool there. It was demolished years ago but I have many happy memories of it. Almost all weekends I spent with Nigel, and I'll never forget the first time I was invited to tea at his parents'.

His mother, a slender lady with snow-white hair, answered the door. She looked down at Lucy and held out her hand. 'Come in, Lucy. I always wanted a little girl,' she said.

I was so touched that she could be nice to Lucy whatever she thought of me. His father was a sweetheart, and took me on a tour of his beautiful garden. I owe my passion for gardening to Ralph, I learned so much from him. I came to love him far more than I had my own father.

Lucy started school in September 1975 and I began work at the nursery in Clifton. But I also got a cleaning job. It was for a bunch of student-type lads and their house was a tip. The floor in the kitchen was cork, which was already out of style with smart people, but I liked it. This one, however, was in terrible shape, black with ingrained dirt, and I resolved to get it back to showroom condition.

I was on my knees one day, scrubbing at it with a Brillo pad, when one of the guys came up behind me. I used to wear shorts like hot pants then and a halter top. Not your usual cleaner clothes.

'You are a very odd cleaner,' he remarked.

To which I retorted, 'Well, what do you do for a job?'

'I make hot-air balloons,' he said. I can't remember

if I laughed or said something rude about that hardly being a proper job, but I found out later he did just that and his name was Don Cameron.

Fast-forward many years: he had become mega-famous, and a friend of mine was working in his Bristol offices. He came through her office one day and she had a book of mine on her desk. He made a good-natured joke about not reading on his time and she told him to look at the picture of the author. He was puzzled: he knew the face but couldn't place me. My friend told him I used to clean for him.

He roared with laughter. 'I always knew there was something special about her,' he said. 'And she made our kitchen floor beautiful.'

Remarks like that always make me glow with delight. I also love it when old friends remark that I've never changed. They probably mean I'm as talkative and batty as I was back in the day, but I'd hate anyone to claim I was stuck-up, arrogant or mean-spirited.

Around the middle of September John contacted me out of the blue, and said he thought he'd like to come to Bristol to make a new start and be nearer Lucy. I was surprised, as I hadn't heard a word from him since he arrived in Lytham on my thirtieth birthday. (He didn't pay back his return fare either.)

Under the circumstances, I pointed out that I wasn't going to look after him, or be his lady again.

He said that was fine, but would I help him find a flat?

I found a tiny one in Clifton for him, just around the corner from Joan's place. John was thrilled with it, and he soon settled into Clifton life. People were such snobs there, they would turn up their aristocratic noses at a lorry driver, plumber or any kind of manual worker, but a musician or artist could be penniless and that was cool. In no time at all John got a few gigs, mostly with jazz bands, and he didn't hang on my coat tails. Yet he would babysit Lucy whenever I asked. So it was all good. He even came to a fete at the playgroup and met Nigel's mother. She thought him charming, although she was a little worried that he was my ex.

Shortly after this John met Jeanne, a married American from Indiana. She was in England on a sabbatical. She was pregnant, a little accident enroute. John had met her at a party, and just after that she came round to meet me. I liked her on sight, and over a cup of tea, quickly followed by a bottle of wine, we discussed John. She said he was too much of a gentleman for her. I agreed he could be. But as I talked about our life together, I could see she was getting far more enthusiastic about him by the minute. I even told her about the night he'd been so crazy that I picked up a pillow and thought seriously about smothering him. Nothing put her off, but I suppose she heard affection rather than spite in my voice. Soon they were an item, and they moved into a flat together. She asked me how much it would cost to have her baby in England. I said, 'Do what I tell you and there'll be no charge.'

I took her to my doctor's, and she was then given an antenatal appointment at St Michael's Maternity Hospital. Her baby was due around December, I think. Always a bossy person, and because I really liked Jeanne and wanted John to be happy, I kind of supervised them, acquiring a cot and other things for the baby. In turn she liked having Lucy to stay and suddenly we were a team of four.

When baby Tessa was born I felt I had to keep an eye on all three of them, remembering how difficult things were when I had Lucy. As their flat was close to the nursery, I would pop in most days to see what I could do to help, or just give moral support as the weather was awful, the flat cold and draughty and I suspected they were struggling financially.

Around this time Nigel suggested we move in together, and he found a nice little house in Whitchurch, Bristol, quite close to his mum and dad's. It would mean that I'd have to give up my job at the nursery, and also the visits to see baby Tessa and

Jeanne. Lucy would go to the village school Nigel had attended.

I was glad to be getting out of the house in Cotham as there were a couple of nasty women upstairs, who were giving me a hard time. Heaven knows why they were unpleasant, but if I hung washing in the garden, they'd chuck it on the ground. They spilled rice and other things outside my door and complained Lucy made a lot of noise, when in fact she was a very quiet little girl. They even wrote a letter to our landlord as if it was from me, threatening to tell his wife he was having an affair. He called on me, and I proved it wasn't written by me by showing him my distinctive, terrible handwriting. He was all for evicting the girls, but I said I was leaving anyway.

The house Nigel had found was nice, semi-detached, built in the forties with a lot of empty pre-fabs just across the quiet road: three beds, two interconnecting rooms and a galley-style kitchen downstairs, plus a large garden, with school playing fields beyond.

I blithely told Nigel I was going to give up smoking when we moved in. He said it would never happen. Little did he know that that was the best way to encourage me to stop. I didn't find it very hard as he didn't smoke, and anyway I had a whole house to decorate.

What a joy it was to have so much room at last. Lucy kicked up a fuss at first about not sleeping with me, but as soon as we'd got her bedroom decorated and made pretty, she was fine. The neighbours' children became her friends and for the first time ever she could play in the street as it was a cul-de-sac.

Jeanne sometimes came on the bus with Tessa to see us – in those days Nigel was often away Monday to Friday – so I was very glad of the company. But Jeanne was worried, knowing her visa was due to expire and she'd have to go back to America. She didn't want to leave John, and as she was still married to someone in the States, she couldn't claim John was her fiancé. Also John's passport stated that he was a musician, which, to American officials, was like having 'drug addict' emblazoned across it, so it was doubtful he'd get a holiday visa.

I said I would come up with a cunning plan, and after thinking hard on it for a couple of weeks, I did. I won't go into the finer details but the crux was that I got Jeanne to write a letter as if from her parents inviting John and me to come out for a holiday in Georgia with Jeanne. They wanted to thank us for putting their daughter up in our home and supporting her while she had her baby. This Jeanne did. My plan was that John and I would go as a couple to the embassy, me with a cushion down my tights, claiming my pregnancy was too advanced for me to fly, and I couldn't take our daughter out of school either, but we felt John should escort our friend and her baby safely to her home.

It so happened that that day in early May was very warm. When John and I got to the embassy I was sweltering with the cushion in place. John looked anxiously at the armed guards and wondered if they would shoot us if they found out we were lying.

Nerve-racking doesn't come close to describing how scared we were. A long wait in an intimidating, vast hall with too much time to consider what the punishment might be for attempted fraud. John was worried that, if they flatly refused to let him go, Jeanne wouldn't cope on her own.

Yet despite the terror I could also see how funny and bizarre my position was. I had adored John, would have walked over hot coals for him, and now I was party to something illegal to enable him to leave the country with the woman he now loved. Had anyone told me about this six years earlier I would have claimed I'd kill any woman who tried to take him from me. But Jeanne was now like a sister to me, I was a sort of auntie to Tessa, and I really did love all three of them.

I hadn't dared tell Nigel what I was going to do. He would have been horrified. While we were sweltering in that vast hall, Jeanne was back in Bristol, meeting Lucy from school and taking her home to my house to give her some tea. No doubt she was on tenterhooks awaiting either a call from the police to say John and I had been arrested, or one from us to say whether or not John could go with her.

One of my biggest assets is that I can tell a convincing story. I didn't know then that one day this gift would enable me to make a living at it. My storytelling ability had got me out of difficulties many a time – though, of course, my stepmother would have called it 'lying'.

When we were called, I waddled in to see the officer, holding John's arm, having told him to leave me to do the talking. I said the officer that day would probably stamp his visa because he looked like a hen-pecked husband. I told the story, heavy on my disappointment at not being able to go myself, and my fear that our baby would arrive early before John got back.

The craggy-faced officer studied us for what seemed for ever without speaking. It was a good job it was so hot that day as John's face was glistening with a terror sweat, and I expect mine was too. I'm told Customs officers look for that. A clear sign of guilt. But all at once the man rubber-stamped John's passport and told him to hurry home from America in time to greet his own new baby.

He shook our hands as he showed us out of his office.

Once we were well away from the embassy, we rang Jeanne with the good news and I slipped into a pub toilet to remove the cushion. Now they could book their flights and go.

They came to stay with Nigel and me for the last week before they left for America. They departed in early June 1976, and the night before their departure Nigel and I took Tessa's nappies to the launderette to wash and dry them. We didn't have a washing-machine.

It was pouring with rain the next morning and as Nigel, Lucy and I went out to see them off in a hired car, John said, 'Rain is the one thing I won't miss about England.' Ironically, the sun came out the next day and stayed until the end of August. We all cheered when it finally rained.

Once John had got Jeanne and Tessa into the car he turned to Nigel. 'I can't think of a better man to leave my two favourite ladies with. Thank you.'

Another man might have thought that patronizing, but not Nigel. I looked at him and saw tears in his eyes. As we went back indoors he said, 'He was a silly bastard, but I couldn't help liking him.'

It struck me then how much I would miss Jeanne. I thought once she got home, I'd be forgotten, and she and John would get on with their new life without a backward glance.

But it wasn't like that. She and John had a daughter called Eleanor, a sister for Tessa. Jeanne became a playwright. Sadly, Eleanor became seriously ill with major organ failure when she was about eight. It was an awful time, and Jeanne and John split up eventually, John coming back to live in Barking.

Years later Jeanne told me she sold her home to pay the medical bills and slept in her car. I've had so many hard times but nothing as bad as that. Eleanor had years of dialysis before she finally got a kidney transplant. She was a bit wild, driving Jeanne to distraction, disappearing in her car, her portable dialysis machine in the boot, and having a little boy. But she married a lovely guy with good health insurance to pay for what she needed.

Meanwhile John had died of a heart attack at only fifty-five.

Before she became ill, Eleanor had been learning to play the trumpet. Years later, with Eleanor and Lucy grown up, I managed to track down John's trumpet. (He did get another one!) He'd always said he wanted Eleanor to have it, and I arranged for Jeanne and her new husband, Eleanor and her husband and son, to meet Lucy and me in New Orleans. I said it was so the two half-sisters could meet, but really it was to hand over the trumpet to its rightful owner. That was pretty emotional for us women.

But getting back to the summer of 1976, it was golden. One hot day after another. I had my first attempt at gardening at our little house, planted masses of seeds but didn't think to water them. When it finally rained in September, they sprouted, but it was too late for flowers.

Nigel took us to Butlin's in Minehead. But it wasn't a place to go when temperatures were in the high twenties and there was no air-conditioning. The accommodation was pretty basic and it didn't have any ensuites. We had to go to the facilities three blocks away.

I entered a beauty contest, egged on by Nigel. *She* magazine was sponsoring it, but I failed to notice it was to find Miss Personality. Which, of course, meant being loud, naughty and over the top. I could have done that easily, but however good I looked that night, and many said I looked gorgeous, I was beaten to first place by a lady with a calliper on her leg. She showed her knickers and did some high kicks with her good leg. Afterwards Nigel delighted in saying I was beaten by a woman of fifty with a wooden leg.

I had spent a week or more making Lucy a mermaid costume for the fancy-dress competition. I sewed the sequins on her tail one by one, but it turned out there were about twenty mermaids. Who knew mermaids were popular in fancy dress?

We also had to share a table in the restaurant with a milkman and his wife. They were without doubt the dullest couple in the entire world. We escaped from the camp one day and Nigel took me to the Valley of the Rocks, Lynmouth, Lynton and many other pretty places he knew. We really didn't want to go back to Butlin's, but it had been expensive so we felt we had to stay.

On the way home our car broke down on a country lane. Nigel had borrowed it from a friend as his rally car was having some repairs. He walked to a phone box and rang his friend, who had a garage, and he promised to come and get us when he'd finished work. We made the best of it: we got a couple of lilos out of the boot and sunbathed. Suddenly, and I promise I'm not making this up, a man in flowing orange robes with a shaved head appeared and asked if we had some matches. We said no and he disappeared into the woods. About half an hour later we smelt smoke and, to our horror, the wood was on fire. Nigel legged it to the phone box again to ring the fire brigade.

They duly turned up, as did the police, and when we told our story of the orange-robed man, we could see they didn't believe us. I thought we were about to be arrested. Fortunately it transpired the same man had been into a village shop and asked for paraffin to be put in a lemonade bottle. So we were off the hook.

The second holiday we had that year was at Rhossili on the Gower coast. We had the ancient Baden-Powell tent again, held together with safety pins. We also took Afro, Nigel's large, beautiful and very stupid Afghan hound. It was the best holiday I've ever had, gorgeous weather, fantastic scenery. There was nothing more than a water tap in the field where we were camping but we brazened it out, going to a caravan park for a shower each afternoon. Afro was very funny, lying down like a water buffalo in rock pools. I felt like I was in Heaven.

I get the pictures of that holiday out quite often and smile to see Lucy in the orange bikini we'd bought in a charity shop a year before. She lived in it.

After the wonderful summer of 1976, it was hellish when the rain and cold came back. But sometime in that autumn or winter, Nigel suggested we get married. Not a romantic proposal – in fact, he always said it was my idea. I didn't get an engagement ring either. This is probably why I don't know the date, or even the month, but for anyone reading this who hasn't already guessed that Nigel and I got married and I became Lesley Pearse, it's out of the bag now!

Nigel and his mum, Lorna, were a bit tight and Lorna suggested we save money with three old wedding rings she had, which had belonged to various relatives. We took them to a craft market in Bristol, and the jeweller melted them down, then did some kind of hocus-pocus in wax, and behold the rings emerged as one beautiful wide lacy one. I was thrilled. It cost sixteen pounds, and everyone who saw it was amazed.

The ring set the tone of the wedding. It was a very low-key affair on 4 March 1977 in the same Quakers Friars register office where my brother had got married. We had a family-and-close-friends reception at Nigel's parents' house.

I had spent weeks making the dress I was married in, very seventies with a frill round the bottom, Laura Ashley voile, a small brown and white print with a high neck and long sleeves. I was delighted with it until Dad and Hilda arrived. I had been astounded they accepted the invitation to the wedding after their disinterest in me for so long. But I accepted it as an olive branch and I'm glad I did. The first thing Hilda said on arrival was 'That dress is lovely, Lesley, very demure.'

I knew in that instant it was the second thing I'd got badly wrong. The first tragedy was my hair: I'd had it permed the day before and I looked like Mrs

Thatcher. As for the dress being demure, that wasn't my style at all. What was I thinking? However, I had made Lucy a pretty Laura Ashley red and white dress, and she looked gorgeous. As did Nigel in a brown velvet jacket and pin-striped trousers. He told me afterwards that he nearly ran away when he saw my hair.

However glad I was that Hilda and Dad had agreed to travel to Bristol for the wedding, it would have been too much to expect her to buy a nice outfit. She wore an old navy blue number with what looked like a soup stain down the front. My new mother-in-law in contrast looked so elegant, and she'd made a wonderful buffet. Fortunately one of Nigel's aunts had been a nurse so she got on famously with Hilda.

I remember that Hilda's words, as Nigel was preparing to drive them back to the station, amused me. 'Thank goodness you haven't found another broken reed,' she said. I ought to have been indignant. She had never met David and only seen John for about five minutes. But she was right about Nigel. He was an oak tree, unbreakable.

We had a disco at the local pub in the evening and I put on a long, black velvet, low-cut, slinky number, my real style, and I was brave enough to brush out my hair so at least I resembled a 1940s Hollywood starlet. I think Nigel was relieved to see me looking a bit racy.

We had no money for a honeymoon, so I went with Nigel in his truck to Devon and Cornwall, ending up in Plymouth where he'd been stationed while in the navy. We went to the pictures on the final night, and about half an hour into the film all the lights came on. We had to leave as there was a bomb scare.

We had beautiful warm spring sunshine on our wedding day, but on the way back from Cornwall it was snowing. English weather is as unpredictable as I am.

13

We decided to buy a house. Well, I did, and drip-fed the idea to Nigel so he believed he had instigated it. He had to sell the V8 engine in his rally car for a deposit. Such a mammoth sacrifice meant he really did love me. I saw dozens of houses and, believe me, in our price range most were horrendous. There was only one I really liked. It was extremely neglected, and empty as the couple who had lived there had split up.

But, sad as it was, it cost only six thousand pounds. End of terrace, no front garden, like the houses in *Coronation Street*, two up, two down, kitchen and bathroom in an extension at the back. No central heating, of course, just some very ropy electric radiators. Out the back, beyond a yard and a garage, there was the overgrown Arnos Cemetery, which to me was rather lovely.

I have the imagination to see beyond muck and neglect, and I'd had plenty of practice at turning fleapits into palaces. Besides, it had the bones of a house that could be gorgeous. There was a school for Lucy just around the corner, a park nearby, and you could walk into central Bristol or to the main station. I got Nigel to come with me to see it and just hoped he could look beyond the décor, and delight in that it was two thousand pounds less than all the others. I was thrilled when he shared my enthusiasm. Whether it was the side gate onto a cul-de-sac, or the garage beyond the rubbish-strewn yard that lured him, I don't know. I like to think he sensed I wanted it and that was enough.

I realized I was pregnant at about the same time. I was convinced it was a boy and I called him Sam. We moved into 1 Clyde Terrace at the end of May, in a heatwave. We had no furniture to speak of. Nigel's godmother gave us a double bed but the mattress sank in the middle, and Pete Budd of the Wurzels, who had grown up with Nigel, gave us a dining table and chairs. He'd just hit the big-time with 'I've Got A Brand New Combine Harvester' and was moving out of his rented flat. It was a cheap fake-wood affair, but I painted it matt black and reupholstered the seats of the chairs with a pink Welsh tweed. They looked very Habitat.

I got a job as a barmaid, too, lunchtimes only, in the Naval Volunteer in Bristol's King Street, just off the docks. I worked in the old bar, frequented by dockers. Back then ships still came into the docks and had to be unloaded. I loved it there, and as my tummy got bigger the other barmaid, who worked with me, had a job to get past me. As a result, the manager sent me to work in the cocktail bar upstairs.

I wasn't happy about this, expecting it to be very quiet and boring, but on my first session to my shock and delight all the dockers trooped up to drink with me serving them. The manager didn't approve of rough men in the smart bar, so he said I could go back down, but I had to stay at the far end of the bar, and Gloria, the other barmaid, at the other. I was there when Elvis died, and I'll never forget coming in to find Gloria not just crying but keening, like a wounded animal. 'The King is dead,' she sobbed. I had loved Elvis too but, sad as it was, I couldn't join in her grief fest.

One day a chap asked for a pint of Bass, then refused to pay. I took the pint away. We were so busy that day that I didn't notice if Gloria had served him afterwards or he had left. But at almost closing time he came up to the bar and beckoned to me to come closer. I thought maybe he was going to apologize for earlier. However, I didn't put my head right over the bar, which was just as well as he threw the contents of his glass at me. It wasn't beer but urine and it stank. Fortunately it didn't hit my face or head, only soaked my dress.

In a second the whole bar went mad, they shouted

abuse at him and a couple of men caught hold of his arms, took him to the doors of the bar and threw him out into the street. Some of the customers went out to give him a pasting, which he richly deserved.

Awful as it was to have that thrown at me, I was touched by the regular drinkers' loyalty to me. They were always teasing me about my posh voice, and tried to make me speak Krek Bristle. But it was lovely that they defended me.

Meanwhile one man, a real sweetheart who lived nearby, ran home to get me a clean dress. When they heard I'd had my baby, a month or two later, some came to visit me in hospital.

In the late afternoons and evenings, I was decorating the new house, at first just the bedrooms as everything else needed doing downstairs, such as the electrics and plumbing. One of Nigel's friends was a builder and would come round on Sundays to do jobs when Sue, his wife, was working. He always used to say, 'What's the budget on this job, Nige?' Nigel invariably said it was a fiver and a Sunday roast was thrown in.

I got two kitchen units at an auction for four pounds. Over the next few years I painted and repainted them so often it was surprising we could shut the drawers. I also found stuff in skips. I couldn't walk past one without checking what was in it.

Just before I started wallpapering the dining room

with a very elegant dark red paper that had little gold motifs, Nigel drew a felt-tip picture of me in profile on one of the walls. He was no artist, but the big tummy was authentic. Years later when I redecorated that room we laughed so much to see my image revealed again.

At times when Nigel was away working overnight, I was extremely reckless. I wanted to wallpaper the hall and stairs, and there was a huge drop on the stairs. I propped a ladder at one end and put a plank across to rest at the top of the stairs on a wooden toy box. Then I walked the plank, to hang the paper. Lucy was only coming up for seven, but she was alarmed, saying it was dangerous. Bad enough when I was slender and fit. But I looked like an egg on legs. When Nigel came home he wasn't amused and asked why I was in such a hurry. During the next few years he discovered that when I have a plan it has to be executed immediately.

We used to argue a lot about decoration. In those days I was a stripped-pine-and-Laura-Ashley person, but Nigel liked black ash. He bought a couple of second-hand display units and I hated them. As I began to strip pine doors and other bits of furniture, though, he finally came round to my way of thinking. Ralph, my father-in-law, used to take me for my ante-natal appointments as the hospital was at the top of a steep hill and I couldn't waddle up it. He, too, was constantly telling me I wasn't to climb ladders or lift heavy stuff. I ignored such advice.

We saw in the new year of 1978 with a friend, Barry, who used to navigate for Nigel when he was rallying. I remember dancing in the street at eight months pregnant. It would be a while before I got out again in the evening after that night.

Some friends dropped by on the evening of 1 February. Lucy was spending the night with Nigel's parents — I'd taken her there because the new baby was due the next day. As a punctual person, I expected my babies to be so too. On cue, contractions began soon after the friends had arrived. I said nothing as it was good to see them. When they finally got up to leave at about ten, saying they imagined I'd be wanting an early night, I said I'd be getting Nigel to drive me to the hospital. They had five kids between them, yet they hadn't guessed what was happening, even when I was squirming in the chair.

It was a very wild night, high winds and heavy rain. Nigel remarked when we got to the hospital that this baby would be a wild child born on such a night.

She turned out to be seven pounds thirteen, born at 3.20 a.m. on 2 February. Lucy suggested the name Samantha as it was her best friend's name. I thought of my old friend Dorothy's baby Samantha and it seemed perfect, though we never called her that. Only Sammy. She wasn't a wild child: she was shy, sweet and cuddly. An open door to her wasn't an escape route, as it had been to Lucy. To Sammy it was just a place where she could look at the view. She saved the wildness till she was a teenager!

When Lucy was born, I felt such extreme happiness, but this time with Sammy it was even more blissful because now I was in a little home of my own, and Nigel was a good provider with the best work ethic I've ever known, reliable, kind and funny.

Mind you, it was perishing cold that winter, and I used to put a hot-water bottle in the pram with Sammy when I went to the shops. I was the proud owner of a second-hand Silver Cross model, which I loved. One of the first jobs I insisted had to be done when we moved in was knocking a hole in the wall of the garage at the back of the house so I could keep the pram in there. Nothing worse than a pram taking up the whole hall.

I used to take Lucy to dancing classes on Saturdays and one icy morning we set off down the steep hill through the cemetery behind the house to get there. Suddenly I was sliding down, my boots squeaking as I tried to resist. I remained clutching the pram's handle and yelled at Lucy to help – I was like a runaway train. All she could do was laugh, and I'm sure it was hysterically funny to see her mum being dragged down a hill on her bottom. Over the years we had many incidents in that cemetery, some funny like when I was blackberrying and disappeared into an ancient, rotting coffin, again with Lucy laughing her head off. But some incidents were more worrying, such as when Sammy and her friends started a fire in the summer that got out of control.

But in the main that period of my life was serene, happy and very good.

There were moments, too, that stand out, such as when my father asked if he could come to see us. I had written to him and Hilda, but there was little response, so I was close to giving up on him altogether. But he came in September 1978 when Sammy was seven months old. The gods smiled on us, with warm, sunny weather, and because I couldn't drive we walked miles, Dad delighting in pushing the pram. The SS *Great Britain* had just been brought back to Bristol to be restored and, as Dad loved ships and knew all about this one, we went to see it. We had picnics on the Downs, and Dad fed Sammy, which made me well up. He also did lots of little woodworking jobs at our house, building a cupboard round the electricity and gas meters, and repairing a beautiful old tool chest given to Nigel by an uncle. Nigel also got a lecture for not taking care of his tools.

But they got along famously as both had been in Hong Kong and Singapore, Dad as a Royal Marine, Nigel in the navy. They talked about places they both knew. But best of all Dad told me a few stories about my real mum. He said he often got her back late to the nurses' home in Plymouth, but she'd shin up the ivy and climb in through an open window. He said he would smile at her beautiful long legs and remarked that I had inherited them. I understood then why so often in the past he'd shaken his head and said, 'You are so like your mother.' It seemed she had been an incorrigible daredevil too, and no respecter of authority.

His visit opened the doors to keeping in touch. A couple of years later, at only seventy-two he became ill and was in hospital from April until September with a heart problem that affected his circulation. I went to see him as often as possible, though it was difficult with a small child. The last time I took Sammy she was about two. He was in a coma but she climbed onto the bed and commanded him to wake up. He did too. And I was able to tell him I was expecting another baby the following May.

He died a week later. At the funeral I cried, not so much for Dad exactly but because I'd hardly known him and that was so sad. I loved my father-in-law, Ralph, and could tell him anything. On the way home with Hilda, Selina, Paul and Michael, I began to cry again and Hilda told me off. To my surprise, Michael rounded on her and asked, 'If she can't cry at her father's funeral, when can she cry?' I loved Michael for that. We'd seen so little of each other for years, through misunderstandings and Hilda dripping poison into his ears, but that day I saw the spark of the kind brother who had held my hand all the way to school in the snow.

Jo came along in 1981, nine and a half pounds of delight. Well, not so much delight at her birth as she had an arm in the wrong place. It took for ever and a whole lot of agony to get her out. Plus the momentary disappointment that she wasn't a male Joe, but another girl. She is officially Joanne, but back then she was Jojo and later she decided to be Jo.

As with Sammy, I instantly forgot about wanting a boy and she made up for that tiny twinge of initial disappointment by proving to be placid and super-smiley. Sammy and Lucy adored her too.

My decision to become a writer came when Jo was only a few weeks old. It was a warm June night and I was feeding her upstairs, and reading *The Thorn Birds* at the same time. I was so engrossed in the wonderful story that I didn't notice the sun coming up, or that Jo was still in my arms at an empty breast. I put her into her cot then, but as I went downstairs to make a cup of tea, I thought that if I could write a book as good as that one, I could die happy.

I didn't tell anyone, least of all Nigel, that I'd decided to write, and to test the water I wrote humorous letters to the local paper and magazines, and to companies complaining about their products. I often got apologies and vouchers back from the companies, and a couple of my letters to local papers were accepted. But when I got twenty-five pounds from a magazine for a letter about the contents of my fridge, or lack of contents, I knew where I was going.

Nigel was my biggest fan with the letters, but he was lukewarm about giving me sixty pounds for a home-study course in short-story writing. He thought it was a waste of money and wouldn't take me anywhere. He hadn't learned then how persistent I could be.

Meanwhile, aside from dreaming about becoming a writer, as hard up as we were back then, we usually managed a holiday somewhere warm, camping or an apartment, and travelling by coach because it was so much cheaper. The last time we did that we went to Rosas, in Spain, close to the French border, with Jo aged about two, being sick again and again. She went through all the clean clothes I'd taken onto the coach, and in the end she wore a T-shirt of mine, which made her look like a refugee child. Sammy, on the other hand, could sleep anywhere, and got under the seat at one point.

Nigel had decreed that, as he carried the luggage, we could take just one case between the five of us. Into that went an inflatable boat and oars. But the girls had so much fun in it. Nigel would row them around, with his legs over the side, until he tipped them out into the sea, with shocked squeals from them all. I have to say he was good with them on holiday, playing with them constantly.

I loved those days when the girls were small, the happiest in my life. I made the tiny backyard very pretty and in the summer I'd have a paddling pool out, and invite round other mums I'd met through the playgroup at the end of the road with their little ones. In turn they'd invite us to their houses so no one had the chore of clearing up all the time. Or we'd meet in the park.

Around this time Roneen, up in Aberdeen, wrote and said Jo her daughter had moved to Cardiff and married a man called Ron Prosser. I was delighted at the thought of catching up with Jo – the last time I'd seen her was in London in 1970 just after Lucy was born.

I'd no sooner written to say how much I'd like to see her again than she swept in one day wearing a fabulous silver-fox coat, and smelling like heaven. I had nappies drying around the fire, so I doubt she was equally impressed by me. It was super to catch up again. I think it was soon after that that she had her son, Grant, and I went over to Cardiff to see her and her mum, who was staying there. Around that time Toots came back to England. She was living in Thailand, as she still is, and brought her daughter Padma, who was about five. She had followed Mark, the American she met when I met John, and lived in India with him and then went back to the USA. Sadly he was killed in a motorbike accident, and Toots had become a Buddhist.

I remember we went to Bath for the day when she came and it was freezing. But meeting up with these old friends was good. I wrote to Toots for years, but our friendship fizzled out. It's still going strong with Jo. We don't get together often now – children and grandchildren see to that – but when we do it's always fun and she will always have a special place in my heart.

While real life went on all around me I still had my mind set on becoming a writer. I absolutely loved the home-study course I'd bought despite Nigel's objection. In fact, I couldn't wait for the next lesson to arrive and the tutor's comments on the previous one. Then one day the tutor told me to write a short story connected with somewhere I'd worked.

By then I was leader at the playgroup at the end of the road. I got a pittance for it, but the added bonus was that I could take Jo, who was too young at eighteen months to be there officially. But I loved it and made so many friends among the other mothers. One of them, Julia, was a partner in crime, sharing a bottle of cheap wine in either her or my garden. She was about ten years younger than me and had two children, Daniel and Vicky, who were roughly the same ages as Sammy and Jo. We had grown-up girls' nights out quite often. Her husband, Martin, and Nigel got on well, and in summer we all went to a beach together.

I chose to set the story in the playgroup, starring Julia and me. The main thrust was the romance between me and an ex-naval chap. In the story I fell down the stairs of the old church hall. Julia rescued me and I told her I was falling in love. In the original version I woke one morning beside him and considered his proposal of the night before.

My tutor liked it, and suggested sending it to *My Weekly*. I did and they offered me sixty pounds for it: the exact cost of the course. But they said I would have to change it slightly, so the heroine muses over the man's proposal after a date, not in bed with him. I agreed, of course, and I still smile at the prudish attitude, but it was about thirty-eight years ago.

Feeling justified in daydreaming that I could now rival Jackie Collins, I began my first book. I can't remember what I called it, only that it was huge and mainly autobiographical. But completing a writing course certainly wasn't a fast track to being published. I worked on the novel every night once the girls were in bed (which was always by seven). Nigel was still away Monday to Friday, and even when he was home, I'd stay typing in the dining room, pausing briefly at nine to watch the news with him. I finished it in six months, despite typing with just a couple of fingers. The manuscript was daubed with Tipp-Ex blots.

In my naivety I sent it to Virago Press. I should have researched them and discovered they were a publisher of the literary kind. But I felt I was something of a virago and therefore had found my obvious home. The huge pile of paper came back very quickly. But inside there was an arty postcard with a note: 'You have enough material here for three books, but you can write. Good luck.'

Somehow I knew that didn't mean they'd be happy to see a shortened version, but being told I could write was enough. I binned it and began another.

14

I can't remember what instigated my friend Julia and me to sell china ornaments at parties. I have to assume it was a way of getting out to have fun together, and we would justify it by making a few bob. I'd had my shop years before so I knew how to find companies that sold interesting stuff. One was called Devon Ceramics, here in Torquay where I live now. Vernon, the owner, designed and made a range of animal-themed household items, including toothbrush holders, soap dishes and plant-pot holders. They came in a range of pastel colours. My favourite was a rabbit with a hole in its bottom for cotton wool. I believe it was a copy of a rabbit Vernon's grandfather had made and marketed back in the thirties. I remember that when I was a child nearly everyone had a green rabbit by their fireplace.

Vernon also made tall, slender cats in either black or white. Very stylish during the eighties. And these were to be the stars of our little business. We agreed to take his seconds and sell these big cats for ten pounds each. He packed up boxes of a selection of his wares, and we carried them off to my garage with hope in our hearts.

Julia was quite shy, so it was down to me to browbeat friends and friends of friends into having parties for us. Once there, I did the selling, and Julia handled the money. Mostly we had a lot of laughs at these parties. Our favourites were thrown by ordinary young mums in small houses. When we went upmarket, it was disappointing to find the women picky and mean.

We also expanded the range of stuff we had for sale: at one point we had hand-thrown pottery, white china mugs, teapots and butter dishes, with a cute little yellow teddy bear sitting on them, and gorgeous big jardinières. We wangled visits to the Wills cigarette factory in Bristol's Hartcliffe too. We'd set up a stall by the canteen, and usually we did very well. The money we made we ploughed back into stock.

After some months we were finding it harder and harder to get people to hold parties for us. We were giving the hostess a big discount on whatever she wanted to buy, but that didn't really help. The solution was to expand our business. In my opinion, we needed to get a stall in the Bristol market on Sundays. I thought I could ask customers there if they wanted to hold a party at their house. But Julia didn't want a market stall, so I said I'd do it alone to see how it panned out.

Sadly, that decision was to spoil our friendship. Getting up at six, lugging big, heavy boxes around in all weathers, I was doing all the donkey work. Julia wouldn't budge and do it with me so we divided up the stock and went our separate ways. I was very sad – we'd been so close and had so much fun together.

The market stall was great in the summer, and I was selling stuff hand over fist. But as autumn arrived and the weather grew colder, the crowds began to dwindle. There was a guy selling furry car-seat covers behind me, and I used to make him laugh when the weather was icy by burrowing into them. Everyone predicted I'd make a fortune at Christmas – I even persuaded Nigel into demonstrating some jokey toys – but the closer it got to the festive season the less I was taking. The enthusiastic customers I'd once had were happier to be in warm shopping malls.

One of my suppliers, a lovely man called Brian, suggested I get a shop. My reckless nature took over and I wanted one.

I was still writing, and my dream of being published hadn't gone away, just faded slightly. I rarely mentioned to friends that I was writing because it's a bit like trying to get someone interested in watching grass grow. But I had one friend, Shelagh, an English teacher, who loved books, and we'd talk about writing. At that time there used to be an after-noon sewing club at the infants school and we'd make things to sell at the school fetes. I began a craze among the other mothers for talking in writer-speak, such as '"Pass the thimble," she said, with a toss of her long, golden hair.'

Everyone joined in. Cathy got up from the table one day and said, '"I'm going to the bathroom," she announced, as she sashayed across the gymnasium floor.'

We'd be helpless with laughter sometimes, and it got to the point where we couldn't speak normally. They were happy times – in fact, all of the years my girls were at that school were good ones. I remember when Jo was about six months old one of the male teachers, a lovely, kind man, who had been particu-larly attuned to Lucy's feelings when Sammy was born, picked Jo out of her pram when I'd arrived for a special service and threw her into the air, much to her delight. 'I'm sorry,' he said. 'She's just that kind of baby, born to be fun.'

She was, too – naughty, but there was never a dull moment with her. She and Sammy were best friends from little girls to adulthood.

Lucy moved on to St Bernadette's secondary school just a year after Sammy started at Infants. Jo was at nursery school then, but my thinking was that once both girls were at the same school, literally just around the corner from our house, I could run a shop. And write at night, as I'd always done.

Brian found the shop. He'd gone to see it with the idea of selling cheap framed prints there. He knew immediately it wasn't suitable for his slightly down-market trade, but perfect for me. It was in prestigious Clifton, right across the street from the university, in a listed building called the Berkeley Centre. It was owned by a rather grand company that had converted a few large properties into small upmarket specialist shopping centres in Bath and Cheltenham.

Ours boasted a Saturday-only doorman, who wore tails and a top hat. He was an actor, so he had great presence and drew shoppers into the Berkeley. Most Saturdays we had an entertainer too. It was a lovely place to visit, and the hefty rent and service charge mirrored that. A coffee shop at the back with a gorgeous domed ceiling had been famous in the thirties and forties for tea dances, and in the present it was a well-known meeting place. All the shops were one-offs and interesting – a French brasserie, a handmade-pasta shop, a florist and a lovely hand-bag shop to name just a few. With superb lighting, white marble floors and a fabulous ambience, I felt I couldn't go wrong.

I took a shop right at the back, beneath a hairdresser.

I called it 'A Little Something', after my old shop in Kent. I got a company to decorate the windows with a bear and a honey pot, and took my Victorian rocking horse there for children to ride on. It would be easier to tell you what I didn't sell than what I did! The ceiling was full of pretty mobiles, any wall without shelves had sets of flying birds, frogs, cars, teddies and anything weird I could find. The floor-to-ceiling shelves were full of animal-themed china. Then I had card racks and badge racks I put outside the shop every morning. I remember one badge that used to crack me up: 'If the whole world is a stage, I want better lighting.'

I did all the setting up of the shop, painted it, put up the shelves and the lighting, though I asked an electrician to check it. I had an ancient, second-hand till, on which the largest single item you could ring up was £9.99. Nigel had found it somewhere. I discovered the counter on a skip and painted it yellow and white. Luckily the shop was already carpeted. Nigel was completely uninterested in it at this stage, which was hurtful. I suspect he thought it was as barmy as imagining I could get a book published.

I loved the shop so much, though on hot days in summer it was very quiet. I used to hope that on Saturdays it would be fine first thing to bring shoppers out, then rain later to drive them into the Berkeley

Centre. Fortunately, in term-time the students flocked in and I got a name for having the best funny cards in Clifton. Sadly they disappeared in June until early October.

I advertised for a part-time assistant from three to five thirty so I could ride my bike home to be there when the girls came out of school. During the middle of the eighties there was high unemployment and I had about a hundred young people call for an interview. I despaired of finding anyone suitable as so many strolled in chewing gum, inappropriately dressed and in some cases spoke so badly I couldn't imagine anyone employing them.

But then a girl rushed in like a hurricane, half an hour ahead of her slot. 'I'm sorry I'm early,' she said breathlessly. 'I just want to work here so bad!'

Well, that was it, love at first sight for me. Enthusiasm is the most important thing for a salesperson, and she had that and charm by the bucketful. Her name was Georgia, and she was nineteen. Needless to say I snatched her up. She's still a friend to this day, and I never regretted taking her on. True, her arithmetic was rubbish when the till broke down, and she was a bit clumsy, but she was honest, loyal and reliable, and she made me and the customers laugh. With her flair for display, and boundless energy, she was just lovable.

One afternoon I was working alone when I spotted a woman pop a 99p teddy bear into her bag. It was baking hot, I'd taken about ten pounds all day, and my blood began to boil at someone stealing from me. I grabbed the woman's bag and tipped it out on my counter. To my shock, the little bear wasn't the only thing in it. There were dozens of other items, not just from my shop but others too.

I was livid. I hauled back the curtain that hid my handbag and stuff for the children's tea and, with my hands on my hips, like John Cleese in *Fawlty Towers*, I suggested she take my purse and shopping too. Finally I told her to get out of my shop and never come back. With that I kicked her up the backside. As I stood there, flushed with rage, a boy student, who I hadn't noticed behind the pillar in the shop witnessing everything, ran out laughing.

The next day he came back, this time bearing a laminated sign he'd made. It read, 'Shoplifters will not only be prosecuted, but publicly humiliated.'

I'm sure that shoplifter was too shocked to tell anyone what had happened and I doubt she stole again.

About the same time as the shoplifting incident, I finished a second book, a murder mystery. I wrote to a few literary agents with a sample chapter and a bit about myself. Many didn't reply. But one, a Darley

Anderson, replied to say he wanted to see the complete book.

In great excitement I sent it off, and waited impatiently for his verdict.

When he replied, saying he'd like to meet me for lunch, my excitement knew no bounds. By then I'd got to know all the other shopkeepers in the Berkeley, mostly women like me in their early forties. I had mentioned I was writing and they, too, got excited for me, advising me on what to wear. A couple of them came over to the House of Fraser shop in Clifton and talked me into buying a Jacques Vert number with a swirly skirt. I wasn't convinced it was me, but if they thought that was what a successful novelist wore, I was happy to go along with it.

Darley was utterly charming, a Yorkshireman with a great sense of humour, and a rosy face. I always felt he looked as a vicar should. I didn't know then that the Church had originally been his calling, but I guess God didn't call loudly enough. After our lunch he took my manuscript out of a straw bag and plonked it on the table with a good deal of drama and looked at me intently.

'Lesley, you can write,' he said, 'but this is rubbish. Go home and write about something you know.'

As you can imagine, my balloon had burst, and I rushed off to the loo for a cry.

When I came out I noticed several people staring at me. I looked down and, to my horror, my swirly skirt was caught in my knickers. I was exposing my bottom.

I couldn't get out of there fast enough and rushed to Paddington station, only to find I couldn't get a train back until well after six on the ticket I had. So I sat on a bench sweltering, trying hard not to cry.

Recovering quickly from disappointment is one of my few skills, probably because I've had so much experience. I thought first about Georgia in the shop, wondering how she was coping alone. Then I thought about what I really knew. The answer came back like an arrow. The music world in the sixties and musicians. By the time my train pulled into Bristol I had the whole story of my next book in my head. I would call it *Georgia*.

I cannot adequately describe the joy of knowing without question that you are on the right track. I've been on the wrong track so many times, with relationships and jobs, that I didn't expect to get such an intense and empowering vibe to let me know that, for once, I was right.

Georgia was the only person I talked to about the book. In fact I related it to her as an oral serial while we worked together. Every night when the children were in bed I'd be thundering away on that little manual typewriter, so engrossed in the story that I was often at it until three or four in the morning. I'd often go to bed with Nigel around ten, wait till he was asleep, then get up and creep downstairs again.

Obsessive is, I suppose, the right description for me, but I prefer to be thought of as 'persistent'.

I finished *Georgia* in six months and sent it to Darley. He loved it but pointed out some major faults, including a rather ridiculous coincidence that no one would believe. He also said his heart sank when I took Georgia to New Orleans, because he knew the moment she got off the plane that I had never been there. I was upset at the time but to learn that I couldn't get by on imagination alone was a valuable lesson and one I took very seriously.

So, it was a massive rewrite, and many endless hours of research. Fortunately I have a mind like a sponge. I soak up what most people would consider trivial information or boring historical facts. I can also walk streets, look at houses, sense and picture the past. For many years I thought everyone could do this. I didn't see it as a gift, just as I imagined everyone could write. I thought the only difference between me and others was that I was persistent enough to complete a book.

I have a theory that I can tap into previous lives. How do I know how it feels to be a Victorian kitchen maid? Because I feel it. In my third book, *Charity*, in which I wrote about the pain of giving up a baby for adoption, I also had my heroine looking after a very disagreeable old man who lived in a mansion in a village near Oxford. I would point out that I literally stuck a pin in a map. I had no previous knowledge of the area, and I'd never been there.

I was close to finishing the book when I decided I ought to go and check that there wasn't a housing estate where I had placed the mansion I'd described so lovingly. I was driving along the lane to the village when suddenly, through a gap in some trees, I saw my fictitious house. It was now a country-house hotel.

I pulled into the car park, and although I couldn't see a small lake as I'd described, in every other way it was the same. I went in, ordered a coffee and got into conversation with the owner. He ran murder-mystery weekends there, and loved that I had used his hotel as a setting for a book. He told me it had been a convent until the Reformation and had been owned by his family for some two hundred years. He intrigued me further by telling me C. S. Lewis had come to stay a few times, and had given him a signed copy of *The Lion, the Witch and the Wardrobe*, and said what a fortunate boy he was to have grown up in such an enchanted place.

I said that, aside from the missing lake, his hotel

was exactly the same as my fictional country house and the old man in the story had an oak-panelled bedroom. He took me upstairs, opened a door with a flourish, saying, 'There you are,' and, to my astonishment, it was oak-panelled and the mullioned windows were also as I'd described.

Blown away by the magic power I seem to possess, I trust it now. I always check out places, and I research anything I want to put in as a fact. There is no doubt in my mind that I once held a below-stairs job. I can see myself scrubbing slate floors, up to my elbows in hot water rubbing stains out of the master's shirts, or spitting on a flat iron to check it's hot enough to press a blouse.

I wrote and rewrote *Georgia* so many times. Each draft Darley sent off to a different publisher because, bless him, he believed in the story and me. Finally, though, when I'd written *Tara* and *Ellie* too, he said there was nowhere else to try and sent the manuscript back to me.

In the eighties what they called sex-and-shopping books were popular, titles like *Lace*, *Scruples* and novels by Jilly Cooper and Sally Beauman. I have to admit I loved them too. But I couldn't write with any authority about rich people and designer labels. It seemed sex and drugs and rock and roll in the sixties wasn't bestseller stuff.

But I continued to write, run my shop and be a good mum for another six years, convinced the tide would turn.

Then a young couple came to live in the little cul-de-sac by our house, Donna and Tim. She was the production secretary for *The House of Eliott* TV series, which was being filmed in the square behind my shop, and Tim was the set designer for *Casualty*. They were young and beautiful. Nigel and I took them to our hearts, delighted that such a glamorous pair would move into our sphere.

I confided in Donna about my writing and she insisted on reading *Georgia*. To my delight she loved it and suggested I send it to the publisher Heinemann. Her mother had a friend who was published by them, and was very successful. I knew Darley had a dim view of that publisher for some reason, and that was why he hadn't tried them. But spurred on by Donna's enthusiasm, I packed up the manuscript and sent it off to them.

Once it had gone, I told Darley what I'd done and suggested he get in touch to try to sell it, but I didn't think he would.

Despite all my efforts with the shop, it had started to fail. There was a recession in the early nineties so the crowds I used to get on Saturdays and during the run-up to Christmas were dwindling fast. I was naive about business and imagined that as I had sixty thousand pounds' worth of stock I couldn't go bust. But that isn't how it works.

I didn't tell anyone my fears, least of all Nigel, but the anxiety was eating away at me. Unfortunately I was tied into a lease I couldn't get out of, so I couldn't just pack up and walk away.

Then one afternoon Darley called me at the shop, and said, 'You'd better sit down.'

Once I had done as he asked, he told me he'd had an offer of eight thousand pounds for *Georgia*.

As you can imagine I was ecstatic. To me, that was all the money in the world. It transpired that when Darley had contacted Heinemann about the unsolicited manuscript I had sent, they had dispatched a new junior editor to go into the slush-pile cupboard, retrieve it and read it. That editor was Louise Moore, and she is still with me after thirty years. She described how she got the huge, crumpled, tea-stained bundle out, and without much hope of it being a gem, sat down to read it. Fortunately for me she loved it so much that she barely moved until she'd finished it.

I remember the day Nigel and I took the girls to South Kensington to meet Louise. Heinemann Books was in Michelin House, the iconic building I had first seen as a child with the world-famous Michelin Man astride it. That seemed like an omen: a building I had always liked was now offering me the possibility of fame and fortune. That day Louise told me I had a lot of work to do on the book, but I didn't mind. She believed in it, and that was enough for me.

These days when I look back at that time, the shop in serious trouble, my marriage with cracks appearing and my three daughters still very dependent on me, I wonder how I kept all the balls in the air. I suppose I must have focused mostly on my writing and hoped all would be well with the other aspects of my life. Certainly when I got my advance for *Georgia*, I used it to shore up the shop. That was a foolish step, as I soon learned nothing could save it.

Christmas of 1992 was completely different from all my previous Christmases. I had always taken 80 per cent of my annual turnover in December, but that year it went so quiet. It is a fact that in lean times people stop spending money on unnecessary things, and my shop was a monument to the frivolous, silly and unnecessary. Normally on Christmas Eve I'd close the doors on a shop with severely depleted stock. True, I normally had a sheaf of unpaid invoices, but also a bulging bank bag of money, cheques and credit card receipts too. But that Christmas the shelves were still well stocked, the money bag less than half full, yet I still had as many unpaid invoices as I'd had in other years.

It was only then that I owned up to Nigel about how bad things were. I remember he said, 'But how could that happen? You're so clever.'

It wasn't true, of course. I was, though I say it myself, a very good salesperson. I also had a vivid imagination and a flair for arranging stuff, but I was and still am useless with money.

15

In early January my old friend and supplier Brian came into the shop to find me sitting at the counter with my head in my hands. I hadn't slept for more than a couple of hours a night since Christmas, and I'd wake in terror knowing I couldn't pay for most of the goods I'd ordered in for Christmas. By day, surrounded by people, I could just about cope, but I dreaded the night when everything pressed in on me.

I didn't attempt to put on a brave face for Brian. I just blurted it all out.

He offered to come the next day and do a stocktake. He also said I must get all the unpaid bills together and that it would be advisable to call my accountant and talk to her.

Things moved very quickly from there. He did the stocktake, counting everything from the smallest sticker to a huge china pelican, and agreed I was going bust. I got all the invoices together and Jane, my accountant, gave me the name of an insolvency practitioner. I made an appointment with them a few days ahead.

The insolvency woman who interviewed me seemed very nice and one of the first things she said to me was 'I'm taking all of this out of your hands now. There is nothing more for you to worry about.'

Of course that lifted my spirits. But I might have known it wasn't going to be so simple, and indeed I never suspected that when I told her about my first book, due out in June of that year, she didn't see a middle-aged woman with a failing shop but a golden goose who would possibly lay a golden egg each year and the proceeds would fall into her hands. Perhaps I should have been flattered that she saw me as some-one who was going somewhere. But very soon I began to feel like prey.

I won't bore you with the depressing saga of debt, and just how she set about fleecing me. All I will say is that I was angry for a very long time afterwards that she purposely misled me, knowing that, in my naivety, I trusted her.

The real tragedy of 1993 was that I should have been on cloud nine. For almost seven years I'd written and rewritten *Georgia* again and again, and dreamed of little else but getting published. Finally it was going to happen, but that joy was almost eclipsed by putting up the 'Closing Down' sale signs, and watching the business I'd built with love be torn apart by human hyenas who came only for the knock-down prices.

Many of them I had considered to be friends, and some I had supported through family and marriage problems, listened to them over cups of coffee. But those same people snatched up the best things, often trying to beat the price down further. I even saw a couple stealing from me. Like this was a 'Take what you want bonanza. She's probably got a small fortune tucked away.'

If only I had! In those last three months I felt just as I had as a teenager: alone and friendless. I was often in tears as I packed goods to send back to suppliers, to make my debt to them less. I felt ashamed that I'd let down some of those good people, because however hard I had tried to pay off the smaller companies, once the insolvency witch had taken over, everything had to go into a pot for the creditors, and there was a pecking order for who got first dibs.

The final war wound came from a woman I considered a friend, someone whose daughter had been with me back in the playgroup days. She came to buy the remainder of my stock with her imbecile of a husband to sell on a stall at an indoor market. There was no compassion in their faces, only greed. They watched me like hawks as I counted out rubbers, pencils and other tiny items, convinced I was going to double the price. To be distrusted when I was giving them hundreds of pounds' worth of goods for next to nothing was the last straw. I never spoke to them again after that day.

Only two people gave me comfort in that grim time. One was an elderly lady called Maureen, who had come to work for me a few years earlier when Georgia had left to get a proper job. Maureen had more than enough of her own problems, but she believed in my writing, supported me in every way, including acting as a stand-in mother to my eldest daughter when she had to be rushed to hospital while I was out of the country. She was steadfast to the end, even lied for me.

The other was Jane, my accountant. I was upset as I owed her seventy pounds and couldn't pay her. She said she'd take 'a few stocking fillers' for her then young children. Absolute junk of no value! Jane made me see life would get better, as it did, and she's still my accountant over thirty years on. She has a smile in her voice, a wonderful sense of the ridiculous (which includes me) and she is my security blanket.

But enough of the trials of insolvency. I hope I can make you smile again at my failure to find a real job when I finally closed the shop doors for the last time.

I owed twenty-three thousand pounds, but I'd gone for a voluntary arrangement in the hope I could pay back all of my creditors. The insolvency witch had made sure this had no end date, having already taken five thousand pounds of mine, and claimed four and a half thousand of that for her expenses.

I could see I'd be swimming in syrup for the rest of my days, unless I could pull something out of the bag.

I've always been good at selling so I applied to British Home Stores. Sadly, at the interview I think they saw the wild look in my eyes and were afraid I'd reorganize the entire shop. Or maybe they thought I'd be a bad influence on other staff. They were probably right on both counts.

Next I became an audio typist at a solicitor's. My first job was a letter to a fireman who was claiming for injuries after falling out of the cab of a fire engine. I felt sorry for him as he had three small children and a new baby on the way. Of course I should just have typed the letter, which was asking him for proof that the Fire Brigade was somehow responsible for his injuries. But, no, I had to read every last word in his file and imagine I was Perry Mason defending him.

The next was to an illegal immigrant, which was unusual at that time. The man came from Ethiopia and wanted to bring his wife and children over. I got swept away reading his backstory of extreme hardship. But in the time I took to read it, another typist would have completed six or seven letters. Between the two letters I chatted too much and made the other women laugh. At lunchtime I was called into the boss's office.

'I'm sorry, Mrs Pearse,' he said, looking at me over his glasses. 'You are a very entertaining lady, but a distraction, and I'm afraid I must let you go.'

I rather liked at forty-eight being considered a distraction.

After that I weighed pick-and-mix at an indoor market. It was a very downmarket area, with grubby, snotty kids intent on stealing sweets. Their dirty hands delving into the boxes made my stomach churn. I suggested to the boss, a greasy, large-bellied man in a stained T-shirt, that maybe I could put a few ounces of sweets into cellophaned beribboned bags to sell as gifts.

He looked at me as if I had two heads. 'My customers want to stick their sweets in their gobs straight away. They wouldn't understand a ribbon,' he said.

Then I saw advertised what I thought was the perfect job, selling lingerie, and it came with a great wage. It was an international company so my hopes were high. But the shop was in a seedy part of Bristol, which seemed odd, but assuming it was like a warehouse, I set off. As I approached the shop's window I saw a pair of stilettos that looked big enough for a man. I wondered what I was getting into.

It was something of a shock to discover that this was a place men paid to come to for four hours, in which time they would be transformed into women, photographed and allowed to relax in their girly outfits.

A wall of before and after pictures showed how huge the transformation was.

I wouldn't have minded so much if these men had liked to dress in fabulous frocks such as Shirley Bassey or the Three Degrees wore. But it seemed most opted for twinsets and tweed skirts, then sat to watch *The Sound of Music*.

My job would be to strap them into waspies to give them a waist, a bit of padding on the hips and, of course, false boobs. Then the make-up. I would have to learn how to conceal the beard line and help with wigs.

Once the client was ready the photos were taken, back then with a Polaroid camera. One copy went to them, and one for the wall. Then they went off to watch a video, mostly musicals.

I had a job not to laugh as Doreen, the manager-ess, explained it all. She was the kind of plump, grey-haired kindly sort of woman you'd expect to find in a knitting-wool shop.

The wage was tempting, as was the thought of dining out on stories about the people I'd meet there, but I didn't think I could cope. I was afraid I'd be wanting to slap them and call them silly boys. Plus I'd seen giant Babygros on one rack and nappies. I'd definitely be smacking those who wanted to go down that road.

So I had to decline the job, much to Doreen's disappointment. She said I was the only applicant she felt could do the job well, and she'd had dozens of women apply. She also admired my smart French-navy suit and said many of the clients would want to dress just like me.

As I left the shop I was looking over my shoulder, afraid people might think I'd gone into the shop earlier as a man, bought new clothes, got my face and hair done and now I was a man in drag. Hopefully, though, I would look like a good advertisement for the shop.

In the absence of anyone wanting to employ me, I took to writing single-mindedly. Lucy had moved out, Sammy was growing up too fast and Jo was at school. I told myself that if I could write back in the day with the kids playing around my desk, now, without interruptions, it should be a doddle

What I didn't take into account until years later was the mental pressure of writing for hours on end in a dark dining room without any company. I'd spent the last seven years in an arcade where I could have little chats with other like-minded shopkeepers. Not to mention the customers, who often told me their life story. There was always something to do, whether that was dusting the china and cleaning the shelves, arranging greetings cards, or unpacking new stock. Before I'd had the shop I'd run the playgroup at the end of the road. I used to do sewing and stripping pine furniture too. And I had the company of other mothers whenever I needed it.

To be truthful, I had felt alone for much of my life, even when surrounded by friends, but I had parted company with that since I'd married Nigel and had the children. Now aloneness was with me day after day, like a dark shadow in the corner of the room. I was forty-eight, I had a big debt to pay off and the only solution was to immerse myself in writing.

To this day I don't know why I felt that running away from Nigel was the answer to everything. I found reasons. I felt like a plant that hadn't been watered for months, that he wasn't interested in my writing. Even that he was a bit of a bully. They were true, but looking back now I don't know why I couldn't see I was suffering from depression. A couple of years later Nigel asked me why I didn't talk about what was wrong. But I had never talked to anyone, ever, when things were bad for me. As a child I didn't dare speak out, and later I discovered that merely removing myself from jobs or relationships in which I wasn't happy saved the day. Of course, if I had a grievance, running away didn't solve it.

So I continued to write fast and furiously that summer of 1993. *Tara* was now in the publisher's hands, and I wrote *Charity* and *Camellia* too. Forgive me if I've got the odd fact wrong here, but it's hard to remember dates and even the responses to my books so long ago. But I will say that writing *Charity* where the title character gives her son for adoption was both immensely painful yet cathartic. As for Camellia, she was probably the only character I've ever written who was like me. In its original state *Camellia* was a confusing story about two young girls, in two different timelines. Louise, my editor, very sensibly decided to hold back from publishing it. Sometime later I took out a great chunk and used that as the book *Ellie*. I think, of the earlier books, *Ellie* is some of my best work, and writing it so that *Camellia* could become the sequel was a brilliant brainwave. I adored writing *Ellie* because I knew exactly where it had to go.

Back to the situation at home and in publishing. In 1993 *Georgia* did reasonably well for a first book. I always remember a journalist insisting on a photograph of me writing at the kitchen sink. Absolutely silly. Does anyone prop a laptop on the draining-board and write between scouring saucepans?

Someone informed me there was a whole shelf of *Georgia* at Heathrow airport, and I drove up there with Jo, who was eleven or twelve at the time, to look at it. The information was correct. Someone at WHSmith loved the book and had ordered lots of copies. I took a sneaky picture of them, while Jo went up to the rather gormless young assistant and said, 'My mummy wrote that book.'

The assistant carried on chewing her gum and yawned. 'Oh, really,' she said, with as much interest as if Jo had said there was a fly in the window display. I was really embarrassed and, giggling our heads off, Jo and I rushed out.

But as any debut novelist will tell you, you soon find out there is no brass band playing, no throngs of people queuing to buy your book. No excitement, as you imagine, at all.

I don't think that had any bearing on why I ran away from home late that summer. I knew what I was doing and I got the video of *The Bodyguard* the night before to watch with Jo and Sammy. Sad to say I think the song 'I Will Always Love You' has probably haunted them ever since. In my head I was doing the right thing in not telling them I was leaving for fear of seeming that I was conspiring with them against Nigel.

So, the next day once they'd gone to school I

packed up the essentials, wrote an explanatory note to them and Nigel, which I put on the table, and left. I couldn't have done anything worse really. But we all know the 'doing the wrong thing for the right reasons' scenario.

I holed up in a small B&B near Bath, and the only person I told was my old friend Julia. You may remember I told you we'd fallen out over the market stall, and hadn't spoken since. But something bad had brought us together again. Coming back from a buying trip in London on a coach, I was set upon by a group of girls who broke my jaw, knocked my front teeth out and left me in a terrible state. The next morning Julia saw my Jo crying in the school playground and asked what was wrong. Jo said I'd been hurt by some bad girls. Big-hearted Julia forgot about our quarrel and came straight to me, insisting on taking me to the police station and on to the hospital. That day she soothed my pain, even made me laugh as she ran, pushing me in a wheelchair. That was why I confided in her about running away from Nigel, and no one else.

But leaving your home, all your treasured possessions and your children, and finding yourself alone in an impersonal room is probably for some a fast track to thinking you might as well end it all. I felt terribly alone in the world but I was never suicidal. I felt I could only find my way back to normality by being alone.

I'd been gone about ten days when Julia rang me and said she'd seen Nigel. She said he'd lost lots of weight suddenly and was in a bad way, as were the girls. I felt I had to go home then. But I was very scared. Nigel could be terrifying when he was angry, which, of course, is probably why I'd got into the habit of keeping my feelings to myself. But he wasn't scary that day, just the opposite, so badly hurt I felt like a louse. I remember Jo saying to me, 'If you feel you've got to run away again, Mummy, please take me with you.'

God knows I tried hard to make everything right again, but I couldn't. I limped through the rest of that year feeling hopeless. Nigel tried so very hard to be nice, but it wasn't him to be smarmy and try to please me.

On Christmas morning the worst thing happened. He'd bought me an eternity ring. It was very beautiful. Three or four years earlier I'd have thought all my dreams had come true to be given such a present. But a ring is a symbol of everlasting love and I couldn't promise that. To make things even worse I put it on and, as often happens with rings, my finger began to swell. By the time it had turned blue, I knew I had to get the ring cut off. I went to the fire station in Bath, rather than Bristol, as Nigel knew quite a few of the local firemen.

I blubbed out the whole story to the guy who cut it off. He was kind and entirely sympathetic. His kindness that day helped, though. However, Nigel's anger in the days that followed made it impossible for me to stay and on 1 January 1995 as my second book, *Tara*, was shortlisted for the Romanitc Novel Awards, I left with Jo for an exceptionally grim flat on the Bath Road.

All the money I had went on advance rent. We had a knife, fork and spoon each, a duvet, bed linen and towels. In the days that followed we trawled through every charity shop close by to get a few things we needed. Peter, the helpful fireman, lent us a single bed for Jo and a TV. We were cold and very miserable, but we had each other. Sammy had opted to stay with her dad and, of course, Lucy wasn't living at home anyway. But money was the biggest problem. On enquiring at Social Services I found that as I was under contract to a publisher, they couldn't give me any financial help. Jo could have free school dinners, and I would get a reduction of council tax, but that was all.

Later, after many pleading conversations, Social Services paid a proportion of the rent. But life was a struggle. I wasn't going to try to get child support from Nigel. I knew that would be like throwing a fire bomb through a window. Finally I went cap in hand to the bank. Thank heavens I didn't owe them any money.

I told the manager I wanted a sizeable overdraft until September, when I would get a new book contract. He looked at me as if I was a Martian. I asked him if he knew what I did and had to practically spell out that I wrote books. He still looked dumb. 'Like this,' I said, putting the paperbacks of *Georgia* and *Tara* on his desk.

'Oh, right,' he said, with the intelligence of an earthworm. 'Real books.'

I just smiled as if I was brimming with confidence. 'The first two of many, and by the way, *Tara* has just been shortlisted for the Romantic Writers Award.'

That wasn't a fib, and it was the most cheering piece of news ever, especially as the letter came just after I'd had a phone call to say my uncle Jim had died. He and his wife, Sybil, had wanted to adopt me when my mother died, and they'd always kept in close touch, the only relatives who had. I loved them both. I had scraped the money together for the petrol to get to Ashford and the funeral, but seeing my aunt look so old, alone and vulnerable was distressing.

Amazingly the bank manager let me have a ten-thousand-pound overdraft and wished me well. I left the bank silently whooping with glee. I think it was the same day I had a call from Georgia to tell me she'd had a baby girl named Ciara. I rushed to the hospital to see them both. Georgia might have stopped working for me several years before, but I'd lost none of my affection for her.

I felt I was on a roll with good news, so I rang Hilda, my stepmother. I had tried to keep in touch with her more often, though she gave me very little encouragement to do so. My brother Michael had moved her into a flat next to her sister, and although she was in her nineties she was still a force to be reckoned with. But in all the time I was writing short stories she'd bought the magazines and praised them. That meant a great deal to me.

To my astonishment that day she said she'd just finished reading *Georgia*. I hadn't given her a copy as there are some rude bits in it. But she said she'd rung the publishers and demanded one. Nervously I asked what she thought of it.

'Very good,' she said thoughtfully. 'But it's a shame you had to exercise the coarser parts of your brain.'

Of all the things I admired about my stepmother, her command of the English language was the greatest. Even the most mundane conversations with her were a feast of unforgettable descriptions and powerful words, such as 'I have net curtains to keep out the vulgar gaze.' It's one of my favourites and I just wish I'd kept a record of all the others.

I had no money to waste that year, so I just worked and worked until long into the night. There was a door in my bedroom leading out onto a small, gravel-covered yard. When it was hot I wanted the door open, but all the cats in the neighbourhood used it as their convenience and the smell was overpowering. Someone recommended mothballs. I bought a few packets and sprinkled them about. The cats stopped coming but I was almost asphyxiated by the smell of the chemical!

Jo seemed happy in the grotty flat with me. I think she had picked up on how unhappy I'd been when we were still at home, and now she felt happier because I was. She's told me since that she had the best time in those summer months as it was warm and she'd meet friends in the park just across the road. We were so hard up I couldn't even give her the bus fare to school, but she walked cheerfully every day.

Sammy didn't communicate much with me. I suspect she was angry with me. In later years she admitted she'd had the time of her life back then as her dad was away from home so much. As for Lucy, she didn't really comment, though she did go to stay at the family home for a time, which was odd.

Of course, like any mother, I've always been convinced that all of the problems that each of them had are my fault. Even now they're grown women I still think that.

Then Hilda died, and within four days of her death Roneen, Toots and Jo's mum, went too . . . Hilda and Roneen. Without Hilda, I would never have developed my love of books, and chilly though she was, I owe her a lot. As for Roneen, she was kind, a great listener, enormous fun, and I loved her. Sadly I couldn't go with Jo to Roneen's funeral as I had to go to Hilda's, and I didn't have any money to go all the way to Aberdeen anyway. Losing those two was like the end of an era.

I think it was later that year when Heinemann decided to up the advertising budget for my new book *Charity*. I remember seeing posters at the station and on bus stops. Jo and I drove around town one night to find them. It was very exciting. I hoped that the new year would be a better one for me.

16

I was so happy when Jo and I finally left the grotty flat on Bath Road in Bristol. Aside from the smell of cats, I had kept planting flowers in the front garden and people would dig them up almost immediately. That to me is a heinous crime.

I had found a three-storey house to rent, with a back garden in a quiet road at Knowle, in Bristol, which meant Sammy and Lucy could come back to live with me if they wanted to. My financial situation was looking better as I had a new two-book contract and had a cunning plan in my head to get the insolvency witch off my back. I wrote to every one of my creditors and offered them sixty pence in the pound as a final settlement, and they agreed.

Charity would be published in January 1995 and *Ellie* was all but finished. As I wrote the cheques to my creditors I felt such relief, but I was a little worried about how the witch would react: I had bypassed her getting any further 'expenses', as she liked to call it.

We all liked the new house, especially Jo, who had

the room right at the top. I remember coming home from London and stopping at IKEA to buy her a lovely rug, a lamp and new bedding. It's a funny thing about memory, I can still picture the dining room, the kitchen and Jo's room, and even my office, when I finally bought a computer and got someone to teach me how to use it. But I don't remember the bedrooms and who slept where.

I do remember Jo and Sammy having a fight in the bathroom, though, and breaking the shower screen. I wanted to bang their heads together. I also remember going to my friend Jo in Cardiff for the weekend and getting a phone call to tell me the girls had thrown a party and a whole lot of gatecrashers turned up. They had opened a crate of champagne, sent by my publisher, and those cretins didn't just drink it, which would be understandable, but smashed the bottles in the road, along with other loutish behaviour. I came rushing back from Cardiff and breathed fire and brimstone over the girls. But they had been so frightened when the party got out of hand I thought that was punishment enough.

The neighbours were not so forgiving. We were the street pariahs until we finally left.

My troubles didn't end there. I went away for a brief holiday, got back and went to get some cash from the machine, to see my card swallowed. On enquiring why this was so, I was told I'd been declared bankrupt. The insolvency witch had taken her revenge for my paying off my creditors by filing for bankruptcy. Apparently, she had offered them twenty-three pence in the pound, clearly intending to make a few more quid out of my misfortune.

I went to the office that dealt with this to be given a form almost as big as a telephone book to fill in with all the people I owed money to. I was in danger of blowing a fuse as I explained I didn't owe anything to anyone. All my utilities had been frozen too, and they were asking about my car, explaining that it could be taken.

It seemed the witch had posted bankruptcy notices in places I would never see, and she also claimed she couldn't find me. Considering I still had the same phone number, publisher and agent that I'd had from when we'd first met, this was an out-and-out lie, and her nasty revenge.

In the end it went to court. I had to pay seven thousand pounds for a barrister to defend me. My old business landlords wrote a letter to the court saying I was honourable to the last, but the witch had lied to them constantly. The judge stated this case should never have been brought to court and awarded costs against the witch.

It was over, but it took an age to lose the stigma,

and I never got a penny back of those court costs, even though I wrote to the Law Society. It transpired that insolvency practitioners have no ombudsman so they can do what they like. How awful. I wonder how many other people have been through that kind of hell.

But to move on to happier things. The new year of 1995 brought forth *Charity* and, as I recall, it got into the bookselling charts, not high but in the top thirty. It was more than I'd ever dreamed of. I started looking for a house to buy later that year, but those I could afford were pretty awful. It was Jo who found the house I ended up with. She had been seeing a boy in a street in Whitchurch, where my mother-in-law still lived. The house in question was being built and she thought it looked ideal.

Only I could find a builder who was in such financial straits that he couldn't afford to put the kitchen and bathroom in. Anyway, I did a deal with him that I would pay for them to be done, and get the house at a drastically reduced price. That deal might have backfired on me, but fortunately it didn't, and I got the kind of kitchen and bathroom I wanted.

I called it Camellia House, as I said my book *Camellia*, due out soon, would pay for it. I then had to learn how to grow camellias: they don't like the limey soil in Bristol and have to live in pots.

I am always in a hurry for everything and, having decided I'd throw a launch party for *Camellia* in early May, I had to get landscapers in to build a pond, a base for a conservatory, a small lawn and flowerbeds in time for the party.

It took seven men seven days to do it, and as I planted pansies in the borders the day before the party, I got an inkling of how God must have felt when He was creating the world in seven days. I had been praying for a sunny day, as the caterers would take up a lot of space indoors. My prayers were answered and the weather was glorious. I had invited everyone who had supported me over the years and believed in my ability to write a bestseller. I don't think I'd ever been happier than I was that day. I had a house of my own, no more financial problems, and my three girls were a delight. I was still seeing the fireman who had helped me through the hard time – in fact we'd been an item for some time, but I was now beginning to suspect he was a fortune hunter. When he snubbed a much-loved old friend of mine that day in favour of a film man who had more kudos, my heart hardened and I knew he would have to go.

The following day the heavens opened, but the party had been a huge success, and the book was climbing in the charts.

I loved Camellia House. The sun came in all day

but it was a rather top-heavy design, with five bedrooms upstairs and a garage beneath, which left only room for the kitchen, a tiny utility room and the sitting room. I got the conservatory finished and intended it to be a dining room but, as most of us discover, they are too hot in summer and too cold in winter.

Much later that year Sammy announced she was pregnant. I was thrilled to become a grandmother but worried that her relationship with Jason, the baby's father, wasn't strong enough to last. It turned out to be the last nail in the coffin for the fireman: I could see he seemed resentful about the baby and perhaps thought it would change his position in the house. Finally I was so fed up with him sulking that I told him to pack his bags and go.

Sammy came back to live with me late in her pregnancy. Jason was a mechanic, and he had a shop to sell car parts, but the flat above it was pretty grim. I wanted him to come with her, as I felt they needed to bond tighter at such a time, but he didn't feel able to do so. I would watch Sammy lying in the sun, her tummy getting bigger and browner by the day, and often found myself thinking back to my pregnancy with Warren. She was the same age as I was then, the baby due at the same time, and it was often said how alike we were.

Thankfully she would never have to experience what I went through.

On 9 July 1998, I was going to a rather smart ladies' lunch at a Michelin-starred restaurant in Bath. I asked Sammy to come too, as I didn't like the thought of her alone at home. She had nothing smart to wear, but I lent her a white cheesecloth outfit. I don't remember much about that lunch other than how beautiful and serene she looked. She had a few sips of champagne, and some smoked salmon, both of which she'd never tried before. One of my friends joked that the baby would be born with champagne tastes.

In the early hours of the morning Sammy called to me that she had a tummy-ache. I suggested she come into bed with me. Once there I rubbed her tummy as I had with all the girls when they were little and had tummy-aches. The baby wasn't due for another ten days or so, but as soon as I laid my hand on her I knew she was in labour.

As we were leaving for the hospital I snatched up a cardigan that had been delivered to me that morning. I thought it might get chilly later. The only thing I remember clearly about the delivery was wishing it was me in pain and not my daughter. Births are never like the ones in films, a few contractions, a push, and there is the baby. If only they were. But, finally, he arrived. I left soon after so Sammy could get some sleep.

I was ecstatic with happiness and called on every-one I could think of to give them the joyous news. I got to a friend's floristry shop about five in the after-noon, and she said to me, 'Have you looked in the mirror today?'

I hadn't, of course. Why would I? But I did then, only to find I'd got blood sprayed right up the back of my new cardigan. I looked like a road accident. And no one had mentioned it.

Sammy came home to me the following day with the baby. She named him Brandon.

I remember that time as one of the very best. The girls and I sat around, passing the baby from willing arms to willing arms. We called it frogging: the way babies lie on your chest, they do look like little frogs.

Chloë, Sammy's little Shih Tzu, had come to live with me and Monty, my West Highland Terrier, and took it upon herself to be baby guardian, lying on the changing mat, in front of his cot or by the buggy. She remained with me and Monty after Sammy had gone to her own home, and kept up the vigil when-ever Brandon stayed with me. She slept with him and even let him snuggle one of her ears as if it was a comfort blanket.

I took it upon myself to do the night feeds. I loved

it. The weather was warm and I would stand at the windows, looking out, while I was getting his wind up. I saw lots of interesting things, from a fox sauntering by to people trying to steal cars.

The latter I reported to the police, and after a few occasions a policeman came to the house. 'May I ask why you are up at two or three a.m.?' he asked.

'I'm feeding the baby,' I said.

He looked very surprised, clearly thinking, She's too old to have a baby. I didn't bother to enlighten him.

When Brandon was six weeks or so, I had to go to America to do the research for my book *Never Look Back*. It was to be based on the early settlers in America. I had written most of it from imagination, but intended to drive from Kansas, the wagon trains' starting point, to the West Coast. I took Jo with me – she was seventeen by then. I left the house and dogs in the care of Amelia, a trustworthy lady I'd got to know.

The trip didn't start too well. We got to Kansas, and picked up a lovely little red Firebird convertible at the airport. But once on the six-lane highway I was terrified. I pulled into a hotel claiming that once I'd had a cup of tea I'd be okay. About an hour later, when I'd had time to take on board that I was intending to drive thousands of miles across America and had better stop being a wimp, I asked the girl on Reception the way into the part of town where the wagon trains had begun their journey into unnamed territories. She said that was a tourist area, and it was basically just a straight road there from the hotel.

We set off. It was around four in the afternoon, I think, and much less scary now I'd got my sensible head on, or so I thought. We had a meal, wandered about looking at the restored historic buildings, and thought we'd come again in the morning to go into the museum. It was dark when we made our way back to the hotel, but after a bit the road appeared to be a lot narrower than we remembered. We kept going, and it got narrower still. At this point I felt we were heading towards Canada but, worse, there was nowhere to turn round. We kept going, optimistic that we might see a turning to the right road. But it got darker and darker, narrower and narrower.

Finally I found a place we could turn round. And back we went until we got to a gas station. I went in to enquire the way, but when asked what hotel we were in I didn't know! What sort of mother with a young daughter leaves a hotel in a huge city in a strange country and doesn't take a card with its address? A very stupid one.

The girl behind the counter suggested lots of different hotels, but none of them rang a bell. And all of our belongings, including money and our passports, were in that hotel. I said in desperation it was only about seven miles from the airport. She suggested we drive back there and retrace our steps. I couldn't even look at Jo I was so ashamed for being such a useless mum. But we did what had been suggested, got to the airport and set out again.

There the hotel was, on our right, now lit up like the Blackpool Illuminations.

What a relief!

It seemed when we were given the instructions for downtown Kansas City, it was indeed a straight road. But we hadn't been told that on the return trip the road forked. We'd taken the wrong fork.

The next morning we set off but decided to get some sweets and probably some cigarettes – I was a smoker in those days. Seeing a small road leading to what looked like a leafy suburb, we took it. Sure enough, there was a little row of shops. We left the car with the roof down, but as we were buying some goodies a man came in. 'Is that your red car?' he asked.

I said it was.

To our astonishment he told us to get into it and drive away quickly. 'It's not safe here,' he insisted. 'Even now there will be people watching, looking to rob you and take your car.'

We didn't need telling twice. We were out of the door at the speed of light. But the mystery was that the area looked so calm, peaceful, clean and safe, like an English suburb built in the 1940s. If that was a dangerous place, I wondered what the ghettos we heard about so often were like.

Fortunately there were no more dramas for a while. We drove three or four hundred miles a day, heading west, and stayed in decent-looking motels, usually with a swimming pool. I did say to Jo, though, that we must find a creepy Bates-style motel that was in the Hitchcock film *Psycho* to stay in one night just so we could say we'd done it.

Empty roads, a lovely car and warm sunshine made the journey a joy, and in each place we stopped there was something to laugh about. Mostly there was only the choice of Burger King or McDonald's to eat at, and in Kansas the restaurants were funny, all done up like backdrops from *The Wizard of Oz*, with gingham drapes and tablecloths. Some of those places had salad bars where you could eat as much as you liked. Not very inspired salad, I might add, but we watched a coachload of old people arrive, all wearing baseball caps and Bermuda shorts. They loaded huge plates with salad, and many ordered the largest burgers on the menu, plus a bucketful of milkshake. We looked on in amazement. I think the average age was seventy-five. But they ate hardly anything, just left it. Shocking waste.

As we left Kansas the scenery became more dramatic, and I found that the Wild West was almost exactly as I'd imagined, possibly because of all the cowboy films I'd watched at Saturday-morning pictures. In some places the wagon-train ruts were still there. Jo and I walked down a hill that at first glance looked like pasture, only to find it was full of rocks, really heavy-going. I knew that the wagons had gone only seven or eight miles a day, but over such rough ground it must have been exhausting. Of course only the very old or the small children rode on the wagons. I had read a couple of diaries kept by women on their journeys, and they'd write things like 'Managed seven miles but had to stop. Delivered a fine healthy boy at 3 a.m.'

I found the terrain was much as I'd imagined, but soon realized what an incredibly hard trip it must have been. I was in awe of those women. I doubt many of them wanted to go west, but had to do what their husbands had decreed. While he at least had Sundays to rest, she would have been washing clothes, preparing bread and other food, and looking after several children. They had to contend with sickness, childbirth, accidents – like kids falling under wagon wheels – and the route must have had hundreds of hastily dug shallow graves along it. They didn't name their babies until they were six weeks old as few survived that long.

I had the luck to meet the curator of a Wild West museum that had been a fort. Fortunately he recognized in me someone who cared and took me into his archives to show me fantastic paintings depicting how Native Americans lived, handwoven rugs, beautiful beadwork, war bonnets and much more.

Never Look Back was my first epic historical novel, and I soon learned the value of real research, stepping into the footprints of people long gone, soaking up the beautiful but harsh terrain, imagining what they must have felt, excitement, despair, fear and a longing for a settled home. Jo and I had some sort of adventure every day in our month-long road trip. Religious fanatics running motels, where every towel was embroidered with godly messages, and I felt I had to hide my bottle of vodka. Fantastic scenery, double standards – you can't buy an alcoholic drink in a bar in Utah, but just down the road in a gas station they've got liquor stacked to the roof. Incredibly ignorant people, and then as I despaired, we'd meet someone kind and intelligent. So many bigots, and then the exact opposite.

We saw a brown bear dip into a river, pull out a big fish and sit back on its haunches to eat it. We swam in a lake that felt like warm bath water, saw views that almost stopped my heart they were so awe-inspiring. But one night in a motel a couple next door made so much noise having sex that Jo thought the man was killing the woman.

We were desperate for fresh fruit and vegetables, but they seemed to be lacking everywhere. One Sunday morning we were driving along a completely empty road. I had my foot down, but I certainly wasn't doing more than seventy. Suddenly there were police cars chasing me. Thinking it was time to have a bit of fun, I speeded up. Jo screamed at me to slow down, and I did eventually. The police got out of their cars, pointed guns at us and shouted for us to put our hands on our car.

To be fair to the men, as soon as they heard my voice they calmed down. But they still gave me a speeding ticket. Seems I'd been spotted from a plane. Why, in the middle of nowhere? I wanted to ask if they didn't have any murderers to catch. But I used as many delaying tactics as I could think of in paying the fine, such as sending them an English cheque. In the end I had to pay or I'd never have been let into the US again.

The day after that we ran out of petrol. We'd had three-quarters of a tank when we left Salt Lake City, but we were driving across desert and it was a firing-range place. Each time we came to a turn-off a notice said 'No Services'. No mobile phones, of course, and I'd been told if you needed help you had to put the bonnet up. But I was scared to stop with Jo in the car. The scenery reminded me of that horror film *The Hills Have Eyes*. And I imagined monster-like men coming out of nowhere to grab two lone women. Finally when the gas indicator was right on empty, I stopped at some washrooms and told Jo to go in and stay there till I called her. It seemed for ever with no one passing. Then I saw two motor-bikes in the distance. I was even more scared then, my knees literally knocking. The only weapon I had was a nail file!

The riders slowed down and stopped. My heart was thumping. Then one took off their helmet and smiled. She was a girl with long blonde hair and was with her husband. Panic over!

They siphoned petrol out of their bikes into a Coke bottle, then followed us to the next gas station. I wrote to them when I got home to thank them, and put a dedication to them in *Never Look Back*. We met dozens of people on our journey, most of whom begged us to keep in touch. I wrote to all of them, but only the two lovely bikers responded. Which just proves you should never make sweeping assumptions about people.

I got something in the ball of my foot, and couldn't stand on it. We holed up in Reno for three days hoping it would get better, but soon my leg began to ache and swell. I went to a hospital, but all they were interested in was who my insurers were. I said I'd pay them in cash. A nurse so huge she could barely walk looked at it and said dismissively that it was a blister. I wanted to deck her.

Back at the hotel, Jo borrowed tweezers, found some antiseptic ointment and, with my glasses perched on her nose, operated on me. She drew out a piece of copper wire some four centimetres long! I would say that was the start of her nursing career, and no patient was ever more relieved than I was.

After three weeks away and thousands of miles driven, we arrived in San Francisco to give back our lovely little red sports car. I rang home from the garage and Sammy answered, sobbing her heart out. 'Something terrible has happened, but I can't tell you now.'

I insisted she did, only to be told that Granny was dead, Monty too. Nigel had been with his mum all night, then came to my house to tell Sammy she'd died and accidentally left the gate open. Monty couldn't stand rattling trucks. One came past while Nigel was there. Monty gave chase and was killed.

That afternoon Jo and I saw San Francisco through

a veil of tears. We'd known Granny was ill – Nigel had moved her into a nursing home – but no one had expected her to die so quickly, and beloved Monty too. In one day. I rang American Airlines, told them we'd had a double bereavement and they changed our flight home to the next morning. Sammy had said Nigel was in a terrible state. He was afraid I would blame him for Monty's death. I wouldn't, of course. He loved dogs, and he'd loved his mum. I could only feel deep sympathy as I loved her too.

One good thing came out of it: after all the bitterness Nigel had harboured towards me, he knew I was the only person who had loved her as he did, which brought us together afterwards. I swear she was looking down and cheering us on.

Now, I'm not going to go on and on telling you family stories, or the highlights of my time spent on computer dating, with the creeps, arseholes and saddos I met there. That would fill a book. I won't even go on about the glee I felt when I finally got to number one in the book charts.

There was terror in Thailand when my girls had gone to Phuket, leaving me with six-year-old Brandon: the tsunami happened. I had two days of not knowing if they were alive. But they were and thankfully came back to me.

But I must tell you about a wonderful reunion in New Zealand. My father was a master model-boat maker, and I knew he'd made a huge model of HMS *Leander*, a sailing ship and the first in New Zealand's navy. He had been seconded to New Zealand in 1938, and as he was a Royal Marine he had time on his hands to make the model. When war broke out in 1939 and he had to set sail, he finished it and gave it to the naval museum in Auckland.

As I was going there courtesy of Penguin Books, with a schedule of talks, television, radio and signings, I thought it would be good to track down the model ship and go to see it. I wrote to the museum and, quite by chance, they were just moving many of its exhibits to a new maritime museum. They still had Dad's ship, and the press picked up on the story because I was so successful in New Zealand.

It felt surreal being in Auckland dockyard, which Dad had often mentioned, to climb the stairs up to what had been a social club for marines and sailors, knowing he must have walked up them countless times. And there in the centre of this almost empty hall was his ship, the red paint on the hull as bright as it must have been seventy years before. I felt so emotional looking at it: it was, after all, the very breath of my father's spirit. The hull was cut away on one side so people could see where the crew slept and goods were stored. The museum people told me it had always been a favourite with visiting children. But they had got Dad's name wrong on the brass plaque – I think they couldn't believe he was really called Sergeant Arthur Sargent, and instead had engraved Sergeant Arthur and the date in 1939.

I left there for my tour around North Island, feeling very happy I'd made the effort to find the ship. I had to give a talk in several places, one at the library in Palmerston North. As I had come to expect of New Zealanders, it was very well attended. I gave my talk, then sat down at a desk to sign books. A couple came up to me but I probably only glanced at them. Then she said, 'Forty-five years ago.'

I looked up and, to my astonishment, it was Linda, my poetry-reading friend from Oak Lodge, my saviour when the Pennyquicks had kicked me out. I had kept in touch with her until she got married and went to East Africa with her husband. But, as so often happens, we lost contact. I certainly didn't know she was in New Zealand.

It was the newspaper article that had done it. She had read that the daughter of Sergeant Sargent had come to see her father's model ship and said to her husband, 'Do you think that's our Lesley?' She read on to find I was the novelist Lesley Pearse, whose books she had read.

We had about fifteen minutes together as my PR people were taking me somewhere else. We could only hug each other and cry. But how lovely it was as Linda was the one person I'd never meant to lose track of. I owed her so much and loved her. Since then we've been in touch and they came to see me the last time they were in England. I really hope that one of these days I'll see her again.

To me, finding Linda after all those years was a miracle, and evidence that Fate or kismet can bring about strange and wonderful things. My Scottish friend Jo often says she's never known anyone experience so many coincidences in their life.

What I want to tell you now, is far more than coincidence. It is about a miracle in Ireland and how it took place. As they used to say on the BBC's *Children's Hour* back in the fifties, 'Are you sitting comfortably? Then I'll begin.'

17

Over the years I've been to Dublin many times, and whenever I've set foot there, I've found myself wondering about my Irish relatives. I suppose because I've moved about so much I imagined everyone does the same and that they would no longer be where I'd last seen them when I was seventeen.

Perhaps if I was ever in Ireland for longer than a couple of days I might have gone to Roscommon and asked around, but I've always been booked on a return flight. Then there is the little voice that whispers, *they wouldn't want to know you anyway.*

Yet each time I was on the radio or being interviewed by a journalist I'd try to bring up the subject of my family. I suppose the interviewers had their own agenda and I never really had a chance. However, the last time I was on the radio I managed to bring the subject round to relatives. Some weeks passed. Then, out of the blue, I had a lovely surprise: an email from Sharon, a second cousin. It seemed someone in the family had heard me talking on the radio, then decided to take the bull by the horns and write to me.

Sharon is the daughter of a cousin I went dancing with in Roscommon back in 1962. Her email was warm and interesting, telling me about various family members. I wrote back eagerly.

It all fell silent then, I assumed because of lack of interest, or that Sharon was too busy with her children to write again. Some time later, when once again I was in Dublin, I had an email from Sharon's younger sister Aisling. She said she was fed up with waiting for Sharon to get more news of me, and that she lived in Dublin. I was so excited. There I was in that city for the night, so I wrote and asked if she'd like to come to the hotel and have dinner with me. She agreed.

Thank goodness I did that. We had the best evening, got on like a house on fire, lots of laughter and catching up. Aisling told me the family met up every summer in Roscommon and I must come. I was overjoyed. The main reason I hadn't kept in touch over the years was because of Warren. My relatives were staunch Catholics, and back in the sixties I was too ashamed to tell them, expecting them to be horrified. Now the old aunties and uncles I remembered had passed away. Ireland had moved on, too, the Church losing its grip. Anyway, I saw this as a long overdue chance to meet the younger members of the family.

But then Covid reared its ugly head with the lockdowns. So there was no reunion.

As so often happens when I can't do something I put it out of my head. I think the lockdowns did that for almost everyone. We became very insular and, I might say, apathetic.

Then, in early 2022, just when I'd almost forgotten, my first cousin Marie, who had been just a little girl when I visited Ireland back in 1962, wrote to me, inviting me to come at Easter to meet the family. I literally jumped for joy that we were back on track and booked my flight eagerly. I'd never wanted anything more in my life.

Marie and her husband Donal met me in Dublin. We had a night at their house in Athlone, then went on to the lovely hotel in Roscommon. On the Saturday night I met the 'boys', my male cousins, all much younger than me but lovely. One, a retired police officer, even remembered me wearing a straw hat back in 1962. He was right – it was a boater. I think I imagined I was in *The Railway Children*. I'm very relieved there are no photos of me wearing it.

The big news, however, was that I wasn't the only special guest. John Glynn, my second cousin, had come over with his wife from America and would be with us the next day. I have an old, faded picture of his father Joe, my mother's youngest brother. I kept it because he was so handsome. I'd never met him as he'd long since emigrated to the US. That, too, seems an omen of what was to come.

On Easter Sunday I sat at a table in the bar with John and Joanne Glynn and opened a book of old photos my brother Michael had given me. Among my father's family pictures, and my stepmother's, there were a few black-and-white pictures of the Glynn family. As I turned the pages, we came to a picture of my father when he was in the Royal Marines with the huge model ship he'd built, the one in Auckland no less. I turned the page, saying, 'Well, that's my dad, of no interest to you except that he was called Sergeant Sargent.'

I saw the couple exchange glances but I got the idea they found that a very weird remark. Then I moved on to talk to other people.

It was the loveliest day, a super meal, and my cousin John Joe, known as JJ, had put together a slide show of old photographs of the family. The previous day I'd been taken to see my grandparents' old house, now derelict, and their grave. I was very touched to see that my mother Marie's name had been added to the headstone. It made me very emotional that she hadn't been cast out and forgotten as I had thought.

I turned at one point during the day to see all the little-girl relatives in a corner doing Irish dancing, which made me tearful too. They were so well behaved, no screaming and shouting, just entertaining themselves.

The jollity went on till late in the evening. When I fell asleep in my comfortable room, had I known what was going on in a bedroom further down the corridor that night I would have jumped out of bed. But I slept in blissful ignorance about what would be revealed the next morning before we left for Dublin airport.

But you'll have to wait a little longer for me to reveal all. After all, I was in deepest ignorance right then surrounded by fifty or sixty relatives.

I had just begun my breakfast the next morning when John and Joanne came into the dining room, holding a small bottle of champagne, with grins as wide as the Irish Sea. I hadn't expected to see them again before I left, much less expected champagne. They sat down opposite me and Joanne told me they had met my son Warren.

Of all the things they could have said, that was the absolute last thing I expected. And the most fantastic. I was struck dumb, unable even to ask how or where.

But Joanne smiled kindly at my tears and stunned expression, took my hand across the table and told me

Warren is now called Martin. He's a marine engineer and living in Houston, Texas. It seemed Martin had done a DNA test, which had pinged John Glynn as a close relative. John and Joanne were in Palm Beach, a long way from Houston, but Martin drove there to see them. He told them I had been Lesley Sargent at the time of his adoption, but his attempts to find me years earlier had failed, almost certainly as I'd married and moved countless times. I don't think Martin even knew I was half Irish. But astonishingly Joanne and John said they were planning a trip to Ireland shortly and would make enquiries about Lesley Sargent.

That moment as I sat beside them and made the joke about my father being Sergeant Sargent was like a small explosion. They couldn't have expected that one of the first people they spoke to in that hotel would turn out to be the very woman they were hoping to find for Martin.

As I'd walked away from them they had apparently had a consultation with Marie, my cousin, who said she thought it best to say nothing for now, but to break the news the following day at breakfast, or I'd be crying instead of enjoying the big reunion.

As it turned out, that moment with John and Joanne can only be described as 'One when two planets collide. Or even the hand of God working to put right a wrong.'

Coincidences again: although I was told my baby had gone to Yorkshire, and always imagined him there, Martin's adoptive parents had in fact moved to Kent. Martin did his apprenticeship in Chatham, where my father had been stationed, and even more amazing, his three daughters were born in the same hospital as I was many decades before. Ships and my father were inseparable, and so it is with his grandson.

Obviously Joanne, like any woman who has just unearthed a fantastic secret, was disappointed to be asked to hold back until the next day. But she phoned Martin later that night to tell him they'd found me, and urged him to google me. He was doing this as they spoke and Joanne said he was overcome at the amount of stuff about me on the internet. He'd had no idea I was a novelist. He said in wonderment, 'She's not just any old mother.'

I've often wondered what 'any old mother' might look like.

When I was in the orphanage and we talked about mothers I imagined them to wear a headscarf and have bright red lipstick. That image came from those I'd seen queuing in the baker's.

One of the articles Martin read that night was a recent one called 'The Lost Boy'. In it I'd written about his birth and the forces that had made me give him up. He said he felt so happy to know I hadn't

351

given him up easily or willingly, and that he was still always on my mind. In fact, I'd written other articles like that, and been a member of the Birth Mothers Association. I'd checked every single list that adopted children put their names on.

But just imagine yourself in my shoes, there at a breakfast table, listening to all this! It was the stuff of my dreams and fantasies. Joanne had some photographs of him as a child, and my heart was nearly bursting that he had been found, just a phone call away. So many questions I wanted answers to, but I couldn't ask them of Joanne, so the only thing I could focus on for now was that he'd be fifty-eight in the coming July and he wanted to see me as much as I wanted to see him.

Like I said, it felt like the hand of God.

Marie and I had to leave for me to get to Dublin for the plane home. I think I could have flown home under my own excitement and steam. It was quite the most thrilling and wonderful day of my life, now that I had the expectation of being able to meet him, to hold this grown man in my arms and give thanks for him being brought back to me.

As you can imagine the excitement spread when I got home. My girls, who had always known about my firstborn, were thrilled at last to have the big brother they had been told about since they were small. Now it was not just a sad story in their mum's past, it was a magical new beginning.

Friends like Paula and Linda, who had cuddled and changed him as a baby, were as joyful as I was, as were the many dear friends, Jo, Bee in Northern Ireland, Jeanne in Vermont, who had all come into my life after Martin, yet had comforted me when I talked about him, and understood the scar I had inside me. So many people cried as I told them. My publishers and agent, friends and neighbours were all so happy for me.

As the days passed in a fabulous dream-like state, I could feel that scar inside me peeling away. I could tell myself that this was my reward for being brave enough to pass him to people who could give him everything I couldn't. And that the intense love I felt for him, which never faltered, despite the agony of giving him up, must have stayed within him, making him need me as much as I needed him.

Martin and I spoke on the phone a few days later. Not a terribly coherent phone call, as I remember, but you can't possibly attempt to fill a gap of fifty-seven years in ten minutes.

I had already started this memoir at the time, and the part about him as a baby was all written, so I sent it to him in an email. I always find it easier to express myself in the written word. It is kinder on the recipient too: they can read a bit, mull it over, read some more and so on, until the whole thing is in front of them, like a finished jigsaw. But I never imagined when I began the memoir that I would have such a mind-blowing story as a conclusion.

It wasn't long before I saw him in the flesh. I had already organized a birthday treat for my friend Jo at the end of April. We were going to the theatre and staying at London's Haymarket Hotel. It so happened that Martin came to the UK on business at the same time and arranged to meet me for lunch at the hotel.

I was waiting in the foyer when he arrived. To my astonishment I could still see the baby face I had engraved on my memory in the grown man. As we hugged I felt weak with emotion. I was so overcome that I had a job to string a sentence together. A million questions in my head, yet it was hard to ask any of them. I learned his three daughters were Vicki, Emma and Aimee, and Vicki has a little boy called Archie. They all live in Kent. Suddenly, overnight, I have four children, seven grandchildren and a great-grandson. It's overwhelming.

So far I've only met Aimee, who I think is very like me when I was the same age. My three girls have met Emma and Aimee and, of course, their brother Martin. I think to get everyone together would be like trying to herd cats. But I'm sure we'll manage it bit by bit.

Last September I flew to Houston with my grand-son Brandon to stay with Martin and his partner Svetlana. I took Brandon because I could sense Martin was an action man, as Brandon is, and I doubted he'd want to sit about with me filling in all the gaps about his childhood. It turned out to be a stroke of brilliance on my part: he and Brandon got on like a house on fire.

I loved Svetlana on sight: she's half Ukrainian, half Russian, and cares for poorly birds, a bit like the RSPB here. I would have loved to help her in her garden, but it was so hot I couldn't even sit in the shade let alone dig. But we did go to a plant sale, and I learned from her about the native plants in Texas. I bought her a huge stone alligator for her garden too. She called him James.

Just recently I celebrated thirty years in publishing. Martin came over from America to a very smart dinner in London's Claridge's, with some dear friends and all the people who support and guide me at Penguin Books. It was a wonderful evening, and so good to be able to introduce my son to them all.

One thing I've discovered in all of this is that I can't possibly fill in all the missing years with Martin. I can find out more about his work, the places he's been to, which is almost the whole world, his friends and family stories. But not everything – and that doesn't matter.

I know from the time I was involved with the Natural Parents Association that, although adopted people are very keen at first to meet their mothers, in the long term they usually relate more to their siblings. I also know that sometimes the mother or the child finds it too hard to keep up with expectations. I might be Martin's birth mother, but he won't want me constantly visiting, phoning and trying to muscle in on his life. I told him that if, after a while, he finds it all too much I'll be fine with a card and a letter at Christmas. I am content to know that he turned into a fine man, a son to be proud of. I know where and how he lives. That is enough for me.

He might not truly believe this, but I lived in fear for him for so many years. Because his adoptive father was in the army I imagined him joining up too and being killed in the Troubles in Belfast. I worried that he might be a drug-user, a criminal, or even have some kind of disability. None of those things happened to him, thank heaven, and my worries are over. He has spoken of retiring next year at sixty and coming to live in Devon because he likes sailing. I do hope that happens, but I won't bank on it. I just want him to be happy.

I have always loved the inspirational book by Kahlil Gibran *The Prophet*, written back in the 1920s. In one of the chapters he speaks of children, and his words move me to tears. But what he says is so true.

> Your children are not your children.
> They are the sons and daughters of Life's longing
>   for itself.
> They come through you but not from you,
> And though they are with you yet they belong not
>   to you.
>
> You may give them your love but not your thoughts,
> For they have their own thoughts.
> You may house their bodies but not their souls,
> For their souls dwell in the house of tomorrow,
>   which you cannot visit, not even in your dreams . . .
> You are the bows from which your children as living
>   arrows are sent forth.
> The Archer sees the mark upon the path of the
>   infinite, and He bends you with His might that His
>   arrows may go swift and far.

I hope that all four of my children will go swift and far, safe in the knowledge of how much they are loved.

Discover the novels written
by Lesley Pearse . . .

WHICH BOOK WILL YOU READ NEXT?

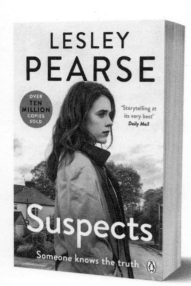

Suspects

When a young couple move into their first home together, a young girl is found murdered nearby. Soon a spotlight is cast on all the neighbours, each hiding their own dark and twisted secrets . . .

Betrayal

Ten years ago she killed her husband. But the past can't stay hidden forever . . .

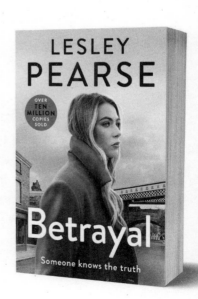

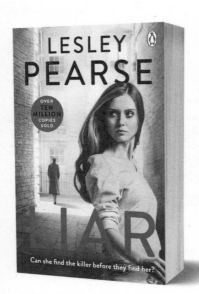

Liar

When Amelia White uncovers a shocking scoop, she begins a desperate search for answers. But to uncover the truth, she must work out who is lying . . .

You'll Never See Me Again

When Betty escapes her marriage, she goes on the run, armed with a new identity. But she never imagined starting again would end in murder . . .

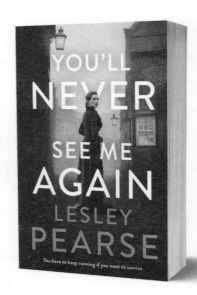

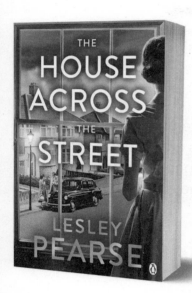

The House Across the Street

Katy must set out to uncover the truth about the mysterious house across the street. Even if that means risking her own life . . .

The Woman in the Wood

Fifteen-year-old twins Maisy and Duncan Mitcham have always had each other. Until one fateful day in the wood . . .

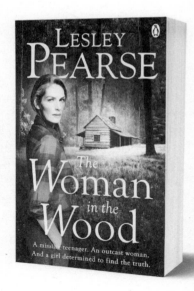

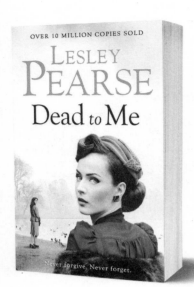

Dead to Me

Ruby and Verity become firm friends, despite coming from different worlds. However, fortunes are not set in stone and soon the girls find their situations reversed.

Without a Trace

On Coronation Day, 1953, Molly discovers that her friend is dead and her six-year-old daughter Petal has vanished. Molly is prepared to give up everything in finding Petal. But is she also risking her life?

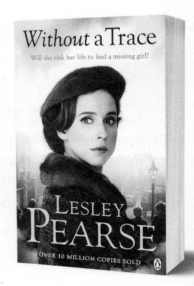

Forgive Me

Eva's mother never told her the truth about her childhood. Now it is too late and she must retrace her mother's footsteps to look for answers. Will she ever discover the story of her birth?

Belle

Belle book 1

London, 1910, and the beautiful and innocent Belle Reilly is cruelly snatched from her home and sold to a brothel in New Orleans where she begins her life as a courtesan. Can Belle ever find her way home?

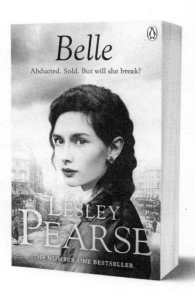

The Promise

Belle book 2

When Belle's husband heads for the trenches of northern France, she volunteers as a Red Cross ambulance driver. There she is brought face to face with a man from her past who she'd never quite forgotten.

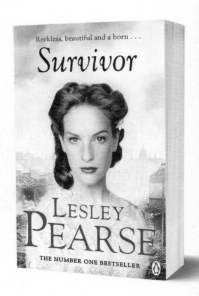

Survivor

Belle book 3

Eighteen-year-old Mari is defiant, selfish and has given up everything in favour of glamorous parties in the West End. But, without warning, the Blitz blows her new life apart. Can Mari learn from her mistakes before it's too late?

Stolen

A beautiful young woman is discovered half-drowned on a Sussex beach. Where has she come from? Why can't she remember who she is — or what happened?

Gypsy

Liverpool, 1893, and after tragedy strikes the Bolton family, Beth and her brother Sam embark on a dangerous journey to find their fortune in America.

Faith

Scotland, 1995, and Laura Brannigan is in prison for a murder she claims she didn't commit.

Hope

Somerset, 1836, and baby Hope is cast out from a world of privilege as proof of her mother's adultery.

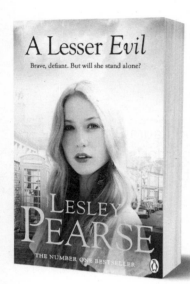

A Lesser Evil

Bristol, the 1960s, and young Fifi Brown defies her parents to marry a man they think is beneath her.

Secrets

Adele Talbot escapes a children's home to find her grandmother — but soon her unhappy mother is on her trail . . .

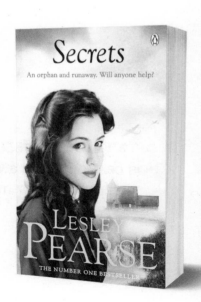

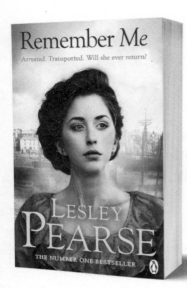

Remember Me

Mary Broad is transported to Australia as a convict and encounters both cruelty and passion. Can she make a life for herself so far from home?

Till We Meet Again

Susan and Beth were childhood friends. Now Susan is accused of murder, and Beth finds she must defend her.

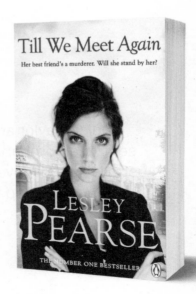

Father Unknown

Daisy Buchan is left a scrapbook with details about her real mother. But should she go and find her?

Trust Me

Dulcie Taylor and her sister are sent to an orphanage and then to Australia. Is their love strong enough to keep them together?

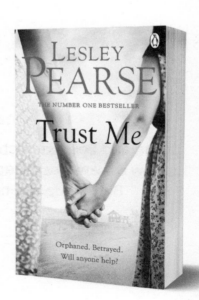

Never Look Back

An act of charity sends flower girl Matilda on a trip to the New World and a new life . . .

Charlie

Charlie helplessly watches her mother being senselessly attacked. What secrets have her parents kept from her?

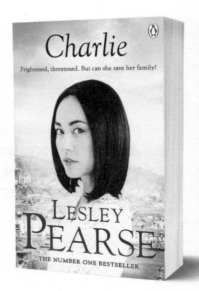

Rosie

Rosie is a girl without a mother, with a past full of trouble. But could the man who ruined her family also save Rosie?

Camellia

Orphaned Camellia discovers that the past she has always been so sure of has been built on lies. Can she bear to uncover the truth about herself?

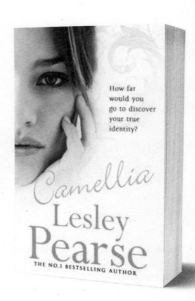

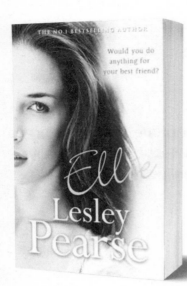

Ellie

Eastender Ellie and spoilt Bonny set off to make a living on the stage. Can their friendship survive sacrifice and ambition?

Charity

Charity Stratton's bleak life is changed for ever when her parents die in a fire. Alone and pregnant, she runs away to London . . .

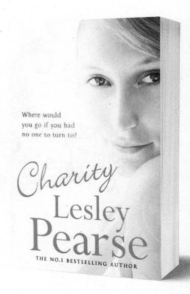

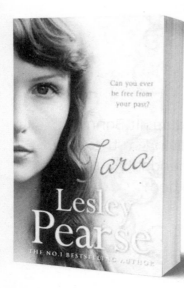

Tara

Anne changes her name to Tara to forget her shocking past — but can she really become someone else?

Georgia

Raped by her foster-father, fifteen-year-old Georgia runs away from home to the seedy back streets of Soho . . .

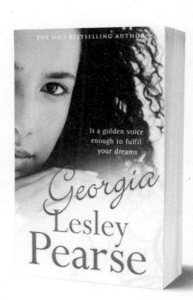